CW00401760

BENELUX
RAILWAYS
LOCOMOTIVES & MULTIPLE UNITS

SIXTH EDITION

The complete guide to all Locomotives and Multiple Units of the Railways of Belgium, the Netherlands and Luxembourg

David Haydock

PLATFORM
5

Published by Platform 5 Publishing Ltd.,
3 Wyvern House, Sark Road, Sheffield S2 4HG, England.

Printed in England by Berforts Information Press, Eynsham, Oxford.

ISBN 978 1 90233696 1

Above: SNCB locomotive 2825 Stands at Amsterdam Centraal with a Benelux train to Brussels Midi on 1 July 2012. This service is expected to be replaced by Fyra V250 high speed trains in December 2012. **Raimund Wyhnal**

Front cover: Rotterdam Rail Feeding shunters 108 and 107 (ex SNCB 7392 and 7390) shunt a TX Logistik coal train, to be hauled by electric loco 189 287 to Oberhausen, at Amsterdam Westhaven on 17 October 2011. **Quintus Vosman**

Back Cover Top: CFL 4002 with four double-deck coaches forming train RB 6710 Luxembourg–Rodange crosses EMU 2217 with train RE 6935 Rodange–Luxembourg at Fentange on 23 March 2011. **Mike Wohl**

Back Cover Bottom: On 26 June 2012 Rail Feeding G2000 diesel 1102 running light engine crosses SNCB 7772 and 7790 working one of the daily freights between Waaslandhaven-Zuid and Antwerpen-Noord yards at Kallo yard in the port of Antwerpen. **Carlo Hertogs**

CONTENTS

INTRODUCTION

This book contains full details of all locomotives and multiple units of the railways of the Benelux countries. The word "Benelux" is cobbled together from the first two or three letters of the three countries concerned, Belgium, the Netherlands and Luxembourg. These three countries had a free trade area with no customs inspection at borders before the European Union was formed. Information is updated to October 2012.

In the Netherlands the language spoken is, of course, Dutch or *Nederlands* to give it is proper name. In Belgium two main languages are spoken. The north of the country, Flanders (*Vlaanderen*) is Dutch speaking with the population referred to in English as Flemings whilst the south, Wallonia (*Wallonie*) is French speaking with the population referred to in English as Walloons. The Flemish people refer to their language as *Vlaams* (Flemish), but it is actually the same as Dutch. Brussels, the capital of Belgium, is officially a dual-language city and is named Brussel in Dutch and Bruxelles in French. In addition there is a small part of eastern Belgium around Eupen where the population's first language is German.

In Luxembourg two languages are in common use. These are French and a low dialect of German known as *Letzeburgisch*. Standard German is also spoken.

English is understood by a large proportion of the population of the Netherlands, a smaller proportion of Dutch-speaking Belgians and even fewer French-speaking Belgians. Common terms used in French and Dutch are detailed in Appendix V on page 176.

INTRODUCTION TO THE SIXTH EDITION

Since the last edition of "Benelux Locomotives & Coaching Stock" was published, there have been many changes mainly due to EU open access regulations and increased cross-border freight operations.

In Belgium SNCB/NMBS is still the only passenger operator whilst open access freight operation is increasing. The SNCB/NMBS fleet is currently going through massive changes following the delivery of 120 new electric locomotives, and the start of deliveries of 305 new EMUs.

In Luxembourg the national operator CFL is expanding outside its borders, but there are no new operators serving the country yet.

In the Netherlands many local passenger services have been contracted to private operators, while freight operations are now by dozens of different companies. Section 6 covers these companies, some of which also operate in Belgium, plus locomotives owned by leasing companies which frequently change hands.

In order to make space for this increasingly complicated information, we have removed hauled coaching stock from this new edition.

LAYOUT OF INFORMATION

For each class of vehicle general data and dimensions in metric units are provided. Vehicle lengths are lengths over buffers or couplers. The following standard abbreviations are used:

km/h	kilometres per hour	m	metres
kN	kilonewtons	mm	millimetres
kW	kilowatts		

Builder codes are shown in Appendix III on page 173, whilst an explanation of codes used for accommodation and multiple units see Appendix I on page 172.

For each vehicle the number is given in the first column. Where a vehicle has been renumbered the former number is generally shown in parentheses after the current number. Further columns show, respectively, the livery (in bold condensed type), the owning company, any detail differences, the depot allocation and name where appropriate. Depot and livery codes are shown in Appendix II on page 172.

For an explanation of the European Vehicle Numbering system see Appendix IV on pages 175.

ACKNOWLEDGEMENTS

We would like to thank all who have helped with the writing of this book, especially Brian Garvin, Michel Van Ussel, Michel Thiry, Carlo Hertogs, Quintus Vosman, Jean-Luc Vanderhaegen, Mike Wohl, Jean-Louis Ottelé, Stojan Mihajlovic, Harrie Peters and Luc Peulen.

ABBREVIATIONS

Standard abbreviations used in this book are:

CFL	Chemins de Fer Luxembourgeois (Luxembourg Railways)
CFR	Compania Nationala de Cai Ferate (Romanian State Railways)
CS	Centraal Station (Central station)
DB	Deutsche Bahn AG (German Railway) or Deutsche Bundesbahn (former West German State Railway)
DR	Deutsche Reichsbahn (former East German State Railway)
EU	Eurostar (UK) Ltd
HTM	Haagsche Tram Maatschappij (Den Haag's public transport operator)
NS	Nederlandse Spoorwegen (Netherlands Railways)
NMBS	Nationale Maatschappij der Belgische Spoorwegen (Belgian Railways – *Dutch language*)
ÖBB	Österreichische Bundesbahnen (Austrian Federal Railways)
PKP	Polskie Koleje Panstwowe (Polish State Railways)
PMPPW	Przedsiebioestwo Materialow Podsadzkowych Przemystn Weglowego
RET	Rotterdamsche Elektrische Tram (Rotterdam's public transport operator)
RU	Railway Undertaking
SJ	Statens Järnvägar (Swedish State Railways)
SNCB	Société Nationale des Chemins de Fer Belges (Belgian Railways – *French language*)
SNCF	Société Nationale des Chemins de Fer Français (French Railways)
STIB	Société des Transports Intercommunaux de Bruxelles (MIVB in Dutch)
SZD	Sovetskie Zheleznye Dorogi

TERSCHELLING

TEXEL

7

ARRIVA

Harlingen
Haven

Sneek

ARRIVA   *MSM*

Stavoren

*Summer
only*

Den Helder

NORTH
SEA

Medemblik

Winkel

Hoogwoud   SHM

Enkhuizen

Heerhugowaard

Broek op Langedok

Alkmaar

Hoorn

NOORD-
HOLLAND

Lelystad

Uitgeest

Purmerend

Beverwijk

CSY

Tata Steel

Ijmuiden   OOU

Zaandam

FLEVOLAND

Almere

Haarlem

Amsterdam

Haarlem works

Zandvoort aan Zee

NZH

Schiphol

Putten

HSL   *Aalsmeer
I*   • *Uithoorn*

Hilversum

Baarn

9

SCHIERMONNIKOOG

AMELAND

Eemshaven

Roodeschool

ARRIVA

Emden

Lauwersoog

Delfzijl

Holwerd

Sauwerd

GRONINGEN

ARRIVA

ARRIVA

Buiten Post

Nieuweschans

Leer →

Groningen

Zuidbroek

Leeuwarden

Waterhuizen

ARRIVA

Winschoten

ON

ARRIVA

ARRIVA

FRIESLAND

Veendam

Wildervank

Tynaarlo

STAR

Heerenveen

Assen

Staadskanaal

Beilen

Musselkanaal

Wolvega

N E T H E R L A N D S

6

Emmen

DRENTHE

EDS

Hoogeveen

ARRIVA
from 12/12

ISM

Meppel

Coevorden

BE

GERMANY

Harden Berg

Kampen

OVERIJSSEL

Mariënberg

Zwolle

ARRIVA
from 12/12

CONNEXXION
ARRIVA from 12/13

Nordhorn

Raalte

Wierden

Almelo

BE

Nunspeet

SRL

Oldenzaal

Bad
Bentheim

Harderwijk

Rijssen

Hengelo

Enschede

Münster →

UTRECHT

Deventer

Goor

Boekelo

Gronau

SYNTUS

MBS

Apeldoorn

Strukton

Haaksbergen

Dortmund
↓

Beekbergen

VSM

Zutphen

10

© 2012 Platform 5 Publishing Ltd.

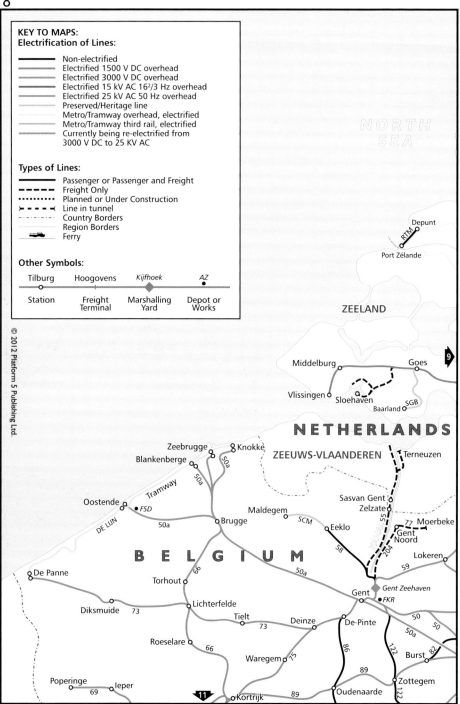

KEY TO MAPS:
Electrification of Lines:

- Non-electrified
- Electrified 1500 V DC overhead
- Electrified 3000 V DC overhead
- Electrified 15 kV AC 16²/3 Hz overhead
- Electrified 25 kV AC 50 Hz overhead
- Preserved/Heritage line
- Metro/Tramway overhead, electrified
- Metro/Tramway third rail, electrified
- Currently being re-electrified from 3000 V DC to 25 KV AC

Types of Lines:

- Passenger or Passenger and Freight
- Freight Only
- Planned or Under Construction
- Line in tunnel
- Country Borders
- Region Borders
- Ferry

Other Symbols:

Tilburg	Hoogovens	*Kijfhoek*	*AZ*
Station	Freight Terminal	Marshalling Yard	Depot or Works

© 2012 Platform 5 Publishing Ltd.

NORTH SEA

Depunt
RTM
Port Zélande

ZEELAND

Middelburg — Goes
Vlissingen — Sloehaven
Baarland — SGB

NETHERLANDS

ZEEUWS-VLAANDEREN — Terneuzen

Zeebrugge — Knokke
Blankenberge
50a

Oostende — FSD
Tramway
50a

Maldegem — SCM
Brugge — Eeklo

Sasvan Gent
Zelzate
77 — Moerbeke
Gent Noord
204
Lokeren

DE LIJN
50a

B E L G I U M

De Panne
66
Torhout — 50a
Gent — Gent Zeehaven
FKR
50

Diksmuide — 73 — Lichterfelde
Tielt — Deinze — De-Pinte
73 — 86 — 50a — 122 — Burst — 82

Roeselare — 66
Waregem — 75
89

Poperinge — Ieper
69 — Kortrijk — 89 — Oudenaarde — Zottegem — 122

9

11

© 2012 Platform 5 Publishing Ltd.

6

SVM●
Leiden ○

Scheveningen
●TS
Den Haag

●LD
Delft ○

Hoek Van
Holland

Maasvlakte

Barneveld ○
Amersfoort ○

Alphen aan
den Rijn ○

Utrecht ○   ●NSM   Woudenberg ○

Woerden ○

Gouda ○

Ijsselstein ○ Nieuwegein ○

UTRECHT   Veenendaal ○

Rhenen ○

●TMR

○ Rotterdam

**ZUID
HOLLAND**

ARRIVA

Geldermalsen ○

Tiel ○   SYNTUS

Kijfhoek ■   BETUWE ROUTE

Gorinchem ○

Dordrecht ○

Oss ○

N E T H E R L A N D S

Lage Zwaluwe ○   ESM ●

's-Hertogenbosch ○

Breda ○

Boxtel ○

Tilburg ○

8

Roosendaal ○

Etten
-Leur ○

BRABANT

Best ○

Bergen
op
Zoom ○

○ Essen
●Wildert

Noorderkampen ○

Eindhoven ○

10

12

12b

HSL

Turnhout ○

15

Hamont ○
Neerpelt ○
To reopen
to passengers

FNND
●
Antwerpen Noord ◆

208

Antwerpen Centraal ○
Antwerpen Berchem ○

Geel ○

Mol ○

15

Balen ○

Leopoldsburg ○

15

Sint
Niklaas ○

59

54

59

Lier ○

15

13

Herentals ○

15

Waterschei ○

Puurs ○

52

SDP

57

25

B E L G I U M

18   21a

Geñk ○
21

21c

FM ●

Mechelen ○

Diest ○

FHS ●   Hasselt ○

53

60

16

35

35

34

Dendermonde ○

Aalst ○

50

Aarschot ○

53

Brussels
National
Aeroport

36

Schaarbeek ○

139

Leuven ○

21

Denderleeuw ○

90

50

50a

Schepdaal ●   ○ Brussels

36   Tienen ○

St Truiden ○

12

© 2012 Platform 5 Publishing Ltd.

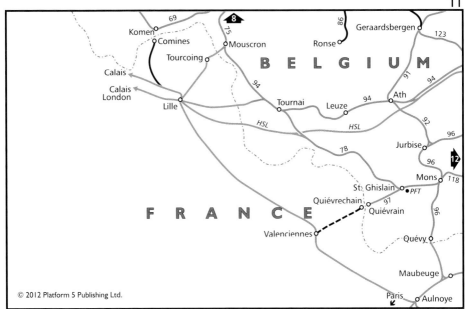

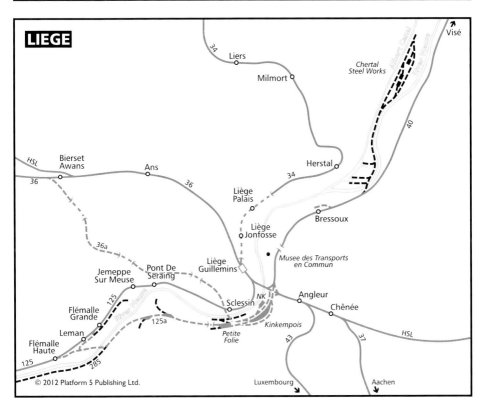

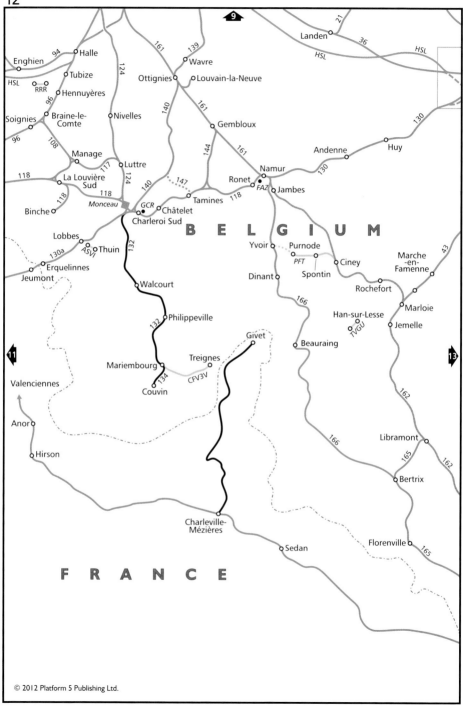

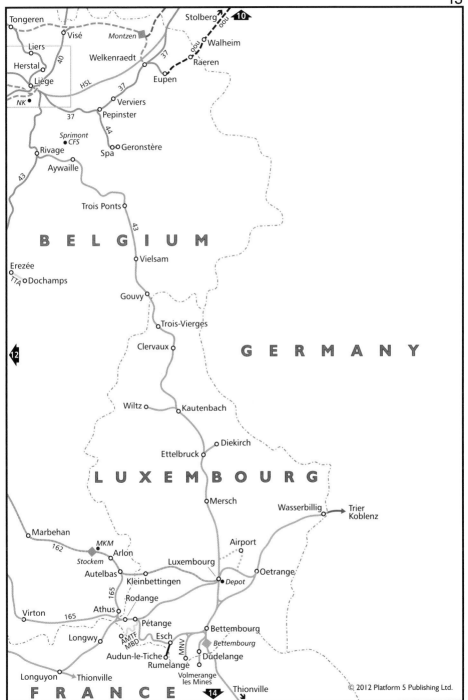

Tongeren
Visé
Montzen
Stolberg **10**
Walheim
Liers
Welkenraedt
Raeren
Herstal
40
37
Liège
Eupen
HSL
37
NK
Verviers
Pepinster
37
44
Sprimont
CFS
Rivage
Spa
Geronstère
Aywaille
43
Trois Ponts
B E L G I U M
43
Vielsam
Erezée
TTA
Dochamps
Gouvy
Trois-Vierges
Clervaux
12
G E R M A N Y
Wiltz
Kautenbach
Diekirch
Ettelbruck
L U X E M B O U R G
Mersch
Wasserbillig
Trier
Koblenz
Marbehan
162
MKM
Airport
Stockem
Arlon
Luxembourg
Autelbas
Kleinbettingen
Oetrange
Depot
165
Rodange
Athus
Virton
165
Pétange
Bettembourg
Longwy
AMTF
MBD
Esch
Bettembourg
MNV
Audun-le-Tiche
Dudelange
Rumelange
Longuyon
Thionville
Volmerange
les Mines
Thionville
F R A N C E
14
Thionville
© 2012 Platform 5 Publishing Ltd.

14

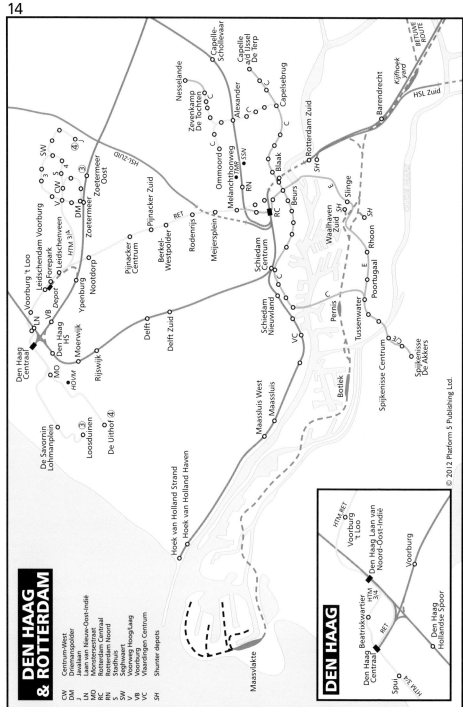

BRUSSELS AREA

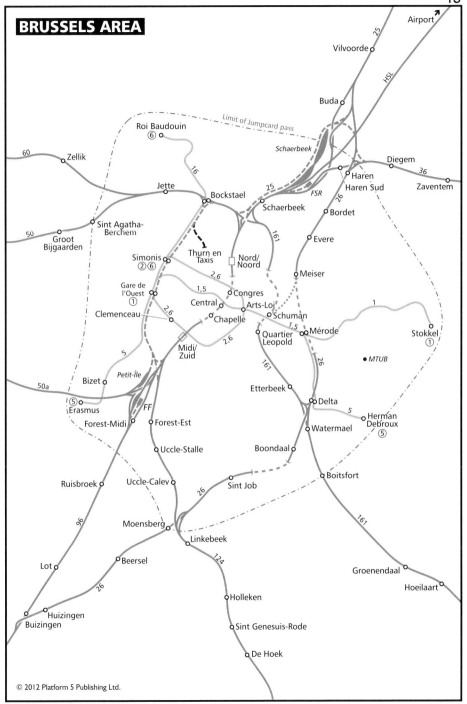

AMSTERDAM

Uitgeest
Hoorn
Koog Bloemwijk
Zaandam-Kogerveld

① Aziëhaven
② Australiëhaven
Zaandam

Buikslotermeerplein

Westhaven

②
①

Australiëhaven yard
Isolatorweg
Amsterdam Zaanstraat Depot

←Haarlem
Sloterdijk
Amsterdam Centraal

Lelylaan
Muiderpoort
Depot
Amsterdam Watergraafsmeer

Haarlemmermeer
Riekerpolder Aansluiting
Zuid WTC
Amstel
Diemen

EMA
RAI

Preserved Tramway
Duivendrecht
Diemen Zuid

Schiphol
Bovenkerk
Bijlmer
Gaasperplas
Weesp
Almere ↗

←Rotterdam
Gein
Amersfoort ↘

Amstelveen Westwijk
Utrecht ↓

© 2012 Platform 5 Publishing Ltd.

▲ HTRS Vossloh G 1206 diesel 1798 is seen at Dordrecht Zuid with a long container train on 4 July 2012.
Raimund Wyhnal

TICKETS & PASSES

Belgium

Single and day return tickets are available, but a return costs twice the single. The maximum second class single in Belgium costs €20.10. The *Billet Week-end* gives a 50% discount off the ordinary return fare. It is valid from 19.01 on Friday to midnight on Sunday.

For €76 in second and €117 in first class, the *Rail Pass* gives ten journeys from any station to any other station in Belgium within a year. The holder (the ticket is transferable) fills in the day, date, origin and destination stations for each journey.

Seniors over 65 pay €5.30 return in second class or €12 in first class for a *Billet Senior* to anywhere in Belgium from 09.00 (all day on Saturdays, Sundays and Public Holidays). This fare is **not** available at weekends in July and August.

SNCB now offers "web deals" at certain times of year. These can be very good value.

Luxembourg

There are three types of ticket, all valid for the whole network in second class on all trains and buses:

- A short duration ticket *(Kuurzzäitbilljee–Billet courte durée)* costs €1.50 and is valid for two hours after validation. For first class travel there is a €0.80 supplement per journey. A carnet of ten tickets costs €12.
- A day ticket (*Dagesbilljee/Billet longue durée*) costs €4 and is valid after validation all day and until 08.00 the next morning. For first class travel there is a €2 supplement per journey. A carnet of five tickets costs €16.
- A weekend ticket (*Billet Weekend*) is valid for up to five people on a Saturday, Sunday or Public Holiday until 03.00 the next morning. It costs €6. Only valid in second class.

Various special day return tickets are issued to nearby stations in Belgium, France and Germany. For details see the CFL website: www.cfl.lu

Netherlands

There are two types of standard ticket, single and day return (*dagretour*). There is also a weekend return which is the same price as a day return except that it is valid from 19.00 on Friday to 04.00 on Monday. Tickets bought from booking offices are €1 more expensive than those from machines. A fine of €35 is added to the fare if bought on the train!

An off-peak discount pass known as the *Voordeelurenabonnement* is available for €60. This is available to anyone and provides a 40% discount on all tickets after 09.00 (all day on Saturdays, Sundays and Public Holidays) for the holder and up to three companions. In addition, Seniors over 60 (*Zestigplussers*) can pay an extra €14 second class or €39 first class and receive seven days unlimited free travel after 09.00 (not on Mondays or Fridays). This consists of one pass every two months (measured from the first day of validity of the ticket) plus one which can be used in any period. Seniors also receive a "Rail Plus" card free of charge which gives a 25% discount on international journeys. To obtain the pass it is necessary to fill in a form obtained from an NS booking office. A passport photo is required.

There is a day ticket (*Dagkaart*) for €48 (second) or €81.80 (first).

Benelux Passes

An InterRail "One Country" pass, which covers **all three** Benelux countries, was priced in 2012 between €119 for any three days and €243 for any eight days in one month in second class. First class costs around 53% more. For five days in a month, the *Benelux Tourrail* pass, not on sale in the Netherlands, costs €165 in second or €258 in first class.

For details of other passes, please see the annual feature in **Today's Railways Europe**, published each spring, plus updates to fare deals in most issues.

GETTING THERE FROM GREAT BRITAIN

By Rail

Eurostar services run from London St. Pancras International to Brussels Midi taking around two hours. Some of these call at Ebbsfleet and/or Ashford. There are onward connections in Brussels to Amsterdam by the hourly "Benelux push-pull" service which also calls at Mechelen, Antwerpen Centraal, Roosendaal, Dordrecht, Rotterdam Centraal, Den Haag HS and Schiphol, and also by *Thalys* services which call only at Antwerpen Centraal, Rotterdam Centraal, Den Haag HS and Schiphol. The Benelux service is expected to be replaced at any moment, possibly from December 2012, by Fyra high speed services between Brussels and Amsterdam.

By Sea

Stena Line offers a Harwich–Hoek van Holland ferry service which takes 6–7 hours. There is a train connection to Rotterdam. Cabins are compulsory on night sailings. P&O Ferries operates overnight Hull to Zeebrugge and Europoort (bus connection to Rotterdam), respectively 12½ and 14½ hours. DFDS Seaways runs daily from Newcastle International Ferry Terminal at North Shields to IJmuiden taking 15–16 hours. There are bus connections to/from Newcastle and Amsterdam.

By Air

There are flights from all London airports and many regional airports direct to Amsterdam and Brussels. Amsterdam airport (Schiphol) and Brussels airport are both rail-connected, as are the London airports of Gatwick, Heathrow, Luton and Stansted and the British regional airports at Birmingham and Manchester. Newcastle Airport is served by the Tyne & Wear Metro. Flights also operate from the UK to Antwerpen, Charleroi (sometimes known as Brussels South), Eindhoven, Groningen, Luxembourg and Rotterdam.

▲ SNCB CityRail EMU 968 is seen in the magnificent "cathedral" that is Antwerpen Centraal station on 5 July 2012. **Raimund Wyhnal**

PLATFORM 5 MAIL ORDER
EUROPEAN HANDBOOKS

The Platform 5 European Railway Handbooks are the most comprehensive guides to the rolling stock of selected European railway administrations available. Each book lists all locomotives and railcars of the country concerned, giving details of number carried and depot allocation, together with a wealth of technical data for each class of vehicle. Each book is A5 size, thread sewn and includes at least 32 pages of colour illustrations. The Irish book also contain details of hauled coaching stock.

EUROPEAN HANDBOOKS CURRENTLY AVAILABLE:
No.1 Benelux Railways (2012) £20.95
No.2A German Railways Part 1: (NEW EDITION IN PREPARATION)
No.2B German Railways Part 2: (NEW EDITION IN PREPARATION)
No.3 Austrian Railways (2012)....................................... £19.95
No.4 French Railways (2011) £19.95
No.5 Swiss Railways (2009)... £19.50
No.6 Italian Railways (2007) £18.50
No.7 Irish Railways (2008) £12.95
No.8 Czech & Slovak Railways (IN PREPARATION)

HOW TO ORDER
Telephone your order and credit/debit card details to our 24-hour sales hotline:
0114 255 8000 (UK) + 44 114-255-8000 (from overseas) or Fax: +44(0)114-255-2471.
An answerphone is attached for calls made outside of normal UK office hours.
Please state type of card, card number, issue no./date (maestro cards only), expiry date and full name & address of cardholder.
Or send your credit/debit card details, sterling cheque or British Postal order payable to Platform 5 Publishing Ltd. to:

Mail Order Department (EH), Platform 5 Publishing Ltd., 3 Wyvern House, Sark Road, SHEFFIELD, S2 4HG, ENGLAND
Please add postage & packing: 10% UK; 20% Europe; 30% Rest of World.

1. BELGIAN NATIONAL RAILWAYS (NMBS/SNCB)

A BRIEF HISTORY OF BELGIUM

The history of today's Belgium, Luxembourg and the Netherlands was closely intertwined until their independence, the territory occupied today by Belgium, Luxembourg, the southern Netherlands, northern France and part of Germany west of the Rhine, the area being given the name Gallia Belgica by the Romans. The Belgae were a group of tribes living in northern Gaul. From 1483 parts of the region were successively annexed to the Burgundian Netherlands, a period when Gent and Brussels became very prosperous. The area successively came under Austro-Hungary then Spain. Protestanism took a hold in the region, leading to the Eighty Years' War which ended in 1648 with the independence of the United Provinces (basically today's Netherlands, Limburg and northern Brabant being annexed later) and the Southern Netherlands, including today's Belgium and Luxembourg, which remained ruled from Spain. There ensued a period of 150 years during which first Austro-Hungary came to dominate the region, then the French revolutionary army conquered the Southern Netherlands, creating the "Batavian state". In 1810 Napoleon made both the Southern Netherlands and United Provinces part of the French empire but the defeat at Waterloo eventually brought about the creation of the United Kingdom of the Netherlands – almost equivalent to today's "Benelux". The differences between the Protestant north and Catholic south brought about a rebellion in 1830 resulting in the Kingdom of Belgium – King Leopold I was installed on 21 July 1831.

In 1815, Luxembourg was granted the status of Grand Duchy by the Dutch King, but was in fact part of the German union. In 1831, Luxembourg chose to be part of Belgium but in a series of developments gradually lost territory to its neighbours until it reached its present size. Full independence came in 1867 when the German union was dissolved.

Belgium boomed during the industrial revolution due to its coal reserves, mainly along a line from Mons through Charleroi to Liège, which are an extension of the seams running from Kent through northern France(Béthune–Lens–Douai–Valenciennes). Coal led to the smelting of steel, especially around Charleroi and Liège. Today, the mines are closed and the steel industry in decline. In contrast, the ports or Zeebrugge, Gent and, above all, Antwerpen are now the major economic power houses. The country's "linguistic divide" has become increasingly political, partly due to the decline of the economy in Wallonie and the rise of Vlaanderen.

Geographically, Belgium is a rather flat country except for the south-eastern Ardennes (south and east of a line Charleroi–Namur–Liège which is hilly rather than mountainous.

THE RAILWAYS OF BELGIUM

The first railway line in Belgium, indeed of continental Europe, opened between Brussels and Mechelen on 5 May 1835. All of the early lines, linking the main cities and centred on the capital Brussels, were built by the State, then private companies were allowed by build their own lines. For a brief period, there were three times as many private than State lines but from 1870, lines were gradually taken over by the State. The railways were finally nationalised as SNCB/NMBS in 1926. Exactly a century after the first line was built, on 5 May 1935, the Brussels–Mechelen–Antwerpen line was electrified. The 3000 V DC system was chosen and remains to this day, although new high speed lines are wired at 25 kV AC as is the Athus-Meuse line and Line 42 from Rivage to Luxembourg, while the Namur–Luxembourg line is being converted to 25 kV. In 1952, a crucial development occurred when a six track link, mainly in tunnel, was opened in Brussels between the northern and southern termini. This is now very congested and extra tracks may be built in future. Many passenger train services in Belgium are now linked via Brussels. In the 1990s and 2000s, Belgium was linked to France, the Netherlands and Germany by high speed lines. Belgium now considers its high speed network complete.

In the period since the fifth edition of this book, Belgian Railways have once again been reorganised. The freight arm B-Cargo was completely separated and renamed SNCB Logistics with the aim of curing the subsidiary's chronic deficit. This seems not to have worked. A subsidiary known as On Site Rail France (OSR France) has been created in order to operate freight trains in France. The initial aim was to "save" wagonload traffic in northern France affected by French Railways cuts in services, but OSR is now expanding both geographically and in types of freight. Some locomotives have been transferred to OSR France while others have moved to Inter Ferry Boats (IFB), another freight subsidiary. Those locomotives not in the freight sector are allocated to "SNCB Technics".

Because of the language situation, Belgian National Railways use their logo rather than initials as these differ according to the language used! In Dutch the railway company is NMBS (Nationale Maatschappij der Belgische Spoorwegen) whilst in French it is SNCB (Société Nationale des Chemins de Fer Belges). For this reason Belgian Railways uses a 'B' in a circle as its logo. For reasons of simplicity rather than linguistic preference, we use SNCB throughout this book.

Belgian railways are going through a sustained period of modernisation. Following opening of high speed lines and major upgrades to Brussels–Leuven and lines serving Brussels airport, an RER network is being built to serve Brussels. Modernisation of passenger trains continues apace with 305 new EMUs ordered and refurbishment of EMUs continuing.

For freight, the arrival of open access operators is also transforming the scene. One wonders how long SNCB Logistics will remain as a national operator.

Data in the Belgian section of this book is updated to 23 September 2012.

PLACE NAMES

Listed below are some of the Belgian towns and cities with their alternative rendering. Lille in France is included since Dutch speaking Belgians refer to it as Rijsel, which can be very confusing! NL. Dutch, F. French.

Local Name	Alternative	Local Name	Alternative
Aalst	Alost (F)	Kortrijk	Courtrai (F)
Arlon	Aarlen (NL)	Leuven	Louvain (F)
Antwerpen	Anvers (F)	Lille	Rijsel (NL)
Ath	Aat (NL)	Liège	Luik (NL)
Brugge	Bruges (F)	Mechelen	Malines (F)
Dendermonde	Termonde (F)	Mons	Bergen (NL)
Gent	Gand (F)	Namur	Namen (NL)
Geraardsbergen	Grammont (F)	Oudenaarde	Audenarde (F)
Ieper	Ypres (F)	Tournai	Doornik (NL)

PASSENGER TRAIN SERVICES

Belgian Railways are mostly electrified with regular interval services over most routes. The principal express services are Intercity (IC) and Inter Regio (IR) which call at principal centres. Local trains (L) serve the other routes and stations. Other types of trains are:

CR	CityRail – Brussels suburban services
EC	EuroCity – high quality international train
Fyra	Dutch high speed train with special fares.
ICE	Inter City Express – German high speed train with special fares
INT	International train
P	Peak hour
ICT	Tourist train
TGV	*Train à Grande Vitesse* – French high speed train with special fares
Thalys	High speed TGV with special fares

INTER CITY SERVICES (IC)

The network has route letters in upper case. Details of the routes and usual traction:

A	Oostende–Gent–Brussels–Liège–Eupen	Class 18 and I11 push-pull stock
B	Brussels–Antwerpen–Amsterdam	Class 28 and HSA Prio stock
C	Oostende–Brugge–Kortrijk–Lille	AM96 dual-voltage
	Antwerpen–Gent–Kortrijk–Lille	AM96 dual-voltage
D	Herstal–Liège–Charleroi–Mons–Tournai–Lille	AM96 dual-voltage
E	Knokke/Blankenberge–Brussels–Hasselt–Tongeren	Class 19 and M6 push-pull stock
F	Quiévrain–Mons–Brussels–Leuven–Liège	Class 21/27 & M4 or M6 push-pull stock and AM80
G	Antwerpen–Gent–Brugge–Oostende	AM96
H	Schaarbeek–Brussels–Tournai–Mouscron	Class 21 and M4 push-pull stock
I	Antwerpen–Brussels–Nivelles–Charleroi	Class 18 and M6 push-pull stock
J	Brussels–Namur–Arlon–Luxembourg	AM96, some Class 13 and M6 stock
K	Genk–Landen–Brussels–Aalst–Gent	Class 27 and M6 stock
L	Poperinge–Denderleeuw–Brussels–St. Niklaas	AM80
M	Brussels–Ottignies–Namur–Dinant/Liège–Liers	AM80
N	Essen–Antwerpen–Brussels–Nivelles–Charleroi	Class 18 and M6 push-pull stock
O	Brussels–Liège–Visé	Class 18 and I11 push-pull stock
P	Antwerpen–St Niklaas–Gent	AM96
Q	Antwerpen–Mechelen–Leuven	AM80
R	Brussels–Mechelen–Turnhout	AM80

INTER REGIO SERVICES (IR)

This network has route letters in lower case. Details of routes and usual traction :

a	St Niklaas–Mechelen–Leuven	AM86
b	Antwerpen–Brussels–Nivelles	AM75 and AM96
c	Antwerpen–Hasselt–Liège	AM80
d	Antwerpen–Brussels–Ath–Geraardsbergen	AM80
e	Antwerpen–Mol–Neerpelt/Hasselt	Class 41 DMUs
f	Leuven–Mechelen–Gent–Kortrijk	Class 21 and M4 push-pull stock
g	Antwerpen–Turnhout	AM80
h	Gent–Aalst–Brussels–Brussels Airport	AM96 and AM80
i	De Panne–Gent–Brussels–Brussels Airport–Landen	AM96
j	Quévy–Mons–Brussels–Brussels Airport	AM96 and AM80
k	Tournai–Mons–Charleroi–Namur–Jambes	AM75
l	Binche–La Louvière–Brussels–Louvain La Neuve	AM75
m	Liers–Liège–Gouvy–Luxembourg	CFL 3000 and I10 stock
n	Brussels–Antwerpen	Class 21 and M5 push-pull stock
o	Leuven–Brussels Airport–Brussels	AM66
q	Liège–Welkenraedt–Aachen Hbf	AM62
r	Charleroi–Couvin	Class 41 DMUs
s	Antwerpen–Noorderkempen	AM08

LOCAL SERVICES

These are mainly two-car EMUs but some lines are served by Class 41 DMUs. Routes worked by DMUs are Antwerpen–Mol–Neerpelt/Hasselt; Gent to Eeklo, Ronse and Geraardsbergen; Charleroi–Couvin; Dinant–Bertrix–Libramont and Bertrix–Virton–Rodange–Arlon.

PEAK SERVICES

In the Brussels area there are many peak hour extras. These bring a lot of variety into the scene with all sorts of locos and stock appearing such as Class 11 as well as Classes 21 and 27 on double-deck sets. Further examination of the timetable will show that "P" trains cover some rare curves and routes!

TOURIST SERVICES

These operate in the summer months to coastal resorts as well as places in the Ardennes. These are indicated in timetables by a sun symbol.

NUMBERING SYSTEM

The SNCB list is quite straightforward although new multi-voltage Classes 28 and 29 do not conform to the system! The present scheme dates from 01/01/71 and is as follows:

0001–0999	Electric multiple units. (Leading '0' not carried).
1001–1999	Electric locomotives. Multi-voltage.
2001–2999	Electric locomotives. 3000 V DC only.
3001–3999	Now used for Eurostar sets.
4001–4999	Diesel railcars (43xx series is also used for Thalys PBKA and 48xx for Fyra high speed sets)
5001–5999	Diesel locomotives. High power.
6001–6999	Diesel locomotives. Medium power.
7001–7999	Diesel shunting locomotives. Heavy duty.
8001–8999	Diesel shunting locomotives. Medium power.
9001–9999	Diesel shunting locomotives. Low power.

With the number of EMUs increasing constantly, the first number series was found to be too restrictive, so the new AM08 units have five figure numbers starting 08.

Many trains now also carry 12-figure European Vehicle Numbers (EVNs) which are a long-hand version of the short number. An explanation of EVNs can be found at the end of this book.

WORKSHOPS

SNCB has two workshops for the general overhaul of locomotives and multiple units. However, most of the main depots can undertake quite heavy repairs. The main works, with codes, are:

FAZ	Salzinnes (near Namur): All locomotives and DMUs.
FM	Mechelen: All EMUs and most coaching stock.

DEPOTS

The SNCB has used codes for depots for many years dating back to the days of the telegraphic system. These codes are still in use today as official abbreviations. However on locomotives the allocation is normally stencilled on in full on the main frame somewhere below the cab. EMUs and diesel railcars do not normally carry their allocations but sometimes the code will be found on them against repair data etc. (S) after the allocation denotes the vehicle is stored.

Depot codes will be found on Page 172.

STABLING POINTS

Apart from the depots shown above, trains are stabled at many points on the Belgian network. The list is far from complete and does not include every station where the odd EMU may be stabled.

Aalst, Aarschot, Antwerpen Schijnpoort, Arlon, Ath, Brugge, Brussels Midi/Zuid station, Châtelet, Denderleeuw, Dendermonde, De Panne, Gent St Pieters, Gent Zeehaven, Geraardsbergen, Huy, Jemelle, Kortrijk, Liège Guillemins, Liers, Mol, Mons, Namur, Ottignies, Oudenaarde, Ronet, St Ghislain, Tournai, Turnhout, Welkenraedt.

LIVERIES

Electric Locomotives: The standard electric locomotive livery was blue with a yellow band. Class 11 are painted in the Benelux livery, as the upper half of the body is painted Bordeaux red, the former SNCB InterCity colour, whilst the lower part is painted yellow, the NS colour. Classes 13, 18 and 19 are in the new Inter City livery of white to match the rolling stock. Classes 28 and 29 are in Alpha Trains' silver grey and green livery

Diesel Locomotives: The main-line diesel locomotive fleet are in yellow with a green band. Exceptions are Class 55 once fitted with electric train heating which are blue with a yellow band.

Diesel Railcars: Class 41 units all carry a white livery.

Electric Multiple Units: Old EMUs and were originally painted plain green. The "Break" and AM86/89 "Snorkel" EMUs were introduced in Bordeaux red, and all remaining old EMUs were repainted in that colour, including Type AM75/76/77 units which were originally grey and orange. "Break" units were then repainted in the silver/red/blue "Memling" livery. AM96 EMUs were delivered in a new standard livery of pale grey with blue bodyside stripes and red doors. EMUs are being refurbished and painted in this new livery.

ACTIVITY CODES

The Belgian Railways locomotive fleet has been divided between passenger, freight and infrastructure activities. Codes used in this book are as follows:

C	SNCB Logistics (freight operator)
F	Inter Ferry Boats (IFB, intermodal freight subsidiary)
I	Infrabel (infrastructure manager)
O	OSR France (SNCB freight operator with activities in France)
T	SNCB Technics (operating department)

▲ SNCB Type AM80 "Break" EMU 308 was one of just a few which had been refurbished and re-liveried in 2012. The unit is seen with sister unit 305, in the old livery, on 3 April 2012, with IR c train 2926 from Liège to Antwerpen near Testelt. **Carlo Hertogs**

1.1. ELECTRIC MULTIPLE UNITS

Belgian EMUs operate in fixed formations and therefore only unit numbers are quoted. All classes of EMU may work in multiple with one another except for Types AM08, AM80/82/83, AM86 and Type AM96, which may work with other members of the same type only. "Type" refers to the year in which the batch of units were ordered. All units have electro-pneumatic braking and disc brakes. All EMUs (and domestic hauled stock) were in a maroon livery lined in white until the 1990s when a much more pleasant white livery highlighted in red and blue was adopted.

TYPE AM08   3-CAR UNITS

305 of these EMUs have been ordered from Siemens which builds them at Krefeld in Germany. 08001 to 08210 will be 3000 V DC only and will work in the whole of Belgium, replacing the old 2-car sets from Type AM62 onwards, and increasing capacity on stopping services. These will be assembled at Bombardier, Brugge. 95 of these will be for the future Brussels RER network, but as yet we know of no difference between these and the other units. 08501 to 08595 will be equipped for both 3000 V DC and 25 kV AC but will otherwise be identical to the first batch. 25 kV AC capability will allow them to operate on the Athus-Meuse route plus into France and Luxembourg, if equipped. Like Class 18, tests of the first sets went on longer than expected but deliveries started to accelerate in mid-2012. A few units started to appear on commercial services at this time but none were regular. Once they enter squadron service, the old 2-car sets should rapidly disappear – at last.

Built: 2011–
Builder: Siemens/Bombardier.
Power rating: 2200 kW.
Wheel Arrangement: Bo-Bo + 2-2 + Bo-Bo.
Accommodation: 16/52 1TD + –/104 + 16/76.
Weight:
Length over couplers: 26.86 + 27.55 + 26.86 m.
Maximum Speed: 160 km/h.

3000 V DC sets:

08001	N	GCR	08029	N		08057	N		08085	N
08002	N	GCR	08030	N		08058	N		08086	N
08003	N	GCR	08031	N		08059	N		08087	N
08004	N	GCR	08032	N		08060	N		08088	N
08005	N	GCR	08033	N		08061	N		08089	N
08006	N	GCR	08034	N		08062	N		08090	N
08007	N	GCR	08035	N		08063	N		08091	N
08008	N	GCR	08036	N		08064	N		08092	N
08009	N	GCR	08037	N		08065	N		08093	N
08010	N	GCR	08038	N		08066	N		08094	N
08011	N	GCR	08039	N		08067	N		08095	N
08012	N	GCR	08040	N		08068	N		08096	N
08013	N	GCR	08041	N		08069	N		08097	N
08014	N	GCR	08042	N		08070	N		08098	N
08015	N		08043	N		08071	N		08099	N
08016	N	GCR	08044	N		08072	N		08100	N
08017	N	GCR	08045	N		08073	N		08101	N
08018	N	GCR	08046	N		08074	N		08102	N
08019	N	GCR	08047	N		08075	N		08103	N
08020	N	GCR	08048	N		08076	N		08104	N
08021	N	GCR	08049	N		08077	N		08105	N
08022	N	GCR	08050	N		08078	N		08106	N
08023	N	GCR	08051	N		08079	N		08107	N
08024	N	GCR	08052	N		08080	N		08108	N
08025	N	GCR	08053	N		08081	N		08109	N
08026	N	GCR	08054	N		08082	N		08110	N
08027	N	GCR	08055	N		08083	N		08111	N
08028	N	GCR	08056	N		08084	N		08112	N

08113	N	08138	N	08163	N	08187	N
08114	N	08139	N	08164	N	08188	N
08115	N	08140	N	08165	N	08189	N
08116	N	08141	N	08166	N	08190	N
08117	N	08142	N	08167	N	08191	N
08118	N	08143	N	08168	N	08192	N
08119	N	08144	N	08169	N	08193	N
08120	N	08145	N	08170	N	08194	N
08121	N	08146	N	08171	N	08195	N
08122	N	08147	N	08172	N	08196	N
08123	N	08148	N	08173	N	08197	N
08124	N	08149	N	08174	N	08198	N
08125	N	08150	N	08175	N	08199	N
08126	N	08151	N	08176	N	08200	N
08127	N	08152	N	08177	N	08201	N
08128	N	08153	N	08178	N	08202	N
08129	N	08154	N	08179	N	08203	N
08130	N	08155	N	08180	N	08204	N
08131	N	08156	N	08181	N	08205	N
08132	N	08157	N	08182	N	08206	N
08133	N	08158	N	08183	N	08207	N
08134	N	08159	N	08184	N	08208	N
08135	N	08160	N	08185	N	08209	N
08136	N	08161	N	08186	N	08210	N
08137	N	08162	N				

▲ One of the early uses for AM 08 EMUs was on the shuttle over the high speed line between Antwerpen and Noorderkempen, thus replacing the weird and expensive combination of a Class 1300 loco plus two M6 driving trailers. 08519, taking advantage of its dual-voltage capabilities and ETCS signalling is seen on the HSL at Brecht on 4 October 2012. **Carlo Hertogs**

Dual-voltage sets:

08501	N	MKM	08525	N		08549	N		08573	N
08502	N		08526	N		08550	N		08574	N
08503	N		08527	N		08551	N		08575	N
08504	N	MKM	08528	N		08552	N		08576	N
08505	N	MKM	08529	N		08553	N		08577	N
08506	N	MKM	08530	N		08554	N		08578	N
08507	N	MKM	08531	N		08555	N		08579	N
08508	N	MKM	08532	N		08556	N		08580	N
08509	N	MKM	08533	N		08557	N		08581	N
08510	N		08534	N		08558	N		08582	N
08511	N	MKM	08535	N		08559	N		08583	N
08512	N	MKM	08536	N		08560	N		08584	N
08513	N	MKM	08537	N		08561	N		08585	N
08514	N	MKM	08538	N		08562	N		08586	N
08515	N	MKM	08539	N		08563	N		08587	N
08516	N	MKM	08540	N		08564	N		08588	N
08517	N	MKM	08541	N		08565	N		08589	N
08518	N	MKM	08542	N		08566	N		08590	N
08519	N	MKM	08543	N		08567	N		08591	N
08520	N	MKM	08544	N		08568	N		08592	N
08521	N	MKM	08545	N		08569	N		08593	N
08522	N	MKM	08546	N		08570	N		08594	N
08523	N		08547	N		08571	N		08595	N
08524	N		08548	N		08572	N			

▲ The new AM08 EMUs will be directly, or by cascade, replacing out-of-date AM62–65 EMUs such as 204, in the old maroon livery, seen at Rixensart on the Brussels–Ottignies line on 14 May 2012.
Thierry Nicolas

TYPE AM62/63/65   2-CAR UNITS

These units are in general use on local stopping services throughout Belgium. They are now being withdrawn. All can operate to Maastricht and Aachen. This type will be withdrawn quickly as Type AM08 are delivered.

Built: 1962–65. 153–210 are Type AM62, 212–250 are AM63 and 252–270 are AM65.
Builder–Mechanical Parts: BN, Ragheno, BLC, ABR, Germain, CWFM.
Builder–Electrical Parts: ACEC.
Traction Motors: 4 x 155 kW.   **Weight:** 50 + 52 tonnes.
Wheel Arrangement: A1-1A + A1-1A.   **Length over Couplers:** 23.71 + 23.59 m.
Accommodation: –/104 1T + 28/48 1T.   **Maximum Speed:** 130 km/h.
EVN: 9488 062 **1531**-c + 9488 062 **1532**-c and so on.

Originally numbered 228.153–270.

153	MKM	185	FSD	216	FSD	241	NK
154	MKM	186	FSD	217	FSD	243	MKM
155	MKM	187	FSD	220	FSD	244	MKM
156	MKM	188	FSD	221	FSD	246	MKM
157	MKM	189	FSD	222	FSD	247	MKM
159	NK	191	FSD	223	FSD	248	MKM
160	NK	193	FSD	224	FSD	250	NK
161	NK	195	FSD	225	FSD	252	NK
163	NK	196	FSD	226	FSD	253	NK
164	NK	197	FSD	227	FSD	255	NK
166	NK	198	FSD	228	FSD	256	NK
174	MKM	201	FSD	229	FSD	257	NK
175	MKM	202	FSD	230	FSD	258	NK
176	MKM	203	FSD	231	FSD	259	NK
177	MKM	204	FSD	232	FSD	260	NK
178	MKM	206	FSD	233	FSD	261	NK
179	FSD	207	FSD	234	FSD	265	NK
180	FSD	209	FSD	235	FSD	267	NK
181	FSD	210	FSD	236	FSD	268	NK
182	FSD	212	FSD	237	FSD	269	NK
183	FSD	213	FSD	238	FSD	270	NK
184	FSD	215	FSD	240	NK		

TYPE AM80/82/83   "BREAK"   3-CAR UNITS

These units, known as "Break" sets, are the EMU version of Type M4 coaches and are thyristor controlled. Built as two-car sets they have all been made up to three-car by the insertion of a trailer with 2+2 second class seating. At the same time units were repainted into a new silver livery. The trailer numbers are out of sequence as the new trailers were built in number order but inserted into any set that just happened to be in works at the time. (e.g. set 428 is formed 4281, 3752, 4283). The units are used mostly on IR services. Some sets have been sold to US companies and leased back. Units are being refurbished. 321 was withdrawn after a accident in 2006. All units can operate to Maastricht.

Built: 1980–85. 301–335 are Type AM80, 336–370 are AM82 and 371–440 are AM83.
Builder–Mechanical Parts: BN.   **Traction Motors:** 4 x 310 kW.
Builder–Electrical Parts: ACEC.   **Wheel Arrangement:** Bo-Bo + 2-2 + 2-2.
Weight: 61 + 43 + 47 tonnes.   **Maximum Speed:** 160 km/h.
Accommodation: –/99 1T + –/83 1T + 32/40 1T. **N** = centre car –/61 (17) 1T.
Length over Couplers: 25.425 + 24.96 + 25.425 m.

Regenerative braking.

b   Brecknell-Willis pantograph.

No.			No.			No.			No.		
301	M	NK	337	M	NK	372	M	FHS	407	M	FHS
302	M	NK	338	M	NK	373	M	FHS	408	M b	FHS
303	M	NK	339	M	NK	374	M	FHS	409	M	FHS
304	M	NK	340	M	NK	375	M	FHS	410	M	FHS
305	M	NK	341	M	NK	376	M	FHS	411	M	FHS
306	M	NK	342	M	NK	377	M	FHS	412	M	FHS
307	M	NK	343	M	NK	378	N	FHS	413	M	FHS
308	N	NK	344	M	NK	379	M	FHS	414	M	FKR
309	N	NK	345	M	NK	380	N	FHS	415	M b	FKR
310	M	NK	346	M	NK	381	M	FHS	416	M	FKR
311	N	NK	347	M	NK	382	M	FHS	417	M	FKR
312	M	NK	348	M	NK	383	N	FHS	418	M	FKR
313	N	NK	349	M	NK	384	M	FHS	419	M	FKR
314	M	NK	350	M	NK	385	M	FHS	420	M b	FKR
315	N	NK	351	M	NK	386	M	FHS	421	M b	FKR
316	N	NK	352	M	NK	387	M	FHS	422	M	FKR
317	N	NK	353	M	NK	388	M	FHS	423	M	FKR
318	M	NK	354	M	NK	389	M	FHS	424	M b	FKR
319	M	NK	355	M	FHS	390	M	FHS	425	M b	FKR
320	M	NK	356	M	FHS	391	N	FHS	426	M	FKR
322	M	NK	357	M	FHS	392	M	FHS	427	M	FKR
323	M	NK	358	M	FHS	393	M	FHS	428	M	FKR
324	N	NK	359	M	FHS	394	M	FHS	429	M	FKR
325	M	NK	360	M	FHS	395	M	FHS	430	M b	FKR
326	M	NK	361	M	FHS	396	M	FHS	431	M	FKR
327	M	NK	362	M	FHS	397	M	FHS	432	M	FKR
328	M	NK	363	M	FHS	398	M	FHS	433	M	FKR
329	M	NK	364	M	FHS	399	M	FHS	434	M	FKR
330	M	NK	365	M	FHS	400	M	FHS	435	M	FKR
331	M	NK	366	M	FHS	401	M	FHS	436	M	FKR
332	M	NK	367	M	FHS	402	M	FHS	437	M	FKR
333	M	NK	368	M	FHS	403	M	FHS	438	M	FKR
334	M	NK	369	M	FHS	404	M	FHS	439	M b	FKR
335	M	NK	370	M	FHS	405	M	FHS	440	M	FKR
336	M	NK	371	M	FHS	406	M	FHS			

TYPE AM96 — 3-CAR UNITS

These sets brought new standards of comfort to Belgian main line services and are the same design as Type I11 carriages. Front end design is based on the successful "rubber nose" of Danish IC3 DMUs. There are two versions with the dual-voltage sets equipped for services into France (Antwerpen–Lille, Oostende–Lille and Herstal–Liège–Lille). 434 was withdrawn after an accident at Mons in 2010.

Built: 1996–99.
Systems: 441–490 3000 V DC, 25 kV AC 50 Hz; 501–570 3000 V DC only.
Builder–Mechanical Parts: Bombardier.
Builder–Electrical Parts: Alstom.
Traction Motors: Four 4EXA3046 asynchronous of 350 kW.
Length over Couplers: 26.40 + 26.40 + 26.40 m.
Wheel Arrangement: Bo-Bo + 2-2 + 2-2. **Weight:** 60 + 50 + 50 tonnes.
Accommodation: –/79 1TD + –/88 1T + 45/– 1T. **Maximum Speed:** 160 km/h.
EVN: 94 88 096 **441** 1-c + 94 88 096 **441** 2-c + 94 88 096 **441** 3-c and so on.

I   Equipped to operate to Luxembourg.

Dual-voltage sets:

No.			No.			No.			No.		
441	N	FSD	446	N	FSD	451	N	FSD	457	N	FSD
442	N	FSD	447	N	FSD	452	N	FSD	458	N	FSD
443	N	FSD	448	N	FSD	453	N	FSD	459	N	FSD
444	N	FSD	449	N	FSD	455	N	FSD	460	N	FSD
445	N	FSD	450	N	FSD	456	N	FSD	461	N	FSD

462	N	FSD	470	N	FSD	477	N	FSD	484	N	FSD
463	N	FSD	471	N	FSD	478	N	FSD	485	N	FSD
464	N	FSD	472	N	FSD	479	N	FSD	486	N	FSD
465	N	FSD	473	N	FSD	480	N	FSD	487	N	FSD
466	N	FSD	474	N	FSD	481	N	FSD	488	N	FSD
467	N	FSD	475	N	FSD	482	N	FSD	489	N	FSD
468	N	FSD	476	N	FSD	483	N	FSD	490	N	FSD
469	N	FSD									

3000 V DC sets:

501	N	I	MKM	519	N	I	MKM	537	N	FHS	554	N	FHS
502	N	I	MKM	520	N	I	MKM	538	N	FHS	555	N	FHS
503	N	I	MKM	521	N	I	MKM	539	N	FHS	556	N	FHS
504	N	I	MKM	522	N	I	MKM	540	N	FHS	557	N	FHS
505	N	I	MKM	523	N	I	MKM	541	N	FHS	558	N	FHS
506	N	I	MKM	524	N	I	MKM	542	N	FHS	559	N	FHS
507	N	I	MKM	525	N	FHS		543	N	FHS	560	N	FHS
508	N	I	MKM	526	N	FHS		544	N	FHS	561	N	FHS
509	N	I	MKM	527	N	FHS		545	N	FHS	562	N	FHS
510	N	I	MKM	528	N	FHS		546	N	FHS	563	N	FHS
511	N	I	MKM	529	N	FHS		547	N	FHS	564	N	FHS
512	N	I	MKM	530	N	FHS		548	N	FHS	565	N	FHS
513	N	I	MKM	531	N	FHS		549	N	FHS	566	N	FHS
514	N	I	MKM	532	N	FHS		550	N	FHS	567	N	FHS
515	N	I	MKM	533	N	FHS		551	N	FHS	568	N	FHS
516	N	I	MKM	534	N	FHS		552	N	FHS	569	N	FHS
517	N	I	MKM	535	N	FHS		553	N	FHS	570	N	FHS
518	N	I	MKM	536	N	FHS							

▲ AM96 set 541 heads a train leaving Brussels Midi on 2 July 2007, with 2727 stabled and a Thalys PBKA set in the background. **David Haydock**

TYPE AM70LH   2-CAR UNITS

These units were built for use on the Brussels Airport service when this was just a shuttle. Since the construction of a new station at the airport, services from the south of Brussels now run through to the airport and Type AM70LH units have been put into the general pool of suburban units. All units can operate to Maastricht.

Built: 1970–71.
Builder–Mechanical Parts: Ragheno.
Builder–Electrical Parts: ACEC.
Traction Motors: 4 x 170 kW.
Wheel Arrangement: A1-1A + A1-1A.

Accommodation: –/74 1T + 32/12 1T.
Weight: 52 + 52 tonnes.
Length over Couplers: 23.71 + 23.59 m.
Maximum Speed: 140 km/h.

595	NK	597	NK	599	NK	600	NK
596	NK	598	NK				

TYPE AM66/70JH   2-CAR UNITS

Used on some IR routes but mostly for local and peak services. Refurbished units were allocated to Brussels CityRail services before a more specific refurbishment was carried out on Types AM70TH and AM73. All the 601–664 batch are now refurbished.

Built: 1966/70–71. 601–640 are Type AM66 and 642–664 are AM70JH.
Builder–Mechanical Parts: BN, Ragheno, BLC, ABR.
Builder–Electrical Parts: ACEC.
Traction Motors: 4 x 170 kW.
Wheel Arrangement: A1-1A + A1-1A.
Accommodation: –/102 1T + 20/58 1T.

Weight: 56 + 52 tonnes.
Length over Couplers: 23.71 + 23.59 m.
Maximum Speed: 140 km/h.

Originally numbered 228.601–664.

601	N	FKR	617	N	FKR	633	N	FKR	649	N	FKR
602	N	FKR	618	N	FKR	634	N	FKR	650	N	FKR
603	N	FKR	619	N	FKR	635	N	NK	651	N	FKR
604	N	FKR	620	N	FKR	636	N	NK	652	N	FSR
605	N	FKR	621	N	FKR	637	N	NK	653	N	FSR
606	N	FKR	622	N	FKR	638	N	NK	654	N	FSR
607	N	FKR	623	N	FKR	639	N	NK	655	N	FSR
608	N	FKR	624	N	FKR	640	N	NK	657	N	FSR
609	N	FKR	625	N	FKR	642	N	FKR	658	N	FSR
610	N	FKR	626	N	FKR	643	N	FKR	659	N	FSR
611	N	FKR	627	N	FKR	644	N	FKR	660	N	FSR
612	N	FKR	628	N	FKR	645	N	FKR	661	N	NK
613	N	FKR	629	N	FKR	646	N	FKR	662	N	NK
614	N	FKR	630	N	FKR	647	N	FKR	663	N	NK
615	N	FKR	631	N	FKR	648	N	FKR	664	N	NK
616	N	FKR	632	N	FKR						

TYPE AM70TH   2-CAR UNITS

The "TH" denotes thyristor control, the first Belgian units so fitted. Timken roller bearings. Use as for AM66/70JH. All units have been refurbished and all except 672 were renumbered 960–970 for CityRail services.

Built: 1971–72.
Builder–Mechanical Parts: CWFM.
Builder–Electrical Parts: ACEC.
Traction Motors: 4 x 170 kW.
Wheel Arrangement: A1-1A + A1-1A.

Accommodation: –/104 1T + 28/48 1T.
Weight: 56 + 53 tonnes.
Length over Couplers: 23.71 + 23.59 m.
Maximum Speed: 140 km/h.

672	N	GCR

TYPE AM73/74/78/79 — 2-CAR UNITS

These are the production series of thyristor-controlled units. All units have been refurbished. 677–683 and 707–730 (excluding 709) received a more significant upgrade and a revised CityRail livery. They were renumbered 971–999 in order as they went through works. Withdrawn 716 donated one car to set 709. 766–771 can operate to Maastricht.

Built: 1972–80. 684–706 are Type AM73, 709 AM74, 731–756 AM78 and 757–782 AM79.
Builder–Mechanical Parts: BN (707–730 CFCF). **Accommodation:** –/102 1T + 28/48 1T.
Builder–Electrical Parts: ACEC. **Weight:** 56 + 52 tonnes.
Traction Motors: 4 x 170 kW. **Length over Couplers:** 23.71 + 23.59 m.
Wheel Arrangement: A1-1A + A1-1A. **Maximum Speed:** 140 km/h.

684	N	GCR	703	N	GCR	745	N	GCR	764	N	GCR
685	N	GCR	704	N	GCR	746	N	GCR	765	N	FSR
686	N	GCR	705	N	GCR	747	N	GCR	766	N	FSR
687	N	GCR	706	N	GCR	748	N	GCR	767	N	FSR
688	N	GCR	709	N	GCR	749	N	GCR	768	N	FSR
689	N	GCR	731	N	GCR	750	N	GCR	769	N	FSR
690	N	GCR	732	N	GCR	751	N	GCR	770	N	FSR
691	N	GCR	733	N	GCR	752	N	GCR	771	N	FSR
692	N	GCR	734	N	GCR	753	N	GCR	772	N	FSR
693	N	GCR	735	N	GCR	754	N	GCR	773	N	FSR
694	N	GCR	736	N	GCR	755	N	GCR	774	N	FSR
695	N	GCR	737	N	GCR	756	N	GCR	775	N	FSR
696	N	GCR	738	N	GCR	757	N	GCR	776	N	FSR
697	N	GCR	739	N	GCR	758	N	GCR	777	N	FSR
698	N	GCR	740	N	GCR	759	N	GCR	778	N	FSR
699	N	GCR	741	N	GCR	760	N	GCR	779	N	FSR
700	N	GCR	742	N	GCR	761	N	GCR	780	N	FSR
701	N	GCR	743	N	GCR	762	N	GCR	781	N	FSR
702	N	GCR	744	N	GCR	763	N	GCR	782	N	FSR

▲ Local train 5579 from Jemelle to Herstal is seen on 19 August 2012 formed of AM70 EMU 654 and AM62 183 just after leaving Jemelle.
Carlo Hertogs

TYPE AM75/76/77 4-CAR UNITS

These thyristor-controlled units are gangwayed within the sets only. Pantographs are fitted to only one of the motor coaches. Pressure ventilation. Used on IR and local services. These units are to be refurbished from 2013.

Built: 1975–79. Units 801–820 are Type AM75, 821–832 are AM76 and 833–844 are AM77.
Builder–Mechanical Parts: BN.
Builder–Electrical Parts: ACEC. **Traction Motors:** 8 x 170 kW.
Weight: 51 + 60 + 60 + 49 tonnes. **Maximum Speed:** 140 km/h.
Wheel Arrangement: 2-2 + Bo-Bo + Bo-Bo + 2-2.
Accommodation: 56/– 1T + –/100 1T + –/106 1T + –/96 1T.
Length over Couplers: 25.11 + 24.40 + 24.40 + 25.11 m.

Disc and tread brakes.

* Can operate to Maastricht.

801		GCR	812		GCR	823	*	GCR	834		GCR
802		GCR	813		GCR	824	*	GCR	835	*	GCR
803		GCR	814		GCR	825		GCR	836		GCR
804		GCR	815		GCR	826		GCR	837		GCR
805		GCR	816		GCR	827		GCR	838	*	GCR
806		GCR	817		GCR	828		GCR	839	*	GCR
807		GCR	818		GCR	829		GCR	840	*	GCR
808		GCR	819		GCR	830		GCR	841	*	GCR
809		GCR	820		GCR	831		GCR	842	*	GCR
810		GCR	821		GCR	832	*	GCR	843	*	GCR
811		GCR	822		GCR	833		GCR	844	*	GCR

▲ SNCB AM76 EMU 830 is seen arriving at Antwerpen Noorderdokken on 18 September 2009 with a local Roosendaal (NL)–Antwerpen Centraal stopping service. **Max Delie**

TYPE AM86/89 2-CAR UNITS

These were the first Belgian EMUs to feature 2+2 seating in second class. Another innovation is the use of polyester sides and front nose which are glued onto the main body. They were designed for eventual one-person operation and rear-view mirrors are fitted which are flush with the side of the vehicle when not in use. They are officially known as "Sprinters", but their unusual front end appearance has led to them being nicknamed "Diving Goggles". Used on local services around Brussels, Antwerpen, Hasselt and Leuven. The first class section in the power car was downgraded to second in 2006. All units will be refurbished from 2013. 932 was withdrawn after an accident.

Built: 1988–91. Units 901–935 are Type AM86 and 936–952 are AM89.
Builder–Mechanical Parts: BN.
Builder–Electrical Parts: ACEC.
Traction Motors: 4 x 172 kW type AE121N.
Wheel Arrangement: Bo-Bo + 2-2.
Accommodation: –/88 1T + –/110.
Weight: 59 + 48 tonnes.
Length over Couplers: 26.40 + 26.40 m.
Maximum Speed: 120 km/h.

901	FSR	914	FSR	927	FSR	941	FSR
902	FSR	915	FSR	928	FSR	942	FSR
903	FSR	916	FSR	929	FSR	943	FSR
904	FSR	917 N	FSR	930	FSR	944	FSR
905	FSR	918	FSR	931	FSR	945	FSR
906	FSR	919	FSR	933	FSR	946	FSR
907	FSR	920	FSR	934	FSR	947	FSR
908	FSR	921	FSR	935	FSR	948	FSR
909	FSR	922	FSR	936	FSR	949	FSR
910	FSR	923	FSR	937	FSR	950	FSR
911	FSR	924	FSR	938	FSR	951	FSR
912	FSR	925	FSR	939	FSR	952	FSR
913	FSR	926	FSR	940	FSR		

▲ SNCB AM86 "Goggles" 2-car EMUs 912 and 905 stand at Etterbeek station on 23 March 2006.
David Haydock

TYPE AM70CR   2-CAR CITYRAIL UNITS

Type AM70TH refurbished for CityRail services and renumbered. For details see 672.

960	(665)	C	GCR	964	(669)	C	GCR	968	(674)	C	GCR
961	(666)	C	GCR	965	(670)	C	GCR	969	(675)	C	GCR
962	(667)	C	GCR	966	(671)	C	GCR	970	(676)	C	GCR
963	(668)	C	GCR	967	(673)	C	GCR				

TYPE AM73/74   2-CAR CITYRAIL UNITS

AM73/74 refurbished for CityRail services and renumbered. For details see 684–709. Units 971–977 are Type AM73 and 978–999 are AM74.

971	(677)	C	GCR	981	(711)	C	GCR	991	(722)	C	GCR
972	(678)	C	GCR	982	(712)	C	GCR	992	(723)	C	GCR
973	(679)	C	GCR	983	(713)	C	GCR	993	(724)	C	GCR
974	(680)	C	GCR	984	(714)	C	GCR	994	(725)	C	GCR
975	(681)	C	GCR	985	(715)	C	GCR	995	(726)	C	GCR
976	(682)	C	GCR	986	(717)	C	GCR	996	(727)	C	GCR
977	(683)	C	GCR	987	(718)	C	GCR	997	(728)	C	GCR
978	(707)	C	GCR	988	(719)	C	GCR	998	(729)	C	GCR
979	(708)	C	GCR	989	(720)	C	GCR	999	(730)	C	GCR
980	(710)	C	GCR	990	(721)	C	GCR				

▲ SNCB CityRail AM74 EMU 978 (formerly 707) stands at St Ghislain station during a special open day rolling stock exhibition on 26 June 2010. **David Haydock**

1.2. ELECTRIC LOCOMOTIVES

All electric locomotives are in the standard blue livery with yellow stripes unless stated otherwise. The standard voltage is 3000 V DC. All electric locomotives are allocated to SNCB Technics unless shown otherwise.

CLASS 11   Bo-Bo

These dual voltage locomotives were a development of Class 21 and were built for the Brussels–Amsterdam "Benelux" service. Originally planned to be numbered 1101–1112, the higher numbers were eventually decided on to avoid conflicting with now defunct NS Class 1100. Due to their unreliability, the class was replaced on Benelux services by Class 186 in 2010/11 and now work only peak passenger services. Will probably be withdrawn in 2013.

Built: 1985–86.
Systems: 1500 V/3000 V DC.
Builder–Mechanical Parts: BN.
Builder–Electrical Parts: ACEC.
Traction Motors: 4 x LE622S frame mounted.
One Hour Rating: 3310 kW.
EVN: 1181 = 91 88 **011 081** 0-c and so on.

Maximum Tractive Effort: 234 kN.
Wheel Diameter: 1250 mm.
Weight: 85 tonnes.
Length over Buffers: 18.65 m.
Maximum Speed: 140 km/h.

Electro-pneumatic braking. Rheostatic braking.

1181	B	FKR	1184	B	FKR	1187	B	FKR	1190	B	FKR
1182	B	FKR	1185	B	FKR	1188	B	FKR	1191	B	FKR
1183	B	FKR	1186	B	FKR	1189	B	FKR	1192	B	FKR

▲ Class 11 have been downgraded from Benelux services to peak hour trains. 1187 is seen at Schaarbeek on 8 October 2010, next to 2156 on another peak service. **Thierry Nicolas**

CLASS 12 Bo-Bo

Another dual-voltage development of Class 21, these locomotives were once used on passenger services but were then downgraded to freight trains from Antwerpen, Gent and Charleroi to Lille, Somain and Aulnoye in northern France. To be withdrawn as soon as possible.

Built: 1986.
Systems: 3000 V DC, 25 kV AC 50 Hz.
Builder–Mechanical Parts: BN.
Builder–Electrical Parts: ACEC.
Traction Motors: 4 x LE622S frame mounted.
One Hour Rating: 3310 kW.
EVN: 91 88 **012 001** 0-c and so on.

Maximum Tractive Effort: 234 kN.
Wheel Diameter: 1250 mm.
Weight: 85 tonnes.
Length over Buffers: 18.65 m.
Maximum Speed: 160 km/h.

Electro-pneumatic braking. Rheostatic braking. Thyristor control.

1201	FKR	1204	FKR	1207	FKR	1210	FKR
1202	FKR	1205	FKR	1208	FKR	1211	FKR
1203	FKR	1206	FKR	1209	FKR	1212	FKR

CLASS 13 Bo-Bo

These dual-voltage locomotives were ordered together with 20 identical Class 3000 for CFL. The first ten were built in Belfort, France and the remainder at the Bombardier plant at Brugge. They are general purpose machines with a capability of 200 km/h but are now divided into two sub-fleets – 1301–1345 work only freight on the "Sibelit" Antwerpen–Luxembourg corridor, with some work to other parts of France. 1346–1360 are allocated to SNCB Technics and work some Brussels–Luxembourg services, the Antwerpen–Noorderkempen shuttle and peak services. The class is expected to lose all or most passenger services once Class 18 is approved to operate in Luxembourg. All locos can operate to Maastricht, Luxembourg and France.

Built: 1997–2000.
Systems: 3000 V DC, 25 kV AC 50 Hz.
Builder–Mechanical Parts: Bombardier.
Builder–Electrical Parts: Alstom.
Traction Motors: 4 x PXA4339B frame mounted.
One Hour Rating: 5200 kW.

Maximum Tractive Effort: 288 kN.
Wheel Diameter: 1160 mm.
Weight: 90 tonnes.
Length over Buffers: 19.11 m.
Maximum Speed: 200 km/h.

Electro-pneumatic braking. Rheostatic braking.

1301	L	FNND	1322	L	FNND	1342	L	FNND
1302	L	FNND	1323	L	FNND	1343	L	FNND
1303	L	FNND	1324	L	FNND	1344	L	FNND
1304	L	FNND	1325	L	FNND	1345	L	FNND
1305	L	FNND	1326	L	FNND (U)	1346	L	FNND
1306	L	FNND	1327	L	FNND	1347	L	FNND
1307	L	FNND	1328	L	FNND	1348	L	FNND
1308	L	FNND (U)	1329	L	FNND	1349	L	FNND
1309	L	FNND	1330	L	FNND	1350	L	FNND
1310	L	FNND	1331	L	FNND	1351	L	FNND
1311	L	FNND	1332	L	FNND	1352	L	FNND
1312	L	FNND	1333	L	FNND	1353	L	FNND
1313	L	FNND	1334	L	FNND (U)	1354	L	FNND
1314	L	FNND	1335	L	FNND	1355	L	FNND
1315	L	FNND	1336	L	FNND	1356	L	FNND
1316	L	FNND	1337	L	FNND	1357	L	FNND
1317	L	FNND	1338	L	FNND	1358	L	FNND
1319	L	FNND	1339	L	FNND	1359	L	FNND
1320	L	FNND	1340	L	FNND (U)	1360	L	FNND
1321	L	FNND	1341	L	FNND			

▲ SNCB locos 1319, 1323 and 1316, the middle one dead – a standard practice in Belgium – head a freight from Antwerpen to Bettembourg at Antwerpen-Luchtbal on 10 August 2012. **Carlo Hertogs**

▼ SNCB loco 1831 heads a train of double-deck M6 stock into Brussels Midi on 5 June 2012.
David Haydock

CLASSES 18 & 19   Bo-Bo

In late 2006, Belgian Railways ordered 60 new dual-voltage electric locomotives from Siemens, rather than four-voltage freight locos as expected. The new locos are equipped with ETCS signalling and for push-pull with Type I11 and M6 stock. They have replaced Classes 13, 21 and 27 on passenger services. A second batch of 60 locos was later ordered. The first 36 are Class 18 and the remaining 24 Class 19 with GF auto couplers for use with sets of M6 stock on the Knokke/Blankenberge–Brussels–Hasselt–Tongeren service. After many delays during testing, the class entered service in large numbers in 2011/12. They now operate most IC services and many peak services with I11 and M6 stock.

Built: 2009–12.
Systems: 3000 V DC, 25 kV AC 50 Hz.   **Maximum Tractive Effort:** 300 kN.
Builder: Siemens. Works numbers 1801–1860 21531–21592; 1861–1896 21701–21736.
Wheel Diameter: 1150 mm.
Traction Motors: 4 frame mounted.   **Weight:** 88 tonnes.
One Hour Rating: 6000 kW.   **Length over Buffers:** 19.59 m.
Continuous Rating: 5000 kW.   **Maximum Speed:** 200 km/h.
EVN: 91 88 018 001 0-c and so on.

1801	L	NK	1825	L	FSD	1849	L	FSD	1873	L	NK
1802	L	NK	1826	L	FSD	1850	L	FSD	1874	L	NK
1803	L	NK	1827	L	FSD	1851	L	FSD	1875	L	NK
1804	L	NK	1828	L	FSD	1852	L	FSD	1876	L	NK
1805	L	NK	1829	L	FSD	1853	L	FSD	1877	L	
1806	L	NK	1830	L	FSD	1854	L	FSD	1878	L	NK
1807	L	NK	1831	L	FSD	1855	L	FSD	1879	L	NK
1808	L	NK	1832	L	FSD	1856	L	FSD	1880	L	NK
1809	L	NK	1833	L	FSD	1857	L	FSD	1881	L	NK
1810	L	NK	1834	L	FSD	1858	L	FSD	1882	L	NK
1811	L	NK	1835	L	FSD	1859	L	FSD	1883	L	NK
1812	L	NK	1836	L	FSD	1860	L	FSD	1884	L	NK
1813	L	NK	1837	L	FSD	1861	L	NK	1885	L	NK
1814	L	NK	1838	L	FSD	1862	L	NK	1886	L	NK
1815	L	NK	1839	L	FSD	1863	L	NK	1887	L	NK
1816	L	NK	1840	L	FSD	1864	L	NK	1888	L	NK
1817	L	NK	1841	L	FSD	1865	L	NK	1889	L	NK
1818	L	NK	1842	L	FSD	1866	L	NK	1890	L	NK
1819	L	NK	1843	L	FSD	1867	L	NK	1891	L	NK
1820	L	NK	1844	L	FSD	1868	L	NK	1892	L	
1821	L	FSD	1845	L	FSD	1869	L	NK	1893	L	NK
1822	L	FSD	1846	L	FSD	1870	L	NK	1894	L	
1823	L	FSD	1847	L	FSD	1871	L	NK	1895	L	NK
1824	L	FSD	1848	L	FSD	1872	L	NK	1896	L	NK

Equipped with Type GF auto couplers:

1901	L		1907	L	NK	1913	L		1919	L	NK
1902	L		1908	L	NK	1914	L		1920	L	
1903	L	NK	1909	L	NK	1915	L	NK	1921	L	
1904	L	NK	1910	L		1916	L		1922	L	
1905	L	NK	1911	L		1917	L		1923	L	
1906	L		1912	L	NK	1918	L		1924	L	

CLASS 20 Co-Co

These thyristor controlled locomotives were once the most powerful in Belgium and have had a chequered career with various defects over the years. Their main use was on the Brussels–Luxembourg artery but they have now been downgraded to freight and will be withdrawn soon.

Built: 1975–77.
Builder–Mechanical Parts: BN.
Builder–Electrical Parts: ACEC.
Traction Motors: 6 x LE772G frame mounted.
One Hour Rating: 5150 kW.
EVN: 91 88 0**20 001** 0-c and so on.

Maximum Tractive Effort: 314 kN.
Wheel Diameter: 1250 mm.
Weight: 110 tonnes.
Length over Buffers: 19.50 m.
Max. Speed: 140 km/h.

Electro-pneumatic braking. Separately excited rheostatic braking.

I   Equipped to operate into Luxembourg.

2001	I	MKM	2009	C	FNND (S)	2017	C	FNND (S)
2002	I	MKM (S)	2010	C	FNND (S)	2018	C	FNND (S)
2003	I	MKM	2011	C	FNND (S)	2019	C	FNND (S)
2004	I	MKM	2012	C	FNND	2021	C	FNND (S)
2005	I	MKM	2013	C	FNND	2022	C	FNND (S)
2006	I	MKM (S)	2014	C	FNND	2023	C	FNND
2007	I	MKM	2015	C	FNND (S)	2024	C	FNND
2008	C	FNND (S)	2016	C	FNND (S)	2025	C	FNND (S)

▲ The last Class 20s, SNCB's only Co-Co electric locos, are likely to be withdrawn in December 2012 following the arrival of Classes 18 and 19 which cascaded other locos to freight. The majority were already stored as this was written. 2001 is seen here at Antwerpen Noord depot on 16 June 2005.
David Haydock

CLASS 21   Bo-Bo

These are very similar to Class 27 but lower powered. Used mainly on push-pull passenger trains. 2130 was converted to prototype dual-voltage (3000 V DC/25 kV AC) loco 1901 as a development stage for Class 13 then converted back to standard.

Built: 1984–87.
Builder–Mechanical Parts: BN.
Builder–Electrical Parts: ACEC.
Traction Motors: 4 x LE622S frame mounted.
One Hour Rating: 3310 kW.
EVN: 91 88 021 0010-c and so on.

Maximum Tractive Effort: 234 kN.
Wheel Diameter: 1250 mm.
Weight: 84 tonnes.
Length over Buffers: 18.65 m.
Maximum Speed: 160 km/h.

Rheostatic braking.

2101	FKR	2116	FKR	2131	FKR	2146	FKR
2102	FKR	2117	FKR	2132	FKR	2147	FKR
2103	FKR	2118	FKR	2133	FKR	2148	FKR
2104	FKR	2119	FKR	2134	FKR	2149	FKR
2105	FKR	2120	FKR	2135	FKR	2150	FKR
2106	FKR	2121	FKR	2136	FKR	2151	FKR
2107	FKR	2122	FKR	2137	FKR	2152	FKR
2108	FKR	2123	FKR	2138	FKR	2153	FKR
2109	FKR	2124	FKR	2139	FKR	2154	FKR
2110	FKR	2125	FKR	2140	FKR	2155	FKR
2111	FKR	2126	FKR	2141	FKR	2156	FKR
2112	FKR	2127	FKR	2142	FKR	2157	FKR
2113	FKR	2128	FKR	2143	FKR	2158	FKR
2114	FKR	2129	FKR	2144	FKR	2159	FKR
2115	FKR	2130	FKR	2145	FKR	2160	FKR

▲ There is no visible difference between 2158 and 2758 seen at Schaarbeek station on 26 June 2006, both waiting to head south with peak period extra trains.   **David Haydock**

CLASS 23 Bo-Bo

Mixed traffic locomotive once used all over the system. All locos were stored at the time of going to press.

Built: 1955–57.
Builder–Mechanical Parts: BN.
Builder–Electrical Parts: ACEC/SEMG.
Traction Motors: 4 x CF729 axle-hung.
One Hour Rating: 1880 kW.

Maximum Tractive Effort: 196 kN.
Wheel Diameter: 1262 mm.
Weight: 92 tonnes.
Length over Buffers: 18.00 m.
Maximum Speed: 130 km/h.

Regenerative braking.

Originally numbered 123.014–075.

2314	C	FNND (S)	2340	C	FNND (S)	2355	C	FNND (S)	2367	C	FNND (S)
2316	C	FNND (S)	2341	C	FNND (S)	2357	C	FNND (S)	2368	C	FNND (S)
2320	C	FNND (S)	2342	C	FNND (S)	2360	C	FNND (S)	2370	C	FNND (S)
2321	C	FNND (S)	2343	C	FNND (S)	2362	C	FNND (S)	2371	C	FNND (S)
2325	C	FNND (S)	2349	C	FNND (S)	2364	C	FNND (S)	2372	C	FNND (S)
2328	C	FNND (S)	2351	C	FNND (S)	2365	C	FNND (S)	2375	C	FNND (S)
2339	C	FNND (S)									

CLASS 27 Bo-Bo

Developed after experience with Class 20, these were the first of the 1980s generation of electric locomotives and heralded a new era, being more powerful than their predecessors. They are used throughout the network on passenger work. All locos are equipped with time division multiplex (MUX) equipment for multiple and push-pull working whilst 2742 to 2760 received Type GF auto couplers at one end for use with Type M6 stock. They have been replaced by Class 18 or 19 on this work and will probably lose their couplers and go back to freight work.

Built: 1981–84.
Builder–Mechanical Parts: BN.
Builder–Electrical Parts: ACEC.
Traction Motors: 4 x LE921S frame mounted.
One Hour Rating: 4380 kW.
EVN: 91 88 **027 001** 0-c B-B and so on.

Maximum Tractive Effort: 234 kN.
Wheel Diameter: 1250 mm.
Weight: 85 tonnes.
Length over Buffers: 18.65 m.
Maximum Speed: 160 km/h.

Electro-pneumatic braking. Rheostatic braking.

a   Type GF auto coupler fitted.

2701	NK	2716	NK	2731		NK	2746	a	NK	
2702	NK	2717	NK	2732		NK	2747	a	NK	
2703	NK	2718	NK	2733		NK	2748	a	NK	
2704	NK	2719	NK	2734		NK	2749	a	NK	
2705	NK	2720	NK	2735		NK	2750	a	NK	
2706	NK	2721	NK	2736		NK	2751	a	NK	
2707	NK	2722	NK	2737		NK	2752	a	NK	
2708	NK	2723	NK	2738		NK	2753	a	NK	
2709	NK	2724	NK	2739		NK	2754	a	NK	
2710	NK	2725	NK	2740		NK	2755	a	NK	
2711	NK	2726	NK	2741		NK	2756	a	NK	
2712	NK	2727	NK	2742	a	NK	2757	a	NK	
2713	NK	2728	NK	2743	a	NK	2758	a	NK	
2714	NK	2729	NK	2744	a	NK	2759	a	NK	
2715	NK	2730	NK	2745	a	NK	2760	a	NK	

CLASS 28 (CLASS 186)   Bo-Bo

These locomotives are on long-term hire from Alpha Trains and mainly used on the Antwerpen–Aachen West route which is electrified at 3000 V DC as far as Montzen then at 15 kV AC 16.7 Hz. The locos also operate as far as Köln Gremberg under an arrangement with DB Schenker known as COBRA, and in the Netherlands, having taken over almost all cross-border services. The locos are Bombardier's TRAXX MS design, version DABNL (Germany, Austria, Belgium, Netherlands). The locos are known as Class 186 in Germany and elsewhere but are numbered as Class 28 by SNCB Logistics. For details see Section 6.1. 13 locos were on loan for passenger services in 2012. Alpha Trains numbers are shown in brackets.

2801	(E 186 123)	C	FNND	2816	(E 186 193)	C	FNND	2830	(E 186 207)	C	FNND
2802	(E 186 124)	C	FNND	2817	(E 186 194)	C	FNND	2831	(E 186 208)	C	FNND
2803	(E 186 125)	C	FNND	2818	(E 186 195)	C	FNND	2832	(E 186 209)	C	FNND
2804	(E 186 181)	C	FNND	2819	(E 186 196)	C	FNND	2833	(E 186 210)	C	FNND
2805	(E 186 182)	C	FNND	2820	(E 186 197)	C	FNND	2834	(E 186 211)	C	FNND
2806	(E 186 183)	C	FNND	2821	(E 186 198)	C	FNND	2835	(E 186 212)	C	FNND
2807	(E 186 184)	C	FNND	2822	(E 186 199)	C	FNND	2836	(E 186 213)	C	FNND
2808	(E 186 185)	C	FNND	2823	(E 186 200)	C	FNND	2837	(E 186 214)	C	FNND
2809	(E 186 186)	C	FNND	2824	(E 186 201)	C	FNND	2838	(E 186 215)	C	FNND
2810	(E 186 187)	C	FNND	2825	(E 186 202)	C	FNND	2839	(E 186 216)	C	FNND
2811	(E 186 188)	C	FNND	2826	(E 186 203)	C	FNND	2840	(E 186 217)	C	FNND
2812	(E 186 189)	C	FNND	2827	(E 186 204)	C	FNND	2841	(E 186 218)	C	FNND
2813	(E 186 190)	C	FNND	2828	(E 186 205)	C	FNND	2842	(E 186 219)	C	FNND
2814	(E 186 191)	C	FNND	2829	(E 186 206)	C	FNND	2843	(E 186 220)	C	FNND
2815	(E 186 192)	C	FNND								

CLASS 29 (CLASS 186)   Bo-Bo

In 2010 SNCB hired five more Class 186, this time for freight operation into France – version FB (France, Belgium – 1500/3000 V DC, 25 kV AC). After a brief spell working right to the Spanish border they now only reach Calais and Valenton near Paris. For details see Section 6.1.

Alpha Trains numbers are shown in brackets.

2901	(E 186 346)	C	FNND	2903	(E 186 348)	C	FNND	2905	(E 186 350)	C	FNND
2902	(E 186 347)	C	FNND	2904	(E 186 349)	C	FNND					

▲ 80% of Class 29 workings are container shuttles between Belgium and France, many of them with their origin or destination in Spain. On 4 September 2012 train 43184 from Antwerpen to Madrid Abronigal will be worked by 2903 to Valenton in France and is seen on Line 53 near Wichelen.

Carlo Hertogs

1.3. DIESEL MULTIPLE UNITS

CLASS 41   2-CAR UNITS

These units brought new standards of comfort to Belgian branch line services as they have air conditioning, good seating, information displays etc. Besides replacing ancient Classes 44 & 45 they also eliminated the last diesel locomotive-operated passenger trains in Belgium. They are used on IR trains Antwerpen–Neerpelt plus L trains Dinant–Bertrix–Libramont, Bertrix–Rodange, Rodange–Arlon, Charleroi–Couvin, Gent–Eeklo. Gent–Ronse, Gent–Geraardsbergen and P trains Aalst–Burst.

Built: 2000–02.
Builder: Alstom.
Wheel Arrangement: 2-B + B-2.
Engine: One Cummins QSK650R of 485 kW per car.
Transmission: Hydraulic. Voith T311 bre.
Length over Couplers: 24.80 + 24.80 m.   **Weight:** 49 + 49 tonnes.
Maximum Speed: 120 km/h.   **Accommodation:** 12/64 + –/78 1T.
EVN: 91 88 **041 001** 1-c + 91 88 **041 001** 2- c and so on.

4101	N	FHS	4134	N	FKR	4166	N	FKR
4102	N	GCR	4135	N	FHS	4167	N	FKR
4103	N	GCR	4136	N	FHS	4168	N	FKR
4104	N	GCR	4137	N	FHS	4169	N	MKM
4105	N	GCR	4138	N	FKR	4170	N	FHS
4106	N	GCR	4139	N	MKM	4171	N	FHS
4107	N	GCR	4140	N	FHS	4172	N	FHS
4108	N	MKM	4141	N	FHS	4173	N	FHS
4109	N	GCR (S)	4142	N	MKM	4174	N	FHS
4110	N	GCR	4143	N	FKR	4175	N	FKR
4111	N	FKR	4144	N	FKR	4176	N	FHS
4112	N	FKR	4145	N	FKR	4177	N	FKR
4113	N	GCR	4146	N	FKR	4178	N	FHS
4114	N	GCR	4147	N	FKR	4179	N	MKM
4115	N	FKR	4148	N	FKR	4180	N	FHS
4116	N	FKR	4149	N	FKR	4181	N	FKR
4118	N	FHS	4150	N	FKR	4182	N	MKM
4119	N	GCR	4151	N	FKR	4183	N	FHS
4120	N	GCR	4152	N	FKR	4184	N	MKM
4121	N	FKR	4153	N	FKR	4185	N	FHS
4122	N	FHS	4154	N	FKR	4186	N	MKM
4123	N	FKR	4155	N	FKR	4187	N	MKM
4124	N	FKR	4156	N	FKR	4188	N	FKR
4125	N	FKR	4157	N	FHS	4189	N	FHS
4126	N	FKR	4158	N	FKR	4190	N	MKM
4127	N	FHS	4159	N	FKR	4191	N	MKM
4128	N	FKR	4160	N	FKR	4192	N	FHS
4129	N	MKM	4161	N	FHS	4193	N	FHS
4130	N	FHS	4162	N	FHS	4194	N	FHS
4131	N	FHS (S)	4163	N	FHS	4195	N	FKR
4132	N	FHS	4164	N	FKR	4196	N	FHS
4133	N	MKM	4165	N	FKR			

1.4. DIESEL LOCOMOTIVES

Note: All diesel locomotives are in yellow and green livery except where stated otherwise.

CLASS 52   Co-Co

Classes 52, 53 and 54 are part of a large European family of locomotives. The design originated from Nohab/GM and similar locomotives were found in Denmark (Classes MX and MY), Hungary (Class M61) and Norway (Class Di.3). After many complaints from crews new cabs were fitted to almost all locos which substantially altered their appearance. Classes 52 and 53 were originally differentiated due to having a train heating boiler or not. None now have a boiler. Although not officially withdrawn, all were stored at Stockem in 2012 and are not expect to work again.

Built: 1955.
Builder–Mechanical Parts: AFB.
Builder–Electrical Parts: GM.
Engine: GM 16-567C of 1265 kW at 835 rpm.
Transmission: Electric. Six axle-hung Smit D19 traction motors.
Train Heating: None.   **Wheel Diameter:** 1010 mm.
Weight: 108 tonnes.   **Length over Buffers:** 18.85 m.
Maximum Tractive Effort: 245 kN.   **Maximum Speed:** 120 km/h.

Rheostatic braking. Multiple working fitted.

The original 5201–13 were originally numbered 202.001–013.

5201	I	MKM (S)	5209	I	MKM (S)	5212		I	MKM (S)
5205	I	MKM (S)	5211	I	MKM (S)	5216	(5317)	I	MKM (S)

▲ SNCB 2-car DMU 4138 arrives empty at Antwerpen Berchem on 16 June 2005 to work a special train for journalists to Antwerpen Noord depot.
                                                                    David Haydock

CLASS 53   Co-Co

These locomotives are similar to Class 52 but were originally numbered differently because of having no train heating. Details as Class 52 except:

Built: 1956–57.   **Weight:** 106.6 tonnes.

The original 5301–19 were originally numbered 203.001–019.

5301		I	MKM (S)	5307	(5206)	I	MKM (S)	5313	I	MKM (S)
5302	(5203)	I	MKM (S)	5309		I	MKM (S)	5315	I	MKM (S)
5303		I	MKM (S)	5311		I	MKM (S)	5316	I	MKM (S)
5306		I	MKM (S)	5312		I	MKM (S)	5320	(5210)	I	MKM (S)

CLASS 54   Co-Co

Similar to Class 52, but no rheostatic braking and an additional headlight. Details as Class 52 except:

Built: 1955–57.

Originally numbered 204.001–007.

5401	I	MKM (S)	5403		I	MKM (S)	5407		I	MKM (S)

CLASS 55   Co-Co

These locomotives are now mainly used on infrastructure trains. A few are fitted with electric train heating and are painted in blue and yellow livery instead of the standard yellow and green. Locos at Schaarbeek are fitted with TVM430 cab signalling and adapter couplers for rescue work on the Brussels–Lille high speed line. They are stationed in Brussels and Ath. Their livery has an extra red band.

Built: 1961–62.
Builder–Mechanical Parts: BN.
Builder–Electrical Parts: ACEC/SEMG.
Engine: GM 16-567C of 1435 kW at 835 rpm.
Transmission: Electric. Six axle-hung ACEC D57 traction motors.
Train Heating: None (e Electric. ACEC 300 kW alternator. Most eth equipment no longer functions).
Weight: 110 tonnes.
Maximum Tractive Effort: 272 kN.   **Length over Buffers:** 19.55 m.
Wheel Diameter: 1010 mm.   **Maximum Speed:** 120 km/h.

Rheostatic braking. Multiple working fitted.
e   Fitted with electric train heating.
t   Fitted with TVM 430 cab signalling.

Originally numbered 205.001–042.

5501		T	t	FSR	5510	Y	I		e	NK	5519	Y	I		e	NK	5532		I		NK
5503		I		NK	5511		T	t	FSR	5523		T			NK	5533		T		NK
5505	Y	I		e	NK	5512		T	t	FSR	5526		T			NK	5535		I		NK
5506		T	t	FSR	5514		T	t	FSR	5528		I			NK	5537		I		NK
5507		T		NK	5515	Y	I		e	NK	5529	Y	I		e	NK	5539		I		NK
5508		I		NK	5517		T		NK	5531	Y	I		e	NK	5540	Y	I		e	NK
5509		P	t	FSR	5518		I		NK										

▲ Class 55 are now restricted to engineering trains and LGV rescue duties. 5505 in the blue/yellow livery meaning it is equipped with electric train heating, waits for the right away from Antwerpen Noord yard on 11 August 2012. **Carlo Hertogs**

▼ SNCB diesel 5703, on hire from Alpha Trains, is seen at Marke on 27 March 2012 with a train of chemicals from Tessenderlo to Bully-Grenay in northern France. **Carlo Hertogs**

CLASS 57 B-B

These are Vossloh G2000 diesel-hydraulics on hire from Alpha Trains. They are used for services from Belgium to France by SNCB Logistics but also by subsidiary OSR France within France itself. The locos are in a variety of liveries reflecting past uses – some were previously with Euro Cargo Rail. 5708 was returned to Alpha Trains. OSR France was expected to return four locos in December 2012.

Class Specific Liveries: **A**   Alpha Trains green/grey.
                                     D   Alpha Trains blue/grey.
                                     E   Euro Cargo Rail light grey.

5701	(5001757)	**D**	FNND	5704	(5001618)	**A**	FNND	5707	(5001669)	**E**	FNND
5702	(5001603)	**A**	FNND	5705	(5001758)	**D**	FNND	5709	(5001640)	**E**	FNND
5703	(5001617)	**A**	FNND	5706	(5001637)	**E**	FNND			

CLASS 62 Bo-Bo

Originally a mixed traffic locomotive whose use on passenger trains ceased when Class 41 DMUs arrived. Most locomotives have now been transferred to Infrabel – the infrastructure department. Five locos were sold to private operator ACTS in the Netherlands. Infrabel locomotives are maintained by the depots concerned but normally stable in the engineers' own yards and sidings or at construction sites. Four locomotives are equipped with TBL2 signalling to rescue TGV or ICE sets on the Leuven–Liège line.

Built: 1961–66.
Builder–Mechanical Parts: BN.   **Builder–Electrical Parts:** ACEC.
Engine: GM 12-567C of 1050 kW at 835 rpm.
Transmission: Electric. Four ACEC DN41.1 axle-hung traction motors.
Train Heating: None.   **Wheel Diameter:** 1010 mm.
Weight: 78.6 tonnes.   **Length over Buffers:** 16.79 m.
Maximum Tractive Effort: 212 kN.   **Maximum Speed:** 120 km/h.
Class Specific Livery: I Infrabel blue livery.

Multiple working fitted.

t   Fitted with TBL2 signalling.
E   Fitted with ETCS.

Originally numbered 212.102–231.

6202		I		FKR	6243		I		NK	6288	I	NK
6203		I		FKR	6244	**G**	I		FNND	6291	I	FNND
6207		I		FNND	6246		I		GCR	6292	I	FNND
6210		I		FKR	6247		I		FKR	6295	I	FNND
6212		I		FKR	6249		I		FSR	6296	I	FNND
6213		I		GCR	6250		I		FNND	6297	I	FNND
6214		I		GCR	6251		I		NK	6299	I	FSR
6215		I		NK	6253		I		FSR	6304	I	FKR
6216		I		NK	6254		I		FSR	6305	I	NK
6217		I		GCR	6255	I	I		GCR	6309	I	NK
6218		I		GCR	6256	**G**	I		GCR	6311	I	GCR
6219	**G**	I		FKR	6257		I		NK	6312	I	FNND
6222		I		FKR	6260		I		FKR	6313	T	t	NK
6223		I		FSR	6261		I		GCR	6315	I	FNND
6225		T	t	NK	6262		I		GCR	6316	I	GCR
6227		T	t	NK	6263		I		GCR	6317	I	FNND
6228		I		FKR	6264		I	E	FNND	6319	I	NK
6229		I		FKR	6267		I		NK	6320	I	GCR
6231		I		GCR	6274		I		NK	6323	I	GCR
6236		I		FNND	6275		I		GCR	6324	T	t	NK
6237		I		FSR	6278		I		GCR	6328	I	GCR
6238		I		FKR	6282		P		FSR	6329	I	NK
6241		I		NK	6283		I		FSR	6330	I	FNND
6242		I		GCR	6285		I		GCR	6331	T	FNND

▲ Infrabel revealed a new livery on 6255 in 2011 but this has not been followed up. The photo was taken at Salzinnes works on 8 February 2011. **Philippe Herbiet**

▼ Class 73 and 74 are very similar in outline. This is 7405 at Antwerpen Noord depot on 15 April 2004. **Max Delie**

NOTE RE CLASSES 73–82

Many of these locomotives carry a name on the cabside. This is the radio call sign for the locomotive when used as a shunter. Names are duplicated within the class but not at individual depots. A locomotive being transferred thus may get a new name if this is already in use at its new depot. The list of "named" locomotives is not complete and in some cases actual observations have shown that the depot records are not correct!

CLASS 73 C

General purpose shunters, also formerly used on trip freights. The introduction of Class 77 and reorganisation of freight services led to the withdrawal of the earlier 7301–7335 batch. Those left are now restricted to shunting in depots and cannot work on main lines. Several of the class have been sold to RRF in the Netherlands and others are now in Italy.

Built: 1973–74.　　　　　　　　　　　**Builder:** BN.
Engine: Cockerill 6T240CO of 550 kW at 950 rpm.
Transmission: Hydraulic. Voith L217u.
Train Heating: None.　　　　　　　　　**Weight:** 56 tonnes.
Maximum Tractive Effort: 211 kN.　　　　**Length over Buffers:** 11.40 m.
Wheel Diameter: 1262 mm.
Maximum Speed: 30 km/h.

n　　Fitted with snowplough.

7338	I		FSR	ALBI	7352	I	GCR	MIMOSA
7340	I	n	MKM	COBRA	7354	I	FSR	JIVARO
7350	I		NK	SAFFIER/JAVA	7355	I	FSR	FLORAC
7351	I		NK	ECHO	7359	I	GCR	ALABAMA

▲ In 2012 SNCB Technics bought 30 redundant Class 77s in order to improve the finances of SNCB Logistics. These include 7709, which heads a batch of stored Class 77s at Antwerpen Noord yard on 11 March 2012. **Carlo Hertogs**

CLASS 74   C

Shunters formerly used in pairs around Antwerpen docks. Now restricted to shunting in depots.

Built: 1977.
Engine: ABC 6DXS of 550 kW at 750 rpm.
Weight: 59 tonnes.
Maximum Tractive Effort: 196 kN.
Wheel Diameter: 1262 mm.
Maximum Speed: 30 km/h.

Builder: BN.
Transmission: Hydraulic. Voith L217u.

Length over Buffers: 11.40 m.

Multiple working within class and with Class 82.

ma   Master unit.
s   Slave unit.

7401	T	s	FNND	POLKA		7406	T	ma	FHS	SIRIUS
7402	T	ma	FNND	MARS		7407	T	s	FAZ	SALAMBO
7403	T	s	FHS	TANGO		7409	T		FNND (S)	KIMONO
7404	T	ma	FAZ	OSIRIS						

CLASS 77   B-B

These locomotives, ordered in two batches – 90 then another 80 – are for freight train and shunting use and completely replaced Classes 70, 71, 75 and 80. The class is based on the Vossloh Type G 1200 but adapted for Belgian conditions with an ABC engine, built in Gent mainly for canal barges! 17 are fitted with radio controls and BSI auto couplers for working at Antwerpen Noord, Kinkempois and Gent Zeehaven yards. 25 have Dutch and German safety equipment. The rest are general purpose locomotives and operate throughout Belgium. In late 2012 SNCB Technics bought 30 of the class, all in store, in order to provide liquidity to SNCB Logistics.

Built: 1999–2005.
Builders: Vossloh/Siemens.
Engine: ABC Type 60DZC-1000 of 1150 kW at 1000 rpm.
Transmission: Hydraulic. Voith L4r4zseU2a.
Train Heating: None.
Maximum Tractive Effort: 264 kN.
Wheel Diameter: 1000 mm.
Weight: 87.4 tonnes.
Length over Buffers: 15.59 m.
Maximum Speed: 100 km/h main line/60 km/h shunting.
Multiple Working: Up to three locos may work in multiple.
Class Specific Livery: S   Pale grey with yellow solebars, handrails and ends, blue stripe at bottom of cab and narrow red stripe on bonnets.
EVN: 92 88 0**077** 001-c B-B and so on.

a   Fitted with auto coupler.
d   Equipped to operate in the Netherlands and Germany.
h   Radio fitted for hump shunting.
r   Radio control fitted.

7701	S	C	ah	FNND	ALIBI		7715	S C	ra	FKR	CHICAGO
7702	S	C	ah	FNND	ALPHA		7716	S C	ra	FKR	COBRA
7703	S	C	ah	FNND	BAKOE		7717	S C	ra	FNND	COLUMBIA
7704	S	C	ah	FNND	BAMAKO		7718	S C	ra	FNND	CORDOBA
7705	S	C	ah	FNND	BANGKOK		7719	S C	r	FNND	DAKAR
7706	S	C	ah	FNND	BARRACUDA		7720	S C	r	FNND	DELTA
7707	S	C	ah	FNND	BILBAO		7721	S C	r	FNND	DIAMANT
7708	S	C	ah	FNND	BORNEO		7722	S C	r	FNND	DOMINO
7709	S	T	ah	FNND (S)	BRAVO		7723	S C	r	FNND	ECHO
7710	S	T	r	FNND (S)	BUFFALO		7724	S C	r	FNND	EDELWEISS
7711	S	C	ra	FKR	CALCUTTA		7725	S C	r	FNND	EL PASO
7712	S	C	ra	FKR	CALYPSO		7726	S C	r	FNND	FLORAC
7713	S	C	ra	FKR	CAPRI		7727	S C	r	FNND	GRANADA
7714	S	C	ra	FKR	CARGO		7728	S T	r	FNND (S)	JAVA

7729	**S**	T	r	FNND (S)		7777	**S**	C	d	FNND		7824	**S**	C	r	GCR
7730	**S**	T	r	FNND (S)		7778	**S**	C	d	FNND		7825	**S**	C	r	GCR
7731	**S**	T	r	FNND (S)		7779	**S**	C	d	FNND		7826	**S**	C	r	GCR
7732	**S**	T	r	FNND		7780	**S**	C	d	FNND		7827	**S**	C	r	GCR
7733	**S**	T	r	FNND (S)		7781	**S**	C	d	FNND		7828	**S**	C	r	GCR
7734	**S**	T	r	FNND (S)		7782	**S**	C	d	FNND		7829	**S**	C	r	GCR
7735	**S**	T	r	FNND		7783	**S**	C	d	FNND		7830	**S**	C	r	GCR
7736	**S**	T	r	FNND		7784	**S**	T	d	FNND (S)		7831	**S**	C	r	GCR
7737	**S**	T	r	FNND		7785	**S**	T	d	FNND (S)		7832	**S**	C	r	GCR
7738	**S**	T	r	FNND		7786	**S**	T	d	FNND (S)		7833	**S**	C	r	GCR
7739	**S**	T	r	FNND		7787	**S**	T	d	FNND (S)		7834	**S**	C	r	FNND
7740	**S**	C	r	FNND		7788	**S**	T	d	FNND (S)		7835	**S**	C	r	FNND
7741	**S**	C	r	FNND		7789	**S**	T	d	FNND (S)		7836	**S**	C	r	NK
7742	**S**	C	r	GCR		7790	**S**	T	d	FNND (S)		7837	**S**	C	r	NK
7743	**S**	C	r	FNND		7791	**S**	T	r	FNND (S)		7838	**S**	C	r	NK
7744	**S**	C	r	GCR		7792	**S**	T	r	FNND (S)		7839	**S**	C	r	NK
7745	**S**	T	r	GCR		7793	**S**	T	r	FNND (S)		7840	**S**	C	r	NK
7746	**S**	T	r	GCR		7794	**S**	T	r	FNND (S)		7841	**S**	C	r	NK
7747	**S**	C	r	FNND		7795	**S**	T	r	FNND (S)		7842	**S**	C	r	NK
7748	**S**	C	r	FNND		7796	**S**	T	r	FNND (S)		7843	**S**	C	r	NK
7749	**S**	C	r	FNND		7797	**S**	T	r	FNND (S)		7844	**S**	C	r	NK
7750	**S**	C	r	FNND		7798	**S**	T	r	FNND (S)		7845	**S**	C	r	NK
7751	**S**	C	r	FNND		7799	**S**	T	r	FNND (S)		7846	**S**	C	r	NK
7752	**S**	C	r	FNND		7800	**S**	T	r	FNND (S)		7847	**S**	C	r	NK
7753	**S**	C	r	FNND		7801	**S**	T	r	FNND (S)		7848	**S**	C	r	NK
7754	**S**	C	r	FNND		7802	**S**	T	r	FNND (S)		7849	**S**	C	r	NK
7755	**S**	C	r	FNND		7803	**S**	C	r	FNND		7850	**S**	C	r	FNND
7756	**S**	C	r	FNND		7804	**S**	C	r	FNND		7851	**S**	C	r	FNND
7757	**S**	C	r	FNND		7805	**S**	C	r	FNND		7852	**S**	C	r	FKR
7758	**S**	C	r	FNND		7806	**S**	C	r	FNND		7853	**S**	C	r	FKR
7759	**S**	T	r	FKR		7807	**S**	C	r	FNND		7854	**S**	C	r	FKR
7760	**S**	T	r	FKR		7808	**S**	C	r	FNND		7855	**S**	C	r	FKR
7761	**S**	T	r	FKR		7809	**S**	C	r	FNND		7856	**S**	C	r	FKR
7762	**S**	T	r	FKR		7810	**S**	C	r	NK		7857	**S**	C	r	FKR
7763	**S**	T	r	FKR		7811	**S**	C	r	NK		7858	**S**	C	r	FKR
7764	**S**	T	r	NK		7812	**S**	C	r	NK		7859	**S**	C	r	FKR
7765	**S**	T	r	NK		7813	**S**	C	r	GCR		7860	**S**	C	r	FKR
7766	**S**	T	r	NK		7814	**S**	C	r	GCR		7861	**S**	C	r	FKR
7767	**S**	C	r	NK		7815	**S**	C	r	GCR		7862	**S**	C	r	FKR
7768	**S**	C	r	NK		7816	**S**	C	r	GCR		7863	**S**	C	r	FKR
7769	**S**	C	r	NK		7817	**S**	C	r	GCR		7864	**S**	C	r	FKR
7770	**S**	C	r	NK		7818	**S**	C	r	FKR		7865	**S**	C	r	FKR
7771	**S**	C	d	FNND		7819	**S**	C	r	GCR		7866	**S**	C	d	FNND
7772	**S**	C	d	FNND		7820	**S**	C	r	GCR		7867	**S**	C	d	FNND
7773	**S**	C	d	FNND		7821	**S**	C	r	GCR		7868	**S**	C	d	FNND
7774	**S**	C	d	FNND		7822	**S**	C	r	GCR		7869	**S**	C	d	FNND
7775	**S**	C	d	FNND		7823	**S**	C	r	GCR		7870	**S**	C	d	FNND
7776	**S**	C	d	FNND												

CLASS 80   C

A version of the DB Class 360 (V60) built under licence. Formerly used in the Brussels area, the last loco is, in principle, used for shunting at Schaarbeek depot but had not moved for a year at the time of writing. Many withdrawn locos have been sold abroad, particularly to Italian track maintenance firms.

Built: 1960–1963.
Builder: ABR.
Engine: Maybach GTO6A of 480 kW at 1400 rpm
Transmission: Hydraulic. Voith L37z Ub.   **Weight**: 52 tonnes.
Maximum Tractive Effort: 173 kN.   **Length over Buffers**: 10.360 m.
Wheel Diameter: 1262 mm.   **Maximum Speed**: 30 km/h.

Originally numbered 260.035.

8035	T	FSR (S)

CLASS 82   C

General purpose shunters, sometimes used for trip workings. OSR locos are used in Strasbourg, France.

Built: 1965–66 8204–52; 1972–73 8256–74.   **Weight**: 57 (59 m, 56 s) tonnes.
Builder: ABR (BN 8242–45/8256–74).   **Maximum Tractive Effort**: 191 kN.
Engine: ABC 6DXS of 480 kW at 750 rpm.   **Wheel Diameter**: 1262 mm.
Transmission: Hydraulic. Voith L217u.   **Length over Buffers**: 11.170 (11.320 n) m.
Maximum Speed: 60 km/h.

a   Fitted with BSI auto coupler.
c   Compressed air drier for shunting Eurostar sets at Forest depot.
m   Fitted for multiple working within class and with Class 74.
n   Fitted with snowplough.

8204–52 were originally numbered 262.004–052.

8204	T	c	NK (S)	NEBRASKA	8243	T		FSR (S)	MIRANDA
8205	T	a	FNND (S)	CAPRI	8247	O		FNND	
8209	O		FNND	ALPHA	8248	O		FNND	ETNA
8210	O		NK	ONTARIO	8250	T		FNND	MEXICO
8211	O		FNND	NAPOLI	8252	I	n	NK	ERATO
8212	T		NK (S)	HERMES	8256	T	m	FNND (S)	KATAR
8214	O		FNND	ATLANTA	8257	T	m	FNND	KENIA
8215	C	a	NK (S)	TIRANO	8258	T	m	FNND (S)	LIMA
8216	O		NK	COBRA	8259	T	m	NK (S)	MALAGA
8217	O		NK	BAKOU	8260	T	m	FNND (S)	MEXICO
8218	T		FAZ	ALBI	8261	T	m	NK (S)	MONACO
8221	I	n	NK	COLIBRI	8262	T	m	FNND (S)	NAPOLI
8223	I	n	NK	BRAVO	8263	O	m	NK	NEBRASKA
8226	O		NK	RUBIS	8264	O	m	FSR	NEVADA
8228	O		NK	DOMINO	8265	C	m	FSR (S)	NEW YORK
8231	T		NK (S)	COLORADO	8266	T	m	FNND (S)	OSAKA
8234	O		FSR		8268	T	m	FNND (S)	PEKING
8235	O		FNND	PALMA	8269	O	m	FSR	PORTO-RICO
8236	T		FAZ	URANUS	8270	O	m	NK	RIMINI
8237	O	a	FSR	KASAI	8272	T	m	FSR (S)	TIRANA
8239	T	a	NK (S)	DAKAR	8273	O		FSR	
8242	T		FAZ	ALBATROS	8274	T	m	FNND (S)	TORONTO

CLASS 91 B

The first ten of this class were originally numbered 9001–10. Locos were rebuilt in the late 1970s with more powerful engines and in some cases lengthened frames (marked §) ready for automatic couplers! Many have been made spare by changes in freight workings and have been transferred to departmental use, sold or scrapped. All remaining locos are used as depot or works pilots.

Built: 1961–64.
Builders: Cockerill (9101–10), ABR (9111–9135), BN (9136–60).
Engine: GM 12V71N of 245 kW at 1800 rpm.
Transmission: Hydraulic. Esco Power Twin Disc 11500 HS390.
Train Heating: None   **Weight:** 33.8 (35§) tonnes.
Maximum Tractive Effort: 96 kN.   **Length over Buffers:** 6.625 m (8.055 m.§)
Wheel Diameter: 920 mm.
Maximum Speed: 20 km/h shunting/40 km/h main line.

Originally numbered 230.001–010/101–150.

9109	T		FKR		9131	B		GCR (S)		9146	T	§	NK
9111	T		FHS		9132	T		FKR		9147	T	§	FAZ
9116	T	§	FHS		9134	T		FHS (S)		9149	T		GCR
9118	B		GCR (S)		9135	T	§	MKM		9150	T		FKR
9119	T		FHS		9136	T	§	FKR		9152	T		FKR
9123	T		FKR		9137	B		GCR (S)		9153	T		MKM
9124	T		FHS		9138	T	§	FKR		9156	T	§	NK
9128	T		GCR		9142	O		FNND		9158	T	§	NK
9130	B		Genk									

▲ 8250, 8272 and 8267 are seen outside Antwerpen Noord depot on 16 June 2005.

David Haydock

1.5. SELF-PROPELLED DEPARTMENTAL STOCK

These consist mainly of overhead line inspection units. Full details of these are not available.

ES400 SERIES

Conversions from Class 43 DMUs. ES409 is preserved by BVS.

ES401 (4307)	FSR	ES403 (4328)	GCR	ES406 (4306)	FKR
ES402 (4325)	GCR	ES404 (4319) Y	MKM	ES410 (4315)	NK

ES500 SERIES

In generally re-equipping itself, Belgian Railways acquired some new overhead line units which are similar to ÖBB Class X552. The arrival of these new units allowed older ES100 and ES200 cars to be withdrawn.

Built: 1996–99.
Wheel Arrangement: B–2.
Auxiliary Engine: Deutz BF6M1012 of 93 kW.
Weight in Full Working Order: 55 tonnes.
Wheel Diameter: 840 mm.

Builder: Matisa.
Engine: Deutz BF8M1015C of 330 kW.
Transmission: Hydraulic. Voith T211 rzz.
Length over Buffers: 16.04 m.
Maximum Speed: 100 km/h.

ES501	Y	GCR	ES506	Y	GCR	ES511	Y	NK
ES502	Y	FNND	ES507	Y	FSR	ES512	Y	FHS
ES503	Y	FKR	ES508	Y	NK	ES513	Y	FHS
ES504	Y	FNND	ES509	Y	FKR	ES514	Y	FKR
ES505	Y	FEO	ES510	Y	GCR	ES515	Y	NK

▲ SNCB 9128, the depot shunter, is seen at Charleroi Sud on 15 September 2007. **David Haydock**

2. LUXEMBOURG RAILWAYS (CFL)

Luxembourg Railways are known by the abbreviation CFL (*Société Nationale des Chemins de Fer Luxembourgeois*). The total length of the system is only 270 km, but this does not mean that the network is uninteresting. CFL operates locomotives and multiple units of types that are also found in neighbouring countries, and Luxembourg Ville station sees through workings of locomotives from the DB, SNCB and SNCF. Electrification is at 25 kV AC 50 Hz and all CFL electric locomotives and multiple units operate on this system. SNCB 3000 V DC electrics can also run into Luxembourg Ville station.

A BRIEF HISTORY OF LUXEMBOURG

The early history of Luxembourg was closely linked to that of Belgium and the Netherlands – the main details can be found in the section of this book about Belgium. Before reaching full independence, Luxembourg had been a much larger territory but was partitioned several times. One reminder of this is that Belgium has the "province of Luxembourg" in its south-east.

Luxembourg is generally a hilly country, particularly the north-east. Like Belgium, the country experienced rapid industrialisation, with major steelworks springing up in the south, close to the border with France. As is the case in Belgium, this industry is now in decline due to local raw materials being worked out and the country's distance from ports.

Luxembourg is now a service-based economy which is so strong that it employs hundreds of thousands of workers from neighbouring countries. Their commuting is a major headache and the railways are constantly increasing capacity to carry more by train and reduce traffic congestion. The Luxembourg government has been planning a tram-train project for the city for several years but there has been no news of this since 2009.

THE RAILWAYS OF LUXEMBOURG

With Luxembourg being such a small country, almost all lines are international and were built with cross-border services in mind. Indeed, Luxembourg Railways itself (CFL) is jointly owned with French and Belgian Railways. The line from Brussels via Namur is thus operated mainly by SNCB stock and is electrified throughout at Belgian 3000 V DC, although the current modernisation of this line will see it re-electrified at 25 kV AC as far as Namur. The line from Liège is more important for local than for international passenger traffic and now carries little freight. Most freight traffic between Belgium and Luxembourg passes over the Athus-Meuse line which enters Luxembourg near Rodange. Cross-border passenger traffic is light. Within Luxembourg the Rodange–Esch–Luxembourg line is very important for both passenger and freight traffic, the latter generated by several steel plants. The direct line from Pétange to Luxembourg is more important for passengers and was doubled in December 2012. The line from Luxembourg to Thionville and Metz in France is a major international artery for freight traffic and also carries heavy local passenger traffic plus TGVs to Paris and the Brussels–Strasbourg–Basel service. The line from Luxembourg to Germany (Trier and Koblenz) is still mainly single track and for this reason, some trains operate via the mainly freight line via Bettembourg.

Luxembourg electrified most of its network from the 1960s at 25 kV AC – the same as SNCF lines on the other side of the border. Luxembourg's 25 kV meets Germany's 15 kV AC at Wasserbillig. Freight traffic almost all revolves around the marshalling yard at Bettembourg which has a growing intermodal terminal.

NUMBERING SYSTEM

The CFL locomotive numbering system was based on the horse power of the locomotives. 1801 is an 1800 hp locomotive, for example. However, some new and smaller locomotives and multiple units are not numbered in accordance with this system.

DEPOTS AND WORKSHOPS

With such a compact system there is no need for many depots. All locomotives and units are allocated to Luxembourg shed which has recently been modernised. There are stabling points at Ettelbruck, Wasserbillig, Troisvierges, Bettembourg yard, Pétange and Esch sur Alzette. Locomotives also stable overnight at branch termini as required. There is only one workshop for locomotives and multiple units and this is located next to Luxembourg station.

DEVELOPMENTS

In 1993, CFL completed electrification of its main lines at 25 kV AC 50 Hz, except for the line to Arlon (B), electrified at 3000 V DC and short freight branches Kleinbettingen–Steinfort and Schieren–Bissen, which remain diesel worked. The Luxembourg–Arlon line is currently being re-electrified at 25 kV AC.

CFL owns two Class 628.4 2-car DMUs – 628 505 and 506 – which are maintained by DB and shown in the Platform 5 book "German Railways". CFL Class 2200 are identical to SNCF's Class Z 24500 and the classes interwork, CFL sets reaching Nancy.

In the five years since the previous edition of BENELUX RAILWAYS, CFL cargo has largely renewed its locomotive fleet. Class 800 (802 was still officially in stock in mid 2012 but stored), 850 and 900 have been eliminated, many of the latter having been sold to French operator RDT13. Class 1150 are not used in Luxembourg.

Like other railways, CFL has been divided into activities and rolling stock with it. In 2006, the company created freight subsidiary CFL cargo with steel producer ArcelorMittal which generates much of the domestic rail freight in Luxembourg. The steel company's shunters are now part of the joint fleet. In recent years CFL has expanded outside its borders and now has subsidiaries in Denmark, France, Germany and Sweden. Class 1500 can operate into Germany and locos in the 1580 series into France. Class 3000 operates to Antwerpen within the Sibelit partnership and Class 4000 operates as far as Lübeck and München in Germany. There are occasional "loans" of Luxembourg locos to Germany and Denmark but, for example, CFL cargo Deutschland Class 185 locos do not work into Luxembourg. The latter are not, therefore, included in this book.

CFL will shortly receive new KISS double-deck EMUs from Stadler in order to operate an improved service from Luxembourg to Trier and Koblenz, under contract to the Rheinland Pfalz Land. DB Class 628.4 DMUs will be replaced on the Trier route.

PASSENGER SERVICES

Loco-hauled passenger trains and EMUs tend to mix on all routes. Class 2100 EMUs work the short routes to Volmerange and Rumelange while Class 2200 operate most trains into France including to Thionville, Metz and Nancy, and Longwy. Class 4000 is not approved in France, but currently works passenger trains as far as Koblenz. Only Class 3000 can work to Kleinbettingen and Arlon.

LIVERIES

CFL locomotives, multiple units and hauled stock are generally painted in bordeaux red with yellow highlights on older locos and white on more recent stock.

2.1. DIESEL LOCOMOTIVES

Note: Self-propelled departmental vehicles are also numbered in this series.

CLASS 100   B

These shunters were part of the ArcelorMittal internal fleet which became part of CFL cargo in 2007. They are now seen outside Belval steel works. Originally delivered with numbers 11 to 14. Works numbers 220091 to 220093 and 220097. Originally in yellow livery.

Built: 1968–71.   **Builder:** MaK. Type G 320 B.
Engine: Mercedes-Benz MB 846 Ab of 259 kW or Scania DSI 1441 of 276 kW.
Transmission: Hydraulic. Voith L320 U.   **Weight:** 40 tonnes.
Maximum Tractive Effort: **Length over Buffers:** 8.54 m.
Wheel Diameter: 1000 mm.   **Maximum Speed:** 33/60 km/h.

101	102	103	104

CLASS 300   B-B

These heavy shunters were delivered new to Arbed, now ArcelorMittal, and became part of the CFL cargo fleet in 2007. They are used mainly within steel works, where they sometimes operate in multiple. However, some locos now operate outside these plants. Delivered numbered D 11 to D 24 (301 to 314) and D 38, 40, 41, 5, and 5, the last being at various different steelworks in Luxembourg. Works numbers are respectively 800154 to 800160, 800163, 800182, 800173 to 800176, 800170, 800177, 800184, 800185, 800188, and 800189. Originally in yellow livery. 303 has been withdrawn.

Built: 1966–77.   **Builder:** MaK. Type G 850 BB.
Engine: MaK 6 M 282 A of 626 kW.
Transmission: Hydraulic. Voith L 306 r or L 5r4.   **Weight:** 80 tonnes.
Maximum Tractive Effort: **Length over Buffers:** 12.20 m.
Wheel Diameter: 1000 mm.   **Maximum Speed:** 36/60 km/h.

301	305	308	311	314	317
302	306	309	312	315	318
304	307	310	313	316	319

CLASS 500   B

30 of these locomotives were ordered by Danish State Railways (DSB) as Class MJ but were refused after 16 (501 to 519, there is no 508, 515 or 517) had been built. They are now all hired out by the manufacturer, and considered very good by users. CFL's infrastructure department has hired up to five of the class but at the time of writing had three on hire.

Built: 1993–96.   **Builder:** CMI.
Engine: Caterpillar 3408 BTA of 386 kW.
Transmission: Hydrostatic.   **Weight:** 40 tonnes.
Maximum Tractive Effort: 120 kN.   **Length over Buffers:** 8.90 m.
Wheel Diameter: 950 mm.   **Maximum Speed:** 60 km/h.
EVN: 99 82 9482 **502**-6, **516**-4, **518**-2 L-CFLIF

502	516	518

▲ CFL cargo loco 101 shunts at Pétange wagon works on 18 March 2009. **Mike Wohl**

▼ CFL cargo (formerly Arbed) diesel loco 316 shunts at Belval on 10 August 2011. **Mike Wohl**

CLASSES 700, 710, 720, 730, 750, 760, 770 & 780

In 2010/11 CFL's Infrastructure department purchased 22 permanent way trolleys from Robel of similar designs, but fitted with different types of equipment. They all have a large cab unit, with room for numerous staff, at one end, with cranes and other equipment at the other end. The first 14 of these are Robel Type IIF 54.22 trolleys. 701–706 are standard, with a Palfinger PR220C crane; 711–714 have a PR220C and are pre-equipped for use with a vegetation "mulcher"; 721/722 have a cab-top pantograph and a Palfinger PKR200D crane, which can be fitted with a "basket" for overhead line inspection and maintenance; 731/732 have a PR220C crane, pre-equipped for fitting a "basket".

The remaining vehicles are Type 54.54 vehicles which look very similar but are longer, and have a smaller engine, used only for local movements. They can be used in multiple with the more powerful types. 751–753 have PR220C crane; 761/762 carry welding equipment (this is the only vehicle which is covered); 771/772 have a large crane; 781 has a PR220C, an inspection platform and a cab-top pantograph.

CLASSES 700, 710, 720 & 730   B

Built: 2010/11.   **Builder:** Robel.
Engine: Deutz Type TCD 2015 V8 4V of 500 kW. **Transmission:** Hydraulic. Voith T212 bre+ HA.
Weight (loaded): 43 tonnes (Class 700, 710, 730); 41 tonnes (Class 720).
Length over Buffers: 15.10 m.
Wheel Diameter: 920 mm.   **Maximum Speed:** 80 km/h.

Class 700

| 701 | 702 | 703 | 704 | 705 | 706 |

Class 710

| 711 | 712 | 713 | 714 |

Class 720

| 721 | 722 |

Class 730

| 731 | 732 |

CLASSES 750, 760, 770 & 780   B-2

Built: 2010/11.   **Builder:** Robel.
Engine: Deutz Type TCD 2013 L06 4V of 217 kW. **Transmission:** Hydrostatic.
Weight (loaded): 80 tonnes.   **Length over Buffers:** 19.80 m.
Wheel Diameter: 920 mm.   **Maximum Speed:** 30 km/h (100 km/h hauled).
EVN: 99 82 9210 **751**-c to **781**-c L-CFLIF

Class 750

| 751 | 752 | 753 |

Class 760

| 761 | 762 |

Class 770

| 771 | 772 |

Class 780

781

▲ Robel permanent way trolley 722 is seen during a test trip from Bettembourg to Wasserbillig at Mertert on 25 March 2011. **Mike Wohl**

▼ CFL 1004 plus 516 on hire from CMI are seen at Livange running light from Bettembourg to Luxembourg on 4 April 2005. **Mike Wohl**

CLASS 1000   B

Owned by the CFL infrastructure department and used for light shunting duties.

Built: 1972.
Builder: Jung.
Engine: Deutz F12 L413 of 186 kW at 2150 rpm.
Transmission: Hydraulic. Voith L2r4SU2.
Weight: 32 tonnes.
Maximum Tractive Effort: 94 kN.   **Length over Buffers:** 7.20 m.
Wheel Diameter: 950 mm.   **Maximum Speed:** 30/60 km/h.

| 1001 | 1002 | 1003 | 1004 |

CLASS 1020   B

Owned by the rolling stock department. 1024 is fitted with auto couplers.

Built: 1952–57.
Builder: Deutz.
Engine: Deutz A8 L614 of 100 kW at 1800 rpm.
Transmission: Hydraulic. Voith L33Y.
Weight: 22 tonnes.
Maximum Tractive Effort: 64 kN.   **Length over Buffers:** 7.57 m.
Wheel Diameter: 850 mm.   **Maximum Speed:** 53 km/h.

| 1022 | 1023 | 1024 |

▲ 1022 is seen at Luxembourg depot on 9 May 2009.   **Stojan Mihajlovic**

CLASS 1030   B

Owned by the infrastructure department. 1031 is fitted with remote control.

Built: 1988.
Builder: Jenbach.
Engine: MTU 8V 183 TA12 of 267 kW at 2200 rpm.
Transmission: Hydraulic. Voith L2r4SV2.
Weight: 36 tonnes.
Maximum Tractive Effort: 117 kN.   **Length over Buffers:** 8.55 m.
Wheel Diameter: 950 mm.   **Maximum Speed:** 60 km/h.

1031 | 1032 | 1033

CLASS 1050   PERMANENT WAY TROLLEYS

Owned by the infrastructure department, these permanent way trolleys have a large cabin at
one end for the driver and staff and a hydraulic arm at the other. 1051 was formerly numbered
10. 1053 has been withdrawn.

Built: 1980–82.
Builder: Donelli/Geismar.
Engine: Deutz F8 L413F of 173.5 kW at 1500 rpm.
Transmission: Hydraulic. Clark R 28624-9.
Length over Buffers: 9.90 m.   **Weight:** 36 tonnes.
Wheel Diameter: 850 mm.   **Maximum Speed:** 80 km/h.

1051 | 1052 | 1054

▲ CFL shunters 1033 and 1031 top and tail DB ultrasonic test train 719 001 between Esch-sur-
Alzette and Audun-le-Tiche (France) and pass under the viaduct taking this line to Fontoy on
26 March 2011.   **Mike Wohl**

CLASS 1060   OVERHEAD LINE TROLLEYS

Owned by the infrastructure department. They have a dummy pantograph and a working area above the crew accommodation. They are used for overhead line inspection and maintenance. The two vehicles have quite different cab designs, 1061 being more boxy, and different equipment to lift crews. 1062 is in the recent CFL red and grey livery.

Built: 1985/1992.
Builder: Donelli/Geismar.
Engine: Deutz F8 L413F of 173.5 kW at 1500 rpm.
Transmission: Hydro-mechanical. MHR 28628-2.
Length over Buffers: 12.14 m.   **Weight:** 27 tonnes.
Wheel Diameter: 850 mm.   **Maximum Speed:** 80 km/h.

1061 | 1062

CLASS 1100   B-B

These are standard Vossloh G1000 locomotives on long-term hire from Alpha Trains. Although carrying Vehicle Keeper Markings for CFL cargo, they are used for station pilot as well as light freight duties. Numbering below shows works numbers in brackets. All are in standard Alpha Trains livery of white with a blue cab. All are equipped to operate in Luxembourg and Germany.

Builder: Vossloh.
Engine: MTU 8V4000 of 1100 kW.
Transmission: Hydraulic. Voith L4r4.   **Wheel Diameter:** 1000 mm.
Maximum Tractive Effort: 259 kN.   **Length over Buffers:** 14.13 m.
Weight: 80 tonnes.   **Maximum Speed:** 100 km/h.
EVN: 92 82 0001 **101**-5 to **106**-4 L-CFLCA

| 1101 | (5001483) | 1103 | (5001529) | 1105 | (5001531) | 1106 | (5001532) |
| 1102 | (5001484) | 1104 | (5001530) | | | | |

▲ CFL inspection vehicle 1062 is seen on 18 March 2009 at Noertzange.   **Mike Wohl**

CLASS 1500   B-B

These are standard Vossloh G1206 locomotives on hire from Alpha Trains, MRCE, B&V of Leipzig. They are used for freight duties. Numbering below shows works numbers in brackets. All are equipped to work in both Luxembourg and Germany, the 1580 series also being able to operate in France. CFL cargo's other subsidiaries may also hire G 1206 locos but as they cannot operate in Luxembourg, they are not included here. CFL cargo may hire in additional locos, or subhire locos to cooperating companies if necessary. 1509 was returned to the hire firm. At the time of writing, 1588 could only be used in France and Germany and is based at Hagondange.

Built: 2000–11.
Builder: Vossloh.
Engine: Caterpillar 3512 B DI-TA of 1500 kW.
Transmission: Hydraulic. Voith L5r4 zU2.   **Wheel Diameter:** 1000 mm.
Maximum Tractive Effort: 254 kN.   **Length over Buffers:** 14.70 m.
Weight: 87.3 tonnes.   **Maximum Speed:** 100 km/h.
EVNs: 1501–1508 (for others see below) 92 80 0001 **501**-6 to **508**-1 L-CFLCA.
Class Specific Livery: A   Alpha Trains livery of white with a blue cab.
                      M   MRCE black livery.
                      R   All over red livery.
                      V   Vossloh lime green and grey.

1501 **R**	(1001115)	1503 **R**	(1001129)	1505 **R**	(1001025)	1507 **R**	(1001117)
1502 **A**	(5001476)	1504 **R**	(1001131)	1506 **R**	(1001116)	1508 **R**	(1001127)

1510 **V**   (5001991)   92 80 1275 016-4 D-BUVL

1581 **A**	(5001513)	92 80 1276 001-5 D-ATLD	1585 **M**	(5001684)	92 80 1276 018-9 D-DISPO
1582 **A**	(5001665)	92 80 1276 002-3 D-ATLD	1586 **M**	(5001636)	92 80 1276 016-3 D-DISPO
1583 **M**	(5001649)	92 80 1276 034-6 D-DISPO	1587 **A**	(5001692)	92 80 1276 042-9 D-BUVL
1584 **M**	(5001731)	92 80 1276 037-9 D-DISPO	1588 **V**	(5001693)	92 80 1276 045-2 D-BUVL

Names

1585   Chimène   1586   Phaedra

▲ CFL cargo G 1206 1585, in multiple with Spitzke locomotive G1206-SP-022, head a permanent way train at Differdange on 24 May 2011.   **Mike Wohl**

CLASS 1800 Co-Co

Identical to SNCB Class 55 except for the coupling of traction motors. Used on a variety of freights within Luxembourg and to Ehrang near Trier in Germany. The last locos are expected to be withdrawn by the end of 2012 – a "final" passenger train ran on 23 June 2012. 1801 and 1806 have been sold to Power Rail in Magdeburg, Germany. 1802, 1805, 1807, 1810, 1814, 1816 and 1820 have been transferred to Padborg for use by CFL cargo Danmark. 1815 has already been sold to Ascherslebener Verkehrsgesellschaft.

Built: 1963–64.
Builder–Mechanical Parts: BN.   **Builder–Electrical Parts:** ACEC/SEM.
Engine: GM 16-567C of 1435 kW at 835 rpm.
Transmission: Electric. Six ACEC DS7 axle-hung traction motors.
Weight: 110 tonnes.
Maximum Tractive Effort: 272 kN.   **Length over Buffers:** 19.55 m.
Wheel Diameter: 1010 mm.   **Maximum Speed:** 120 km/h.
EVN: 92 82 000 **1815**-c L-CFLCA and so on.

Rheostatic braking. Equipped with Indusi safety equipment for operation in Germany.

1815	KAUTENBACH 1881–1981	1818
1817		

▲ CFL cargo 1817 and 1818 head a heavy train of scrap at Dippach, having been diverted between Bettembourg and Differdange via Luxembourg, Dippach-Reckange and Rodange on 1 August 2011.
Mike Wohl

2.2. ELECTRIC MULTIPLE UNITS

CLASS 2000   "Z2"   2-CAR UNITS

These EMUs are similar to SNCF Class Z 11500 (also known as Z2 units) and used to interwork with the latter into France. Units operate on all lines in Luxembourg.

Built: 1990–92.
Wheel Arrangement: Bo-Bo + 2-2.
Accommodation: 24/60 1T + –/80 1T.
Weight: 64 + 40 tonnes.

Builders: De Dietrich/ANF/Alsthom.
Traction Motors: 4 x TAB 676 B1 of 305 kW each.
Length over Couplers: 25.10 + 25.10 m.
Maximum Speed: 160 km/h.

All equipped with ETCS.

2001	2005	2009	2013	2017	2020
2002	2006	2010	2014	2018	2021
2003	2007	2011	2015	2019	2022
2004	2008	2012	2016		

Names:

2001	MERSCH		2018	TROISVIERGES
2004	PETANGE			

▲ CFL EMUs 2022 and 2012 form train RB 6666 Luxemburg–Pétange at Noertzange on 21 May 2011. **Mike Wohl**

CLASS 2200   3-CAR DOUBLE-DECK UNITS

These EMUs, built in two batches, are near identical to SNCF Class Z 24500 and they interwork with the latter on services from Luxembourg to Metz and Nancy. 2207 was severely damaged in a head-on crash at Zoufftgen in November 2006 and 2223 was built using parts of 2207. Units operate on all lines in Luxembourg and on almost all services between Luxembourg and France. Cars in 2201 are numbered 22011, 22013 and 22015, and so on. Units carry the last two digits of their numbers on their front ends.

Built: 2005–2007 (2201–12), 2010/11 (2213–2223).   **Builders:** Alstom/Bombardier.
Wheel Arrangement: Bo-2 + Bo-2 + Bo-2.
Traction Motors: 2 x FXA 2851 of 425 kW each per car. Total 2550 kW per unit.
Accommodation: 41/298 3T 1TD.
Total Length over Couplers: 27.35 m + 26.40 m + 27.35 m.
Weight: 190 tonnes.   **Maximum Speed:** 160 km/h.

All equipped with SNCF's KVB automatic train control system.

2201	2205	2210	2214	2218	2221
2202	2206	2211	2215	2219	2222
2203	2208	2212	2216	2220	2223
2204	2209	2213	2217		

Names:

2206   BETTEMBOURG | 2222 DIPPACH / LANDIRAS

▲ CFL EMU 2222 is seen at Mertert running empty from Wasserbillig to Luxembourg on 23 May 2011.   **Mike Wohl**

CLASS 2300   KISS   3-CAR DOUBLE-DECK UNITS

CFL has ordered eight dual-voltage units of the Stadler KISS design to operate an improved Luxembourg–Trier–Koblenz service. They will be introduced on Luxembourg–Trier from December 2013, ousting Class 628.4 DMUs, then from December 2014 will operate through to Koblenz. They will be able operate in multiple with DB FLIRT EMUs from Koblenz to Trier, the DB units going forward to Saarbrücken. There is an option for 31 more units. The outer cars of these units will be identical, the intermediate car housing the first class accommodation upstairs, plus two toilets, disabled spaces and space for cycles and push chairs downstairs.

Built: 2013.   **Builder:** Stadler.
Wheel Arrangement: 2-Bo + 2-2 + Bo-2.   **Power Rating:** 2000 kW.
Accommodation: –/82 (12) + 29/44 (23) 1T 1TD + –/82 (12) = 29/208 (47) 1T 1TD in total.
Total Length over Couplers: 79.84 m.   **Total Weight:** 170 tonnes.
Maximum Speed: 160 km/h.   **Wheel Diameter:** 920 mm.
Systems: 15 kV AC / 25 kV AC.

All equipped with ETCS Level 1 safety and signalling system.

2301	2303	2305	2306	2307	2308
2302	2304				

2.3. ELECTRIC LOCOMOTIVES

CLASS 3000   Bo-Bo

These dual-voltage locomotives were designed to operate in a pool with SNCB/NMBS Class 13 which are identical. They are used mainly on Luxembourg–Liège passenger trains and on Antwerpen–Namur–Bertrix–Rodange–Bettembourg freights over the "Athus-Meuse" line. Otherwise they are used on local passenger services with the recent double-deck stock. Also operate to Antwerpen and Thionville within the Sibelit partnership and to Bressoux and Lérouville in open access. 3001 was withdrawn after a serious fire.

Built: 1998–2000.
Systems: 3000 V DC/25 kV AC 50 Hz (1500 V DC at reduced power).
Builder–Mechanical Parts: Alstom, Bombardier.
Builder–Electrical Parts: Alstom (ACEC).
Traction Motors: Four PXA 4339B frame mounted.
One Hour Rating: 5200 kW.   **Weight:** 90 tonnes.
Maximum Tractive Effort: 288 kN.   **Length over Buffers:** 19.11 m.
Wheel Diameter: 1160 mm.   **Maximum Speed:** 200 km/h.
Train Protection: ETCS, KVB, MEMOR, TBL.
EVN: 91 82 000 **3002**-c L-CFL and so on.

Multiple working fitted. Equipped with rheostatic and regenerative braking.

All equipped for push-pull operation.

3002	3007	3012	3017
3003	3008	3013	3018
3004	3009	3014	3019
3005	3010	3015	3020
3006	3011	3016	

Name:

3002   BLANKENBERGE

▲ CFL 3016 hauls train 90 to Brussels during diversions via Dippach-Reckange and Athus because of work on the Luxemburg–Arlon line on 1 October 2011. The train is seen at Bettange-sur-Mess.
Mike Wohl

▼ CFL loco 4002, sporting a "Unicef" advertising livery, heads train RB 4736 Athus–Luxemburg near Belvaux-Soleuvre station on 21 May 2011.
Mike Wohl

CLASS 4000   Bo-Bo

These are Bombardier's TRAXX design and were ordered together with the recent double-deck stock. The locos are very similar to a DB Class 185 (first generation) but also have equipment to operate passenger trains. The locos are used all over the CFL network with push-pull double-deck stock. In 2012 the class worked passenger trains as far as Koblenz but this working will probably be taken over by the new KISS EMUs. CFL cargo hires locomotives to operate Bettembourg–Lübeck and München services and can hire others as necessary. Many Class 4000 carry bodyside advertisements.

Built: 2004–06.
Systems: 15 kV AC 16.7 Hz/25 kV AC 50 Hz.
Builder–Mechanical Parts: Bombardier.
Builder–Electrical Parts: Bombardier.
Traction Motors: Four axle hung.
One Hour Rating: 5600 kW.
Maximum Tractive Effort: 300 kN.
Wheel Diameter: 1250 mm.

Weight: 84 tonnes.
Length over Buffers: 18.90 m.
Maximum Speed: 140 km/h.

4001	4006	4011 ETTELBRUCK	4016
4002	4007	4012	4017
4003	4008	4013	4018 WILTZ
4004	4009	4014	4019
4005	4010	4015	4020

OTHER TRAINS OPERATING INTO LUXEMBOURG

Luxembourg is such a small country that there is a very large degree of cross-border operation. From Belgium, SNCB Class 13 locomotives work passenger services from Brussels (Class 18 may take these over when they are approved for use in Luxembourg) as do Class AM96 EMUs. Class 13 also work freight over the Athus-Meuse line via Virton to Rodange and Bettembourg. Class 41 DMUs operate the Virton–Rodange–Arlon passenger service.

DB Class 181.2 work IC services from Germany and Class 628.4 DMUs operate the frequent service to Trier. Freight generally changes to CFL cargo traction at Ehrang (Trier).

From France, TGV Réseau sets work the service from Paris, Class BB 26000 electric locos work other long distance passenger services while suburban services are mainly operated by Z24500 double-deck EMUs. Most freight is now worked by Fret SNCF Class BB27000 and its tri-voltage version BB37000.

Surprisingly, no open access freight operators have yet to venture into the country. On the other hand track renewal work is often handled by German companies which bring their exotic types of traction with them.

3. NETHERLANDS RAILWAYS (NS)

A BRIEF HISTORY OF THE NETHERLANDS

The "Low Countries", including Belgium, have had a very closely linked history (see sections on Belgium and Luxembourg above). The Netherlands was settled by Germanic peoples who developed their own language, derived from a dialect from Franken, which is now in Germany. The nation is well-known for having a long coast, very low-lying flat land and being criss-crossed by many rivers – this led to the people being great traders and learning how to tame the sea and rivers, as well as reclaiming land. Independence came in 1648 after the Eighty Years' War which was fought to free the area from Spanish Catholic domination.

Although the new country was, in principle, Protestant, it was also extremely tolerant of other creeds and religions and remains so today. The Netherlands became extremely rich thanks to its trading and the establishment of an empire. Wars with the English and French in the 18th century had no permanent effect and by 1848 the country emerged as a parliamentary democracy.

Today the country is prosperous and outward-looking. International trade, mainly based on the port of Rotterdam and a cluster around Schiphol airport, is extremely important. The Netherlands is for most part very flat; indeed much of the country is below sea level and protected by a network of impressive dykes and dams. Only the south-east is really hilly – by Dutch standards.

THE RAILWAYS OF THE NETHERLANDS

The first railway line in the Netherlands opened from Amsterdam to Haarlem on 20 September 1839. There followed a period when several new lines were built, mainly by the Hollandsche IJzeren Spoorweg-Maatschappij (HSM) and the Nederlandse Rhijnspoorweg-Maatschappij (NSR). The Dutch government produced a plan in 1860 to complete a rail network and formed the Maatschappij tot Exploitatie van Staatsspoorwegen (SS, State Railway Operating Company) which was founded by private investors with concessions for the lines built by the State.

The First World War caused the profitability of private companies to decline and in 1938 the HSM and SS merged to form Nederlandse Spoorwegen (NS), a "private company" owned by the Dutch government. The rail network was damaged considerably during the Second World War but once repairs were completed, main lines were rapidly electrified at 1500 V DC overhead.

The passenger network is now rapidly becoming a multiple-unit railway. Passenger flows are very heavy in the urbanised Randstad conurbations in the west of the country with frequent rail services competing with the very congested road network.

The Netherlands does not have much heavy industry away from the coast and freight traffic between the ports, especially Rotterdam, and their hinterland – which now stretches to Italy, Poland and the Czech Republic – is intense. The Netherlands liberalised rail freight at an early stage and freight traffic has almost doubled in the past decade.

The Netherlands network is relatively small and approximately two thirds of all routes are electrified at 1500 V DC with overhead wire collection. All electric trains in this book are 1500 V DC only unless otherwise shown. Recent electrification – of the HSL Zuid high speed line, *Havenspoorlijn* Rotterdam port line and *Betuweroute* freight-only line from Rotterdam to the German border have all been at 25 kV AC 50 Hz overhead. Conversion of main lines to 25 kV AC has been proposed in the past and VIRM sets are pre-equipped for conversion. However, no progress has been made on this idea.

Infrastructure and train operation are now separated in the Netherlands. The national infrastructure manager is **ProRail** which is owned by the Dutch State. Most track maintenance and renewal is contracted to private companies.

ProRail is also infrastructure manager of the HSL-Zuid high speed line (Hoofddorp–Rotterdam West and Rotterdam Lombardijen–Hazeldonk, the border crossing to Belgium) and the *Betuweroute*. The *Betuweroute* is managed day-to-day by **Keyrail**, whose shares are owned by ProRail, plus the Rotterdam and Amsterdam port authorities.

Most of the sidings and connections between national railway network and industries and are owned by **NS Spooraansluitingen**.

German railway undertaking **Bentheimer Eisenbahn** owns and manages the line between Coevorden and the Dutch/German border at Laarwald. Preserved railways own their own lines.

The former *Zoetermeer Stadslijn* and the Den Haag–Rotterdam *Hofplein* line are now run as the *RandstadRail* light rail system. The infrastructure management is the responsibility of Haaglanden and Rijnmond, the regional transport authorities of the Den Haag and Rotterdam areas.

Inspectie Leefomgeving en Transport (ILT), a department of the Ministry of Transport, is responsible for safety inspections, is the licensing body for railway undertakings, and is also the authority which approves and certifies railway vehicles in the Netherlands.

NEDERLANDSE SPOORWEGEN (NS)

NV Nederlandse Spoorwegen is now a holding company with legally separated business units which are:

NS Reizigers (NS passengers). NS was awarded a concession for the exclusive right to run passenger trains on the *hoofdrailnet* – the "core network", comprising all InterCity (IC) services and Sprinter regional and suburban services.

NS Internationaal operates international passenger train services: IC services between Amsterdam and Berlin via Bad Bentheim, ICE services from Amsterdam to Köln and Frankfurt (and beyond), and the hourly Amsterdam–Brussels *Benelux* IC service. These services are marketed as **NS Hispeed**, which will also include domestic high speed services run by HSA (High Speed Alliance, a joint venture comprising NS and KLM for operation of high speed train services on the HSL-Zuid). These are marketed as *Fyra*. In 2015 the latter will become part of the NS concession. In December 2012, it was expected that the *Benelux* service would be replaced by a *Fyra* high-speed service via the HSL Zuid.

NedTrain is the NS subsidiary responsible for the maintenance, overhaul and refurbishment of rolling stock. NedTrain operates several workshops and depots and has the legal status of a RU. **NedTrain** previously had a department for testing and commissioning rolling stock, activities needed in the framework of approval of rolling stock. This department was turned into another business unit, called NedTrain Consulting, which was awarded the legal status of Notified Body. This business unit has been sold to Lloyd's Register, and is now called **Lloyd's Register Rail**.

NS Stations operates the commercial space in the stations, such as shops.

NS Financial Services is a rolling stock leasing company based in Dublin, Ireland. This company owns the majority of the NS rolling stock fleet. It also owns Syntus rolling stock and DB Schenker Rail Nederland locomotives which were formerly owned by NS.

Abellio was formerly known as Nedrailways and is a subsidiary charged with business development abroad. Abellio operates tendered train services in other countries, making joint bids with strategic local partners. These include two franchises in the United Kingdom, jointly with Serco (Merseyrail Electrics and Northern Rail), and others in Germany.

NS has a subsidiary for special passenger transport, such as charter trains, and other events, known as **NS Chartertrains**.

RegioNS is a subsidiary for the operation of tendered regional train services for which NS Reizigers itself is excluded from tendering. The company operates train services between Apeldoorn and Zutphen as franchised by the province of Gelderland. Arriva was due to take over this concession in December 2012.

NS PASSENGER TRAINS

The NS timetable is almost entirely regular interval with most routes having half-hourly services and many routes four trains per hour. There are now two categories of train – *Intercitytrein*, and *Sprinter*. *Sprinters* are stopping trains and are operated by EMUs. Intercity trains are generally VIRM or *Koploper* EMUs or are loco-hauled. Loco-hauled services are:

Amsterdam–Den Haag HS–Rotterdam–Dordrecht–Roosendaal–Antwerpen Centraal–Brussels. SNCB Class 28 electric locos and ICR stock. This service is expected to be withdrawn in December 2012 when V250 sets start to operate a high speed Amsterdam–Brussels service. Through trains to Brussels and Paris are operated by Thalys PBA or PBKA units.

Den Haag CS–Rotterdam–Dordrecht–Breda–Tilburg–Eindhoven–Venlo. Class 1700 plus ICR push-pull stock or *Koploper* EMUs.

Amsterdam/Hoofddorp–Amersfoort–Enschede. *Koploper* EMUs.

Roosendaal–Breda–Tilburg–Nijmegen–Arnhem. Class 1700 plus ICR push-pull stock or *Koploper* EMUs.

Trains to Germany are formed of loco-hauled DB IC stock or are operated by ICEs.

NEDTRAIN DEPOTS & WORKSHOPS

Depots (*onderhoudsbedrijven*) are responsible for day-to-day maintenance of vehicles and the particular depots which normally carry out such maintenance are shown as allocations in this section. There are no official NS depot codes. Unofficial codes used in this publication will be found in Appendix II on page 172.

The main workshops (*revisiebedrijven*) are at Haarlem for all passenger locos, units and coaching stock. Work on freight locomotives and wagons is now outsourced to Shunter Tractie.

There are many places where EMUs stable, but the main locations where units and some locos will be found are: Alkmaar, Amersfoort, Amsterdam Dijksgracht, Arnhem, Botlek*, Den Haag, Den Helder, Eindhoven, Groningen, Heerlen, Hengelo, Hoofddorp, Kijfhoek yard*, Lelystad, Maastricht, Maasvlaakte*, Nijmegen, Roosendaal, Rotterdam CS, Sittard, Utrecht, Venlo, Vlissingen, Waalhaven Zuid* and Zwolle. Those locations with an asterisk are not on passenger lines.

NS NUMBERING & LIVERIES

Different numbering series were used for locomotives and multiple units, but with renumbering and condemnations, numbers do not now duplicate.

Liveries of most vehicles are based on yellow. Please see Appendix II on page 172 for details of liveries and livery codes used in this section.

OTHER PASSENGER TRAIN OPERATORS

At the end of the 1990s, legal powers and finance for most "loss-making" regional lines in the Netherlands were shifted to the regional transport authorities which then carried out tendering procedures to select suitable "franchise" operators. Details of these operators can be found in Section 4. Further services are to be put out to tender in the near future.

FREIGHT TRAIN OPERATORS

NS relinquished its freight activities in 2000 when NS Cargo merged with DB Cargo to form Railion. This later became DB Schenker. In the same period, rail freight in the Netherlands was liberalised and there are now almost 30 RUs operating freight trains in the country.

3.1. DIESEL LOCOMOTIVES

CLASS 700   B-B

These shunters, owned by NedTrain, are used for moving rolling stock around at depots and works.

Built: 2003–04.
Engine: MTU 8V183 TD 13 of 390 kW at 2100 rpm.
Transmission: Hydraulic. Voith L2r4z(s)e U2.
Length over Buffers: 9.645 m.
Weight: 40 tonnes.

Builder: Vossloh. Type G400B.
Tractive Effort: 130 kN.
Driving Wheel Diameter: 1050 mm.
Maximum Speed: 40 km/h (80 km/h when pulled).

701	G	705	G Willem	708	G	711	G
702	G	706	G Martin	709	G	712	G
703	G	707	G	710	G	713	G
704	G						

▲ NedTrain shunter 708 is seen inside Leidschendam depot with DB ICE 3 set 4610 on 2 November 2007.   **Quintus Vosman**

3.2. ELECTRIC LOCOMOTIVES

CLASS 1700 — B-B

This class is identical in outline and similar technically to Class 1800, (see below) the main differences being that they have thyristor control and upgraded ATB. As built 28 locos had auto-couplers on one end for use with the double-deck DDAR stock as "virtual EMUs". The braking system is not suitable for freight train use. 1735 was withdrawn after a fire.

Built: 1991–94.
Builder: GEC-Alsthom.
Traction Motors: 2 x Alsthom TAB 674 C4 monomotor, frame mounted.
One Hour Rating: 4400 kW.　　　　　　　**Weight:** 83 tonnes.
Maximum Tractive Effort: 294 kN.　　　**Length over Buffers:** 17.48 m.
Driving Wheel Diameter: 1250 mm.　　**Maximum Speed:** 160 km/h.

k　　Fitted with auto-coupler at one end.
§　　Equipped to operate with DDM stock.

1701	k	LD		1742	MT	
1702	k	LD		1743	MT	WOLVEGA
1703	k	LD		1744	MT	WIJCHEN
1704	k	LD		1745	MT	
1705	k	LD	DALFSEN	1746	MT	CASTRICUM
1706	k	LD		1747	MT	
1707	k	LD		1748	MT	T'HARDE
1708	k	LD		1749	MT	
1709	k	LD		1750	MT	
1710	k	LD		1751	MT	
1711	k	LD	EMMEN	1752	MT	
1712	k	LD		1753	MT	
1713	k	LD		1754	MT	DIEMEN
1714	k	LD	VEENENDAAL	1755	MT (S)	
1715	k	LD		1756	MT	
1716	k	LD		1757	MT	
1717	k	LD		1758	MT	
1718	k	LD		1759	MT	BEST
1719	k	LD	VOORHOUT	1760	MT	HOLTEN
1720	k	LD	BEILEN	1761	MT	
1721	k	LD		1762	MT	
1722	k	LD		1763	MT	
1723	k	LD		1764	MT	
1724	k	LD	Anna Paulowna	1765	MT	
1725	k	LD		1766	MT	
1726	k	LD		1767	MT	
1727	k	LD		1768	MT	AKKRUM
1728	k	LD		1769	§	MT (S)
1729		MT		1770	§	MT
1730		MT		1771		MT (S) Abcoude
1731		MT	PURMEREND	1772	§	MT
1732		MT	ZEVENBERGEN	1773	§	MT ENKHUIZEN
1733		MT	BOXTEL	1774	§	MT GRAMSBERGEN
1734		MT		1775	§	MT
1736		MT	GILZE-RIJEN	1776	§	MT (S)
1737		MT		1777	§	MT
1738		MT	DUIVENDRECHT	1778	§	MT
1739		MT	DALEN	1779	§	MT
1740		MT	BAARN	1780	§	MT
1741		MT	PUTTEN	1781	§	MT

CLASS 1800   B-B

These locomotives are based on SNCF Class BB7200. They were originally numbered as Class 1600 but NS Reizigers locos have been renumbered in the 1800 series (1623 becoming 1823 and so on) leaving DB Schenker locos in the 1600 series. None of Class 1800 is still in service with NS Reizigers, most being stored at Dijksgracht and several now in service with freight operators. 1826, 1838, 1841 and 1852 are withdrawn. 1827, 1831, 1834 and 1836 have been sold to LOCON, 1832 to HSL Logistics and 1835 to Bentheimer Eisenbahn. 1856 is reserved for the National Railway Museum.

Details the same as Class 1700 except:

Built: 1981–83.   **Builder:** Alsthom/MTE.

All push-pull fitted.

1823	(S)	HILVERSUM		1846	(S)	LEEUWARDEN
1824	(S)	ALKMAAR		1847	(S)	DELFT
1828	(S)	APELDOORN		1848	(S)	VALKENBURG
1829	(S)	EDE		1849	(S)	OSS
1830	(S)	ZWOLLE		1850	(S)	DEN HAAG
1833	(S)	BERGEN OP ZOOM1837		1851	(S)	TILBURG
1837	(S)	AMERSFOORT		1853	(S)	DEN HELDER
1839	(S)	LEIDEN		1854	(S)	GELEEN
1840	(S)	STEENWIJK		1855	(S)	EINDHOVEN
1842	(S)	WEERT		1856	(S)	HOOGEVEEN
1843	(S)	HEERLEN		1857	(S)	ROTTERDAM
1844	(S)	ROOSENDAAL		1858	(S)	ZAANDAM
1845	(S)	MIDDELBURG				

See Section 6.1 for leased Class 186 locomotives used on the HSA Brussels–Amsterdam service.

▲ 1779 heads NS Internationaal train IC 146 Berlin Ostbahnhof–Schiphol, formed of DB coaches, at Terschuur on the Apeldoorn–Amersfoort line on 8 February 2011.   **Quintus Vosman**

3.3. ELECTRIC MULTIPLE UNITS

All NS EMUs are gangwayed within the unit only. All are disc-braked except for Plan V which have tread brakes. All have power-operated sliding or folding doors.

PLAN V4, V5 & V6   "MAT '64"   2-CAR UNITS

1964 stock. These sets worked *stoptreinen* all over the NS network but are now restricted to a small number of services. They will lose work on Zwolle–Emmen to Arriva EMUs in December 2012 but will probably be retained in reserve in case of bad winter weather which often knocks out more recent types. They operate as a common fleet with all other Plan V stock.

Built: 1969–70.
Builder–Mechanical Parts: Werkspoor (441–458), Talbot (463–482).
Builder–Electrical Parts: Smit.
Traction Motors: 4 x Heemaf of 145 kW each.   **Weight:** 43 + 42 tonnes.
Wheel Arrangement: 2-Bo + Bo-2.   **Length over Couplers:** 26.07 + 26.07 m.
Accommodation: 24/40 1T + –/78.   **Maximum Speed:** 140 km/h.

441–458 are V4, 463–471 are V5 and 474–482 are V6.

441	MT	450	MT	458	MT	474	MT
443	MT	451	MT	463	MT	475	MT
444	MT	452	MT	464	MT	476	MT
445	MT	454	MT	465	MT	478	MT
446	MT	455	MT	467	MT	479	MT
447	MT	456	MT	469	MT	480	MT
449	MT	457	MT	471	MT	482	MT

▲ Few services are now operated by Mat'64 EMUs, but a large number are held in reserve in case of more modern stock breaking down. Unit 471 is seen at Mariënberg on 22 August 2012 with a Zwolle–Emmen service. Arriva was due to take over these services in December 2012. **David Haydock**

PLAN V10–V13   "MAT '64"   2-CAR UNITS

1964 stock. Talbot version of Plan V7, which were similar to other Plan V units, but built with post compartment, most later converted to an open saloon containing 16 seats in a 4+0 layout.

Built: 1972–76.
Builder–Mechanical Parts: Talbot.   **Builder–Electrical Parts:** Smit.
Traction Motors: 4 x Heemaf of 145 kW each.   **Weight:** 45 + 43 tonnes.
Wheel Arrangement: 2-Bo + Bo-2.   **Length over Couplers:** 26.07 + 26.07 m.
Accommodation: 24/40 1T + –/64.   **Maximum Speed:** 140 km/h.

919–920 are V10, 921–935 are V11, 936–950 are V12 and 951–965 are V13.

p   Post compartment converted to passenger accommodation with 12 tip-up seats.

919		MT	931	p	MT	943	p	MT	954	p	MT
920		MT	932	p	MT	944	p	MT	955	p	MT
921	p	MT	933	p	MT	945	p	MT	956	p	MT
922	p	MT	934	p	MT	946	p	MT	957	p	MT
923	p	MT	935	p	MT	947	p	MT	958	p	MT
924	p	MT	936	p	MT	948	p	MT	960	p	MT
925	p	MT	937	p	MT	949	p	MT	961	p	MT
926	p	MT	939	p	MT	950	p	MT	962	p	MT
927	p	MT	940	p	MT	951	p	MT	963	p	MT
928	p	MT	941	p	MT	952	p	MT	964	p	MT
929	p	MT	942	p	MT	953	p	MT	965	p	MT
930	p	MT									

▲ NS 2-car Sprinter 2122 is seen at Venlo on 19 November 2011.   **Luc Peulen**

PLAN Y1 SPRINTER SGM 0 2-CAR UNITS

The earliest batch of 'Sprinter' units from which British Rail's Sprinters took their name, these sets formerly worked on the Den Haag CS–Rotterdam Hofplein line and the *Zoetermeer Stadslijn*. The rapid acceleration from a standing start was especially useful on these lines which have stations at very close intervals. These two lines have now been transferred to *RandstadRail* and have been converted to light rail operation and so the Sprinters have been transferred to other lines, particularly in the south-east of the country. All sets have been modified with first class seating removed, fewer seats and more room for standees and were previously branded "*City Pendel*". They are now all refurbished in a similar manner to the 3-car units. Units were renumbered on refurbishment; former numbers are in brackets.

Built: 1975–76.
Builder–Mechanical Parts: Talbot.
Builder–Electrical Parts: Oerlikon.
Traction Motors: 8 x Oerlikon 160 kW.
Wheel Arrangement: Bo-Bo + Bo-Bo.

Accommodation: –/40 + –/40.
Weight: 52.5 + 52.5 tonnes.
Length over Couplers: 26.10 + 26.10 m.
Maximum Speed: 125 km/h.

2111	(2001)	**Y**	LD		2116	(2006)	**Y**	LD		2121	(2011)	**Y**	LD
2112	(2002)	**Y**	LD		2117	(2007)	**Y**	LD		2122	(2012)	**Y**	LD
2113	(2003)	**Y**	LD		2118	(2008)	**Y**	LD		2123	(2013)	**Y**	LD
2114	(2004)	**Y**	LD		2119	(2009)	**Y**	LD		2124	(2014)	**Y**	LD
2115	(2005)	**Y**	LD		2120	(2010)	**Y**	LD		2125	(2015)	**Y**	LD

▲ 4-car SLT unit 2455 and 6-car unit 2604 are seen at Dordrecht Zuid on 4 July 2012.
Raimund Wyhnal

PLAN Y2   SPRINTER SGM 1   2-CAR UNITS

These sets are similar to Plan Y1, but were built with a toilet and gangways, although the toilets have now been removed. They also previously worked on the *Hofpleinlijn* and *Zoetermeer Stadslijn*. Also refurbished, and renumbered.

Built: 1975–76.
Builder–Mechanical Parts: Talbot.
Builder–Electrical Parts: Oerlikon.
Traction Motors: 8 x Oerlikon 160 kW.   **Weight:** 54 + 53 tonnes.
Wheel Arrangement: Bo-Bo + Bo-Bo.   **Length over Couplers:** 26.10 + 26.10 m.
Accommodation: –/40 + –/40.   **Maximum Speed:** 125 km/h.

2131	(2021)	**Y**	LD	2136	(2026)	**Y**	LD	2141	(2031)	**Y**	LD
2132	(2022)	**Y**	LD	2137	(2027)	**Y**	LD	2142	(2032)	**Y**	LD
2133	(2023)	**Y**	LD	2138	(2028)	**Y**	LD	2143	(2033)	**Y**	LD
2134	(2024)	**Y**	LD	2139	(2029)	**Y**	LD	2144	(2034)	**Y**	LD
2135	(2025)	**Y**	LD	2140	(2030)	**Y**	LD	2145	(2035)	**Y**	LD

TYPE S70   SPRINTER LIGHT TRAIN   4-CAR UNITS

New articulated units based on DB Class 424. They are used mainly in the urbanised Randstad region of the north-west Netherlands.

Built: 2008–2012. Bombardier design.
Builder–Mechanical Parts: Bombardier Aachen.
Builder–Electrical Parts: Siemens (heavy parts), Bombardier (electronics).
Traction Motors: 6 Siemens of 250 kW.   **Weight:** 129 tonnes.
Wheel Arrangement: Bo-2-2-Bo-Bo.   **Length over Couplers:** 69.36 m.
Accommodation: 40/144 (38).   **Width:** 2.84 m.
Floor Height at Entrance: 800 mm.   **Maximum Speed:** 140 km/h.

2401	**S**	LD	2419	**S**	LD	2436	**S**	LD	2453	**S**	LD
2402	**S**	LD	2420	**S**	LD	2437	**S**	LD	2454	**S**	LD
2403	**S**	LD	2421	**S**	LD	2438	**S**	LD	2455	**S**	LD
2404	**S**	LD	2422	**S**	LD	2439	**S**	LD	2456	**S**	LD
2405	**S**	LD	2423	**S**	LD	2440	**S**	LD	2457	**S**	LD
2406	**S**	LD	2424	**S**	LD	2441	**S**	LD	2458	**S**	LD
2407	**S**	LD	2425	**S**	LD	2442	**S**	LD	2459	**S**	LD
2408	**S**	LD	2426	**S**	LD	2443	**S**	LD	2460	**S**	LD
2409	**S**	LD	2427	**S**	LD	2444	**S**	LD	2461	**S**	LD
2410	**S**	LD	2428	**S**	LD	2445	**S**	LD	2462	**S**	LD
2411	**S**	LD	2429	**S**	LD	2446	**S**	LD	2463	**S**	LD
2412	**S**	LD	2430	**S**	LD	2447	**S**	LD	2464	**S**	LD
2413	**S**	LD	2431	**S**	LD	2448	**S**	LD	2465	**S**	LD
2414	**S**	LD	2432	**S**	LD	2449	**S**	LD	2466	**S**	LD
2415	**S**	LD	2433	**S**	LD	2450	**S**	LD	2467	**S**	LD
2416	**S**	LD	2434	**S**	LD	2451	**S**	LD	2468	**S**	LD
2417	**S**	LD	2435	**S**	LD	2452	**S**	LD	2469	**S**	LD
2418	**S**	LD									

TYPE S100 SPRINTER LIGHT TRAIN 6-CAR UNITS

New articulated units based on DB Class 424.

Details as Type S70 except:

Traction Motors: 8 Siemens of 250 kW each. **Weight:** 176 tonnes.
Wheel Arrangement: Bo-Bo-2-2-2-Bo-Bo. **Length over Couplers:** 100.54 m.
Accommodation: 56/208 (68).

2601	S	LD	2619	S	LD	2637	S	LD	2653	S	LD
2602	S	LD	2620	S	LD	2638	S	LD	2654	S	LD
2603	S	LD	2621	S	LD	2639	S	LD	2655	S	LD
2604	S	LD	2622	S	LD	2638	S	LD	2656	S	LD
2605	S	LD	2623	S	LD	2639	S	LD	2657	S	LD
2606	S	LD	2624	S	LD	2640	S	LD	2658	S	LD (U)
2607	S	LD	2625	S	LD	2641	S	LD	2659	S	LD
2608	S	LD	2626	S	LD	2642	S	LD	2660	S	LD
2609	S	LD	2627	S	LD	2643	S	LD	2661	S	LD
2610	S	LD	2628	S	LD	2644	S	LD	2662	S	LD
2611	S	LD	2629	S	LD	2645	S	LD	2663	S	LD
2612	S	LD	2630	S	LD	2646	S	LD	2664	S	LD
2613	S	LD	2631	S	LD	2647	S	LD	2665	S	LD
2614	S	LD	2632	S	LD	2648	S	LD	2666	S	LD
2615	S	LD	2633	S	LD	2649	S	LD	2667	S	LD
2616	S	LD	2634	S	LD	2650	S	LD	2668	S	LD
2617	S	LD	2635	S	LD	2651	S	LD	2669	S	LD
2618	S	LD	2636	S	LD	2652	S	LD			

PLAN Y2/Y3 SPRINTER SGM 1/2 3-CAR UNITS

2036–2080 were built as 2-car units but were strengthened with an intermediate trailer, reclassified from Plan Y1 to Plan Y2 and renumbered 2836–2880. 2881–2895 were built as 3-car units and are Plan Y3. The units work on local stopping trains in the Randstad area such as Amsterdam–Utrecht, Amsterdam–Haarlem–Uitgeest, Amsterdam–Alkmaar and Rotterdam CS–Hoek van Holland. All sets have now been refurbished and renumbered from the 2800 to the 2900 series.

Built: 1978–80 (Plan Y1). 1983–84 (Plan Y3 and centre cars of Plan Y2).
Builder–Mechanical Parts: Talbot.
Builder–Electrical Parts: Oerlikon.
Traction Motors: 8 x Oerlikon 160 kW. **Weight:** 54 + 36 + 53 tonnes.
Wheel Arrangement: Bo-Bo + 2-2 + Bo-Bo. **Length over Couplers:** 26.15 + 26.40 + 26.15 m.
Accommodation: –/72 + 40/40 1T + –/72 1T. **Maximum Speed:** 125 km/h.

2936	(2036)	S	LD	2956	(2056)	S	LD	2976	(2076)	S	LD
2937	(2037)	S	LD	2957	(2057)	S	LD	2977	(2077)	S	LD
2938	(2038)	S	LD	2958	(2058)	S	LD	2978	(2078)	S	LD
2939	(2039)	S	LD	2959	(2059)	S	LD	2979	(2079)	S	LD
2940	(2040)	S	LD	2960	(2060)	S	LD	2980	(2080)	S	LD
2941	(2041)	S	LD	2961	(2061)	S	LD	2981		S	LD
2942	(2042)	S	LD	2962	(2062)	S	LD	2982		S	LD
2943	(2043)	S	LD	2963	(2063)	S	LD	2983		S	LD
2944	(2044)	S	LD	2964	(2064)	S	LD	2984		S	LD
2945	(2045)	S	LD	2965	(2065)	S	LD	2985		S	LD
2946	(2046)	S	LD	2966	(2066)	S	LD	2986		S	LD
2947	(2047)	S	LD	2967	(2067)	S	LD	2987		S	LD
2948	(2048)	S	LD	2968	(2068)	S	LD	2988		S	LD
2949	(2049)	S	LD	2969	(2069)	S	LD	2989		S	LD
2950	(2050)	S	LD	2970	(2070)	S	LD	2990		S	LD
2951	(2051)	S	LD	2971	(2071)	S	LD	2991		S	LD
2952	(2052)	S	LD	2972	(2072)	S	LD	2992		S	LD
2953	(2053)	S	LD	2973	(2073)	S	LD	2993		S	LD
2954	(2054)	S	LD	2974	(2074)	S	LD	2994		S	LD
2955	(2055)	S	LD	2975	(2075)	S	LD	2995		S	LD

ICM1/2 (PLAN Z0/Z1)   KOPLOPER   3-CAR UNITS

These Intercity trains, also known as IC3 units, were built with raised cabs and through gangways. The gangways have been welded shut in the recent refurbishment. The coaches in these sets formed the basis for the loco-hauled ICR stock now familiar over many NS routes. These units and the similar 4-car units can be found on Intercity services to Groningen, Leeuwarden, Enschede and Arnhem plus Zwolle–Roosendaal. Prototype Plan ICM0 units 4001–7 built in 1977 have now been withdrawn. All units were refurbished in 2007–2011 with red leather seats in first class and blue moquette in second class. Following refurbishment units are known as ICMm.

Built: 1983–89.
Builder–Mechanical Parts: Talbot.   **Builder–Electrical Parts:** Oerlikon.
Traction Motors: 4 x Oerlikon of 312 kW each.   **Wheel Arrangement:** Bo-Bo + 2-2 + 2-2.
Accommodation: –/68 + bicycle space + 35/27 (3) 1TD + –/68.
Weight: 60 + 42 + 42 tonnes.   **Length over Couplers:** 27.05 + 26.50 + 27.05 m.
Maximum Speed: 160 km/h.

4011 I	ON	4027 I	ON	4043 I	ON	4059 I	ON
4012 I	ON	4028 I	ON	4044 I	ON	4060 I	ON
4013 I	ON	4029 I	ON	4045 I	ON	4061 I	ON
4014 I	ON	4030 I	ON	4046 I	ON	4062 I	ON
4015 I	ON	4031 I	ON	4047 I	ON	4063 I	ON
4016 I	ON	4032 I	ON	4048 I	ON	4064 I	ON
4017 I	ON	4033 I	ON	4049 I	ON	4065 I	ON
4018 I	ON	4034 I	ON	4050 I	ON	4066 I	ON
4019 I	ON	4035 I	ON	4051 I	ON	4067 I	ON
4020 I	ON	4036 I	ON	4052 I	ON	4068 I	ON
4021 I	ON	4037 I	ON	4053 I	ON	4069 I	ON
4022 I	ON	4038 I	ON	4054 I	ON	4070 I	ON
4023 I	ON	4039 I	ON	4055 I	ON	4071 I	ON
4024 I	ON	4040 I	ON	4056 I	ON	4072 I	ON
4025 I	ON	4041 I	ON	4057 I	ON	4073 I	ON
4026 I	ON	4042 I	ON	4058 I	ON	4074 I	ON

▲ 3-car Sprinter EMU 2938 is seen with a local stopping train at Elst, between Arnhem and Nijmegen, on 22 August 2012.   **David Haydock**

4075 I	ON	4081 I	ON	4087 I	ON	4093 I	ON
4076 I	ON	4082 I	ON	4088 I	ON	4094 I	ON
4077 I	ON	4083 I	ON	4089 I	ON	4095 I	ON
4078 I	ON	4084 I	ON	4090 I	ON	4096 I	ON
4079 I	ON	4085 I	ON	4091 I	ON	4097 I	ON
4080 I	ON	4086 I	ON	4092 I	ON		

ICM3/4 (PLAN Z2)   KOPLOPER   4-CAR UNITS

These units are a four-car version of the IC3s and are used on the same services. All units have been refurbished.

Details as ICM2 except:

Built: 1990–93.
Traction Motors: 6 x Oerlikon of 312 kW each. **Wheel Arrangement:** Bo-Bo + Bo-2 + 2-2 + 2-2.
Accommodation: –/55 + –/80 1T + 59/– 2T + –/63 1T.
Weight: 59 + 50 + 42 + 42 tonnes.
Length over Couplers: 27.05 + 26.50 + 26.50 + 27.05 m.

Note: 4231 was numbered 4444 for a time when it had extra first class accommodation.

4201 I	ON	4214 I	ON	4227 I	ON	4239 I	ON
4202 I	ON	4215 I	ON	4228 I	ON	4240 I	ON
4203 I	ON	4216 I	ON	4229 I	ON	4241 I	ON
4204 I	ON	4217 I	ON	4230 I	ON	4242 I	ON
4205 I	ON	4218 I	ON	4231 I	ON	4243 I	ON
4206 I	ON	4219 I	ON	4232 I	ON	4244 I	ON
4207 I	ON	4220 I	ON	4233 I	ON	4245 I	ON
4208 I	ON	4221 I	ON	4234 I	ON	4246 I	ON
4209 I	ON	4222 I	ON	4235 I	ON	4247 I	ON
4210 I	ON	4223 I	ON	4236 I	ON	4248 I	ON
4211 I	ON	4224 I	ON	4237 I	ON	4249 I	ON
4212 I	ON	4225 I	ON	4238 I	ON	4250 I	ON
4213 I	ON	4226 I	ON				

▲ ICM3 EMUs 4205 and 4211 arrive at Zutphen on 23 August 2012 with a Zwolle–Roosendaal service. **David Haydock**

VIRM   REGIO RUNNER   4- & 6-CAR UNITS

These double-deck units were originally known as IRM (*Inter-Regio Materieel*). They work various Intercity services over a wide area. They were built as 3- and 4-car units, but in 2001–05 all units had an extra intermediate transformer trailer (Type ABv6) added and 4-car units also had an intermediate power car (mBv7) added, so that all are now either 4- or 6-car dual-voltage units. This has been done with possible conversions from 1500 V DC to 25 kV AC in mind. Units are now known as VIRM, V meaning *Verlengte* (lengthened).

Unit numbers were in the 82xx series for 3-car units and 84xx series for 4-car units. They are now 94xx series for the 4-car units and 86xx series for the 6-car units. The set number is determined by the ABv3/4 car. Thus 9403 contains 380 8003 and so on. Set numbers change if a 4-car is converted to a 6-car or vice-versa. So 9408 was renumbered 8608 when it became a 6-car unit and 8643 was renumbered 9443 when it became a 4-car unit.

Further batches were built in 2003–05 and 2008–10. These have unit numbers in the 95xx and 87xx series.

Built: 1994–96, 2001–05, 2008–10.
Builder–Mechanical Parts: VIRM1 – Talbot/De Dietrich, VIRM2/3 Bombardier (Talbot).
Builder–Electrical Parts: Holec.
Systems: 1500 V DC (pre-equipped for 25 kV AC 50 Hz).
Wheel Arrangement: 2-Bo + 2-2 [+ 2-2 + 2-Bo] + 2-2 + Bo-2.
Traction Motors: 2 x Holec DMKT 60/45 of 302 kW continuous rating per power car.
Accommodation: –/97(4) [+ 46/48(4) 1T –/94(5)]+ 46/52 1T + 23/80 1T + –/97(4).
Weight: 62.2 [+ ? + ?] + 52.4 (+ ?) + 62.2 tonnes.
Length over Couplers: 27.28 [+ 26.50 + 26.50] + 26.50 + 26.50 + 27.28 m.
Maximum Speed: 160 km/h.

Note: 290 8611 and 290 8718 (ex 9528) have been scrapped and 290 8539 (ex 9420) has accident damage.

NUMBERING

Set formations vary from time to time. The individual car numbers are listed here together with set formations as far as is known at time of going to press. The individual car numbers are quite small and in one corner at solebar level.

Type mBvk1/2	290 8501 to 8860.
Type mBv7	260 8801 to 8880.
Type ABv3/4	380 8001 to 8198.
Type ABv5	380 8201 to 8280.
Type ABv6	380 8301 to 8478.

SET FORMATIONS

First series. VIRM 1. 81 sets – 49 6-car, 32 4-car. Originally built with GTO thyristors, rebuilt with IGBTs 2011–13.

Set	Liv.	Depot	mBvk	ABv5	mBv7	ABv6	ABv3/4	mBvk
9401	I	ON	290 8571			380 8316	380 8001	290 8658
9402	I	ON	290 8503			380 8355	380 8002	290 8504
9403	I	ON	290 8505			380 8312	380 8003	290 8506
9404	I	ON	290 8507			380 8347	380 8004	290 8508
9405	I	ON	290 8509			380 8308	380 8005	290 8721
9406	I	ON	290 8511			380 8378	380 8006	290 8568
9407	I	ON	290 8513			380 8314	380 8007	290 8514
8608	I	ON	290 8515	380 8240	260 8809	380 8328	380 8008	290 8541
9409	I	ON	290 8517			380 8323	380 8009	290 8518
8610	I	ON	290 8705	380 8227	260 8865	380 8310	380 8010	290 8540
9411	I	ON	290 8521			380 8305	380 8011	290 8522
9412	I	ON	290 8641			380 8303	380 8012	290 8584
9413	I	ON	290 8525			380 8309	380 8013	290 8526
8614	I	ON	290 8527	380 8246	260 8810	380 8329	380 8014	290 8617
8615	I	ON	290 8637	380 8220	260 8846	380 8374	380 8015	290 8530

9416	I	ON	290 8531			380 8306	380 8016	290 8532
9417	I	ON	290 8646			380 8339	380 8017	290 8544
9418	I	ON	290 8535			380 8343	380 8018	290 8536
9419	I	ON	290 8537			380 8307	380 8019	290 8538
9420	I	ON	290 8579			380 8397	380 8020	290 8510
8621	I	ON	290 8516	380 8211	260 8843	380 8371	380 8021	290 8542
9422	I	ON	290 8543			380 8313	380 8022	290 8613
9423	I	ON	290 8545			380 8377	380 8023	290 8546
8624	I	ON	290 8529	380 8214	260 8801	380 8335	380 8024	290 8548
9425	I	ON	290 8551			380 8348	380 8025	290 8577
9426	I	ON	290 8550			380 8376	380 8026	290 8552
9427	I	ON	290 8585			380 8381	380 8027	290 8580
8628	I	ON	290 8555	380 8203	260 8814	380 8334	380 8028	290 8556
8629			Coaches used to form 8728					
9430	I	ON	290 8559			380 8365	380 8030	290 8560
9431	I	ON	290 8561			380 8304	380 8031	290 8562
8632	I	ON	290 8633	380 8204	260 8862	380 8373	380 8032	290 8620
8633	I	ON	290 8565	380 8205	260 8847	380 8418	380 8033	290 8566
9434	I	ON	290 8567			380 8315	380 8034	290 8623
8635	I	ON	290 8569	380 8206	260 8827	380 8352	380 8035	290 8570
8636	I	ON	290 8583	380 8207	260 8802	380 8336	380 8036	290 8572
8637	I	ON	290 8573	380 8208	260 8842	380 8370	380 8037	290 8632
8638	I	ON	290 8575	380 8209	260 8834	380 8361	380 8038	290 8576
8639	I	ON	290 8642	380 8210	260 8841	380 8369	380 8039	290 8578
8640	I	ON	290 8501	380 8247	260 8803	380 8337	380 8040	290 8502
8641	I	ON	290 8581	380 8212	260 8821	380 8344	380 8041	290 8648

▲ VIRM set 8640 is seen at Woerden on 2 July 2012 with an Enschede–Den Haag service.
Raimund Wyhnal

8642	I	ON	290 8622	380 8213	260 8825	380 8349	380 8042	290 8626
9443	I	ON	290 8547			380 8311	380 8043	290 8586
8644	I	ON	290 8587	380 8215	260 8826	380 8350	380 8044	290 8588
8645	I	ON	290 8589	380 8216	260 8831	380 8357	380 8045	290 8590
8646	I	ON	290 8591	380 8217	260 8823	380 8346	380 8046	290 8592
8647	I	ON	290 8593	380 8218	260 8805	380 8322	380 8047	290 8594
8648	I	ON	290 8595	380 8219	260 8807	380 8325	380 8048	290 8596
8649	I	ON	290 8597	380 8221	260 8816	380 8321	380 8049	290 8598
9450	I	ON	290 8636			380 8380	380 8050	290 8600
8651	I	ON	290 8601	380 8222	260 8813	380 8333	380 8051	290 8602
8652	I	ON	290 8603	380 8223	260 8837	380 8364	380 8052	290 8604
8653	I	ON	290 8605	380 8228	260 8828	380 8345	380 8053	290 8640
8654	I	ON	290 8607	380 8225	260 8817	380 8320	380 8054	290 8608
8655	I	ON	290 8624	380 8226	260 8832	380 8358	380 8055	290 8610
8656	I	ON	290 8643	380 8239	260 8818	380 8340	380 8056	290 8599
8657	I	ON	290 8609	380 8224	260 8822	380 8353	380 8057	290 8614
8658	I	ON	290 8553	380 8201	260 8804	380 8338	380 8058	290 8554
8659	I	ON	290 8612	380 8230	260 8811	380 8330	380 8059	290 8628
8660	I	ON	290 8657	380 8231	260 8815	380 8319	380 8060	290 8564
8661	I	ON	290 8627	380 8232	260 8835	380 8362	380 8061	290 8533
8662	I	ON	290 8645	380 8233	260 8839	380 8367	380 8062	290 8634
8663	I	ON	290 8625	380 8234	260 8830	380 8356	380 8063	290 8524
8664	I	ON	290 8528	380 8238	260 8840	380 8368	380 8064	290 8618
8665	I	ON	290 8629	380 8236	260 8844	380 8372	380 8065	290 8630
8666	I	ON	290 8631	380 8237	260 8808	380 8326	380 8066	290 8574
8667	I	ON	290 8621	380 8235	260 8833	380 8360	380 8067	290 8606
9468	I	ON	290 8523			380 8420	380 8068	290 8539
9469	I	ON	290 8653			380 8318	380 8069	290 8512
8670	I	ON	290 8639	380 8241	260 8806	380 8324	380 8070	290 8534
8671	I	ON	290 8519	380 8243	260 8819	380 8341	380 8071	290 8520
8672	I	ON	290 8635	380 8242	260 8812	380 8332	380 8072	290 8644
9473	I	ON	290 8563			380 8331	380 8073	290 8619
8674	I	ON	290 8647	380 8244	260 8836	380 8363	380 8074	290 8582
8675	I	ON	290 8649	380 8245	260 8829	380 8354	380 8075	290 8650
8676	I	ON	290 8558	380 8229	260 8820	380 8342	380 8076	290 8652
9477	I	ON	290 8638			380 8351	380 8077	290 8654
9478	I	ON	290 8655			380 8302	380 8078	290 8656
9479	I	ON	290 8615			380 8359	380 8079	290 8616
9480	I	ON	290 8659			380 8379	380 8080	290 8660
9481	I	ON	290 8661			380 8382	380 8081	290 8662

Second series. VIRM 2. Built with IGBTs. 24 sets – 11 6-car, 13 4-car.

8701	I	ON	290 8689	380 8257	260 8848	380 8395	380 8101	290 8690
8702	I	ON	290 8733	380 8262	260 8845	380 8317	380 8102	290 8663
8703	I	ON	290 8691	380 8258	260 8849	380 8396	380 8103	290 8692
9504	I	ON	290 8665			380 8383	380 8104	290 8666
8705	I	ON	290 8671	380 8259	260 8850	380 8409	380 8105	290 8672
9506	I	ON	290 8673			380 8387	380 8106	290 8674
8707	I	ON	290 8698	380 8248	260 8851	380 8388	380 8107	290 8676
9508	I	ON	290 8677			380 8389	380 8108	290 8678
8709	I	ON	290 8679	380 8256	260 8852	380 8390	380 8109	290 8680
9510	I	ON	290 8670			380 8391	380 8110	290 8682
8711 (U)	I	ON	290 8683	380 8251	260 8853	380 8384	380 8111	290 8722
9512	I	ON	290 8685			380 8385	380 8112	290 8686
8713	I	ON	290 8549	380 8249	260 8854	380 8392	380 8113	290 8688
9514	I	ON	290 8667			380 8393	380 8114	290 8668
8715	I	ON	290 8710	380 8254	260 8855	380 8394	380 8115	290 8717
9516	I	ON	290 8693			380 8327	380 8116	290 8694
8717	I	ON	290 8695	380 8252	260 8856	380 8398	380 8117	290 8696
9518	I	ON	290 8697			380 8399	380 8118	290 8687
8719	I	ON	290 8699	380 8255	260 8857	380 8400	380 8119	290 8700
9520	I	ON	290 8701			380 8401	380 8120	290 8702
8721	I	ON	290 8715	380 8250	260 8858	380 8402	380 8121	290 8704
9522	I	ON	290 8681			380 8403	380 8122	290 8706

8723	I	ON	290 8707	380 8253	260 8859	380 8404	380 8123	290 8708
9524	I	ON	290 8709			380 8405	380 8124	290 8669
9525	I	ON	290 8711			380 8406	380 8125	290 8712

Third series. VIRM 3. 21 6-car sets.

8726	I	ON	290 8713	380 8260	260 8860	380 8407	380 8126	290 8714
8727	I	ON	290 8675	380 8261	260 8861	380 8408	380 8127	290 8716
8728	I	ON	290 8557	380 8202	260 8838	380 8366	380 8128	290 8651
8729	I	ON	290 8719	380 8263	260 8863	380 8410	380 8129	290 8720
8730	I	ON	290 8684	380 8264	260 8864	380 8386	380 8130	290 8664
8731	I	ON	290 8723	380 8265	260 8824	380 8412	380 8131	290 8724
8732	I	ON	290 8725	380 8266	260 8866	380 8413	380 8132	290 8726
8733	I	ON	290 8727	380 8267	260 8867	380 8414	380 8133	290 8728
8734	I	ON	290 8729	380 8268	260 8868	380 8415	380 8134	290 8730
8735	I	ON	290 8731	380 8269	260 8869	380 8416	380 8135	290 8732
8736	I	ON	290 8703	380 8270	260 8870	380 8417	380 8136	290 8734
8737	I	ON	290 8736	380 8271	260 8871	380 8375	380 8137	290 8735
8738	I	ON	290 8737	380 8272	260 8872	380 8419	380 8138	290 8738
8739	I	ON	290 8739	380 8273	260 8873	380 8411	380 8139	290 8740
8740	I	ON	290 8741	380 8274	260 8874	380 8421	380 8140	290 8742
8741	I	ON	290 8743	380 8275	260 8875	380 8422	380 8141	290 8744
8742	I	ON	290 8745	380 8276	260 8876	380 8423	380 8142	290 8746
8743	I	ON	290 8747	380 8277	260 8877	380 8424	380 8143	290 8748
8744	I	ON	290 8749	380 8278	260 8878	380 8425	380 8144	290 8750
8745	I	ON	290 8751	380 8279	260 8879	380 8426	380 8145	290 8752
8746	I	ON	290 8753	380 8280	260 8880	380 8427	380 8146	290 8754

Fourth series. VIRM 4. 51 4-car sets.

9547	I	ON	290 8759	380 8428	380 8147	290 8760
9548	I	ON	290 8761	380 8429	380 8148	290 8762
9549	I	ON	290 8763	380 8430	380 8149	290 8764
9550	I	ON	290 8765	380 8431	380 8150	290 8766
9551	I	ON	290 8767	380 8432	380 8151	290 8768
9552	I	ON	290 8769	380 8433	380 8152	290 8770
9553	I	ON	290 8771	380 8434	380 8153	290 8772
9554	I	ON	290 8773	380 8435	380 8154	290 8774
9555	I	ON	290 8775	380 8436	380 8155	290 8776
9556	I	ON	290 8777	380 8437	380 8156	290 8778
9557	I	ON	290 8779	380 8438	380 8157	290 8780
9558	I	ON	290 8781	380 8439	380 8158	290 8782
9559	I	ON	290 8783	380 8440	380 8159	290 8784
9560	I	ON	290 8785	380 8441	380 8160	290 8786
9561	I	ON	290 8787	380 8442	380 8161	290 8788
9562	I	ON	290 8789	380 8443	380 8162	290 8790
9563	I	ON	290 8791	380 8444	380 8163	290 8792
9564	I	ON	290 8793	380 8445	380 8164	290 8794
9565	I	ON	290 8795	380 8446	380 8165	290 8796
9566	I	ON	290 8797	380 8447	380 8166	290 8798
9567	I	ON	290 8799	380 8448	380 8167	290 8800
9568	I	ON	290 8801	380 8449	380 8168	290 8802
9569	I	ON	290 8803	380 8450	380 8169	290 8804
9570	I	ON	290 8805	380 8451	380 8170	290 8806
9571	I	ON	290 8807	380 8452	380 8171	290 8808
9572	I	ON	290 8809	380 8453	380 8172	290 8810
9573	I	ON	290 8811	380 8454	380 8173	290 8812
9574	I	ON	290 8813	380 8455	380 8174	290 8814
9575	I	ON	290 8815	380 8456	380 8175	290 8816
9576	I	ON	290 8817	380 8457	380 8176	290 8818
9577	I	ON	290 8819	380 8458	380 8177	290 8820
9578	I	ON	290 8861	380 8459	380 8178	290 8822
9579	I	ON	290 8823	380 8460	380 8179	290 8824
9580	I	ON	290 8825	380 8461	380 8180	290 8826
9581	I	ON	290 8827	380 8462	380 8181	290 8828
9582	I	ON	290 8830	380 8463	380 8182	290 8821

9583	I	ON	290 8832		380 8464	380 8183	290 8831
9584	I	ON	290 8833		380 8465	380 8184	290 8834
9585	I	ON	290 8835		380 8466	380 8185	290 8836
9586	I	ON	290 8837		380 8467	380 8186	290 8838
9587	I	ON	290 8839		380 8468	380 8187	290 8840
9588	I	ON	290 8841		380 8469	380 8188	290 8842
9589	I	ON	290 8843		380 8470	380 8189	290 8844
9590	I	ON	290 8845		380 8471	380 8190	290 8846
9591	I	ON	290 8847		380 8472	380 8191	290 8848
9592	I	ON	290 8849		380 8473	380 8192	290 8850
9593	I	ON	290 8851		380 8474	380 8193	290 8852
9594	I	ON	290 8853		380 8475	380 8194	290 8854
9595	I	ON	290 8855		380 8476	380 8195	290 8856
9596	I	ON	290 8857		380 8477	380 8196	290 8858
9597	I	ON	290 8859		380 8478	380 8198	290 8860

▲ The first refurbished NID sets were outshopped in spring 2012. Early teething troubles often took them out of service from the Amsterdam–Rotterdam route. The first set, 7501, is seen here in Haarlem works, power car 8001 forward, on 9 March 2012.　　**Luc Peulen**

NID (DDZ)   4- & 6-CAR DOUBLE-DECK EMUs

These units started to be formed in 2012 from former DDAR (*dubbeldeksaggloregiomaterieel*) double-deck stock. This was built for *Agglo Regio* services and derived from NS first generation DDM-1 double-deck stock. The stock was first introduced as fixed formation sets with an ABv composite, one or two Bv seconds and a Bvk driving trailer second powered by a Class 1700 locomotive. These were "virtual EMUs" which could work in multiple, for which purpose the locomotives were fitted with an auto-coupler at one end.

However, in 1997/98 50 mDDM (*motordubbeldekmaterieel*) power cars were delivered, releasing 50 Class 1700s for use on Intercity services. These power cars were most unusual in having three bogies, in order to transfer enough power, including on lines with tight curves. All of the traction and auxiliary equipment is placed on the lower level, leaving space on the upper level for seats.

Original set numbers consisted of a "7'", a digit denoting the number of coaches and the last two digits of the driving trailer. Thus 7345 would be a 3-car set with driving trailer 7045, 7445 would be a 4-car set with the driving trailer 7045. 7845 would be an mDDM-powered 4-car set with the driving trailer 7045. Trains were used on everything from *Sneltrein* to IC services in the Randstad area.

In February 2012, NedTrain's Haarlem works outshopped the first refurbished version of trains with mDDM power cars, all of them upgraded for Intercity services and known as NID (*Nieuwe Intercity Dubbeldekker*). They are also known as "DDZ" sets. All the mDDMs plus 190 trailers will be refurbished and formed into 30 4-car and 20 6-car sets. The units will first be outshopped as 4-car sets before returning to Haarlem to receive the extra two cars in the case of the 6-car sets. mDDM power cars, formerly with both first and second class accommodation and known as mABk, are rebuilt with only second class seats.

Apart from an overhaul, all refurbished sets will receive air conditioning, seats to IC standard, wireless internet and information displays. Front ends are rebuilt with one-piece windscreens. The all yellow livery will be replaced by the yellow and blue used on IRM sets. Work will be completed in 2014. It is not yet known what will happen to the spare cars – seven ABvs, 32 Bvs and 29 BVks.

The new trains are numbered in the 75xx (4-car) or 76xx (6-car) series, the final two digits being the same as the **power car**, not the driving trailer as before. The new coach numbers conform to the EU numbering system. It is not yet known which routes the units will operate but they will stay in the Randstad area. Details below are all after refurbishment.

Built: 1996–98 (power cars); 1991–93 (trailer cars).
Builder: De Dietrich/Adtranz (power cars); Talbot (trailer cars).
Wheel Arrangement: Bo-Bo-Bo + 2-2 + 2-2 (+ 2-2 + 2-2) + 2-2.
Traction Motors (power car): 6 Adtranz Type 6FBA 4548A asynchronous of 390 kW each.
Accommodation: –/44 (8) + 40/58 (10) 1T + –/114 (5) 1T (+ 40/58 (10) 1T + –/114 (14)) + 27/55 (6).
Length over Couplers: 21.39 + 26.40 + 26.40 (+ 26.40 + 26.40) + 26.89 m.
Weight: 80 + 46 + 46 (+46 + 46) + 53 tonnes.
Maximum Speed: 140 km/h.

NUMBERING

Vehicle	Original numbers	New numbers
mBk	390 7701 to 7750.	94 84 **426 8001** to **8050**.
ABvk	270 7001 to 7079 (7040 and 7079 withdrawn).	94 84 **426 4001** to **4079**.
Bv	280 7201 to 7302 (7208 withdrawn, 7272 stored).	94 84 **426 3001** to **3102**.
ABv	380 7501 to 7577 (7555 stored, damaged).	94 84 **426 2001** to **2077**.

The following formations were current in mid 2012 – the first refurbished sets retained their original formation. All coach numbers begin with 94 84 426. The additional coaches to be inserted into 6-car sets, and taken from former loco-powered sets, were not known at the time of writing. mDDM 7739 was spare in mid 2012.

Unit	mDDM	ABv	Bv	ABv	Bv	ABvk		
7501	8001 (7701)	3007 (7207)	2001 (7501)			4002 (7002)	I	LD
7502	8002 (7702)	3004 (7204)	2028 (7528)			4004 (7004)	I	LD
7503	8003 (7703)	3005 (7205)	2010 (7510)			4021 (7021)	I	LD
7504	8004 (7704)	3062 (7262)	2019 (7519)			4042 (7042)	I	
7505	8005 (7705)	3012 (7212)	2012 (7512)			4007 (7007)	I	LD
7506	8006 (7706)	3021 (7721)	2011 (7511)			4005 (7005)	I	LD
7507	8007 (7707)	3020 (7020)	2007 (7507)			4025 (7025)	I	LD
7508	8008 (7708)	3061 (7261)	2051 (7551)			4039 (7039)	I	
7509	8009 (7709)	3088 (7288)	2047 (7547)			4075 (7075)	I	
7510	8010 (7710)	3085 (7285)	2072 (7572)			4038 (7038)	I	
7511	8011 (7711)	3073 (7273)	2052 (7552)			4059 (7059)	I	
7512	8012 (7712)	3081 (7281)	2048 (7548)			4069 (7069)	I	
7513	8013 (7713)	3001 (7201)	2003 (7503)			4003 (7003)	I	LD
7514	8014 (7714)	3038 (7238)	2059 (7559)			4016 (7016)	I	
7515	8015 (7715)	3011 (7211)	2017 (7517)			4022 (7022)	I	LD
7516	8016 (7716)	3060 (7260)	2044 (7544)			4054 (7054)	I	
7517	8017 (7717)	3076 (7276)	2075 (7575)			4077 (7077)	I	
7518	8018 (7718)	3100 (7300)	2062 (7562)			4074 (7074)	I	
7519	8019 (7719)	3014 (7214)	2057 (7557)			4057 (7057)	I	LD
7520	8020 (7720)	3050 (7250)	2042 (7542)			4048 (7048)	I	
7521	8021 (7721)	3029 (7229)	2065 (7565)			4063 (7063)	I	
7522	8022 (7722)	3097 (7297)	2064 (7564)			4045 (7045)	I	
7523	8023 (7723)	3049 (7249)	2038 (7538)			4019 (7019)	I	
7524	8024 (7724)	3016 (7216)	2041 (7541)			4052 (7052)	I	LD
7525	8025 (7725)	3069 (7269)	2049 (7549)			4066 (7066)	I	
7526	8026 (7726)	3009 (7209)	2006 (7506)			4008 (7008)	I	LD
7527	8027 (7727)	3018 (7218)	2013 (7513)			4006 (7006)	I	LD
7528	8028 (7728)	3027 (7227)	2026 (7526)			4023 (7023)	I	
7529	8029 (7729)	3002 (7202)	2004 (7504)			4024 (7024)	I	
7530	8030 (7730)	3022 (7222)	2009 (7509)			4031 (7031)	I	LD
7531	8031 (7731)	3045 (7245)	2034 (7534)			4067 (7067)	I	
7532	8032 (7732)	3063 (7263)	2040 (7540)			4047 (7047)	I	
7533	8033 (7733)	3066 (7266)	2037 (7537)			4056 (7056)	I	
7534	8034 (7734)	3031 (7231)	2020 (7520)			4053 (7053)	I	
7535	8035 (7735)	3092 (7292)	2067 (7567)			4070 (7070)	I	
7536	8036 (7736)	3003 (7203)	2005 (7505)			4030 (7030)	I	
7537	8037 (7737)	3093 (7293)	2069 (7569)			4065 (7065)	I	
7538	8038 (7738)	3006 (7206)	2002 (7502)			4001 (7001)	I	
7539	8039 (7739)						I	
7540	8040 (7740)	3017 (7217)	2050 (7550)			4071 (7071)	I	
7541	8041 (7741)	3010 (7210)	2045 (7545)			4009 (7009)	I	LD
7542	8042 (7742)	3013 (7213)	2018 (7518)			4028 (7028)	I	LD
7543	8043 (7743)	3023 (7223)	2015 (7515)			4033 (7033)	I	
7544	8044 (7744)	3025 (7215)	2025 (7525)			4024 (7024)	I	LD
7545	8045 (7745)	3083 (7283)	2061 (7561)			4068 (7068)	I	
7546	8046 (7746)	3035 (7235)	2058 (7558)			4049 (7049)	I	
7547	8047 (7747)	3067 (7267)	2063 (7563)			4017 (7017)	I	
7548	8048 (7748)	3024 (7224)	2014 (7514)			4034 (7034)	I	
7549	8049 (7749)	3094 (7294)	2074 (7574)			4061 (7061)	I	
7550	8050 (7750)	3101 (7301)	2046 (7546)			4076 (7076)	I	

3.4. DIESEL MULTIPLE UNITS

CLASS DM'90   2-CAR UNITS

These units were introduced to replace the remaining 1950s and 1960s-built DMUs. Assembly was at the Duewag plant in Germany with Talbot providing the bodies and SIG the bogies. They can only work on lines which have been modified with new generation ATB. 3437–3442 and 3448–3453 are on long-term hire to Syntus and carry Syntus numbers 50–61 (for full details see Syntus). Other units are hired to Syntus according to requirements. 3401, 3402, 3404, 3412 and 3414 are used by RegioNS for the Apeldoorn–Zutphen service and are marked as such. 3403 and 3410 are usually used on Zwolle–Kampen. 3436 carries vinyls for the *Grensland Express* Hengelo–Bad Bentheim, which is operated by Syntus. Although heavy maintenance is carried out at Onnen, units receive lighter maintenance at Hengelo and all units out of use are stored there.

Built: 1995–99.
Engine: Two Cummins NT855R4 of 320 kW at 2000 rpm.
Transmission: Hydraulic. Voith 211 rzze.
Wheel Arrangement: 2-B + B-2.
Accommodation: –/48 1T + 24/37 1T.

Builder: Duewag/Talbot/SIG.

Weight: 47 + 48 tonnes.
Length over Couplers: 26.17 + 26.17 m.
Maximum Speed: 140 km/h.

Disc brakes. Magnetic track brakes.

3401 **Y**	ON	3412 **Y**	ON	3422 **Y**	ON	3432 **Y**	ON
3402 **Y**	ON	3413 **Y**	ON	3423 **Y**	ON	3433 **Y**	ON
3403 **Y**	ON	3414 **Y**	ON	3424 **Y**	ON	3434 **Y**	ON
3404 **Y**	ON	3415 **Y**	ON	3425 **Y**	ON	3435 **Y**	ON
3406 **Y**	ON	3416 **Y**	ON	3426 **Y**	ON	3436 **Y**	ON
3407 **Y**	ON	3417 **Y**	ON	3427 **Y**	ON	3443 **Y**	ON
3408 **Y**	ON	3418 **Y**	ON	3428 **Y**	ON	3444 **Y**	ON
3409 **Y**	ON	3419 **Y**	ON	3429 **Y**	ON	3445 **Y**	ON
3410 **Y**	ON	3420 **Y**	ON	3430 **Y**	ON	3446 **Y**	ON
3411 **Y**	ON	3421 **Y**	ON	3431 **Y**	ON	3447 **Y**	ON

▲ DM'90 DMU 3445, at the time on hire from NS Financial Services to Syntus, is seen at Dodewaard on 16 November 2011 with train 31156 Arnhem–Tiel.   **Quintus Vosman**

4. DUTCH PASSENGER TRAIN OPERATORS

The Dutch Ministry of Transport is responsible for some of the unprofitable services in the Netherlands, but the responsibility, powers and finances for many lines have been delegated to regional authorities. Services have been tendered with some lines continuing to be operated by NS and others by private operators.

4.1. ARRIVA

Arriva Trains Nederland, now part of Deutsche Bahn, operates a large network of non-electrified lines for the Groningen and Friesland provinces in the north of the Netherlands. The company has a recent fleet of Stadler GTWs which are known as *"Spurts"*. It also operates the Geldermalsen–Dordrecht line for Zuid Holland with GTW EMUs, also from Stadler.

Lines operated:
* Groningen–Delfzijl (38 km).
* Groningen–Rodeschool (38 km).
* Groningen–Nieuweschans–Leer (72 km).
* Groningen–Leeuwarden (54 km).

* Groningen–Veendam (29 km).
* Leeuwarden–Harlingen Haven (26 km).
* Leeuwarden–Stavoren (51 km).
* Geldermalsen–Dordrecht (49 km).

Depot: Leeuwarden (operated by Voith). EMUs used on the Dordrecht–Geldermalsen line are maintained at NedTrain's depot at Leidschendam. Units for 2012/13 franchises will be maintained at Strukton's new depot in Zutphen.

From December 2012, Arriva will take over from Syntus on the lines from Winterswijk to Zutphen and Arnhem, Arnhem–Tiel and Apeldoorn–Zutphen (known as the *Achterhoek-Rivierenland* network) for which the company has ordered 24 more GTW DMUs – 13 2-car and 11 3-car. Arriva will also take over the *Vechtdallijnen* from NS Reizigers – the Zwolle–Mariënberg–Emmen line from December 2012 and the Almelo–Mariënberg line from December 2013 in Overijssel and Drenthe provinces. For the Emmen line, the company has ordered 14 GTW EMUs – six 2-car and eight 3-car.

▲ Arriva GTW 2/6 DMU 233 "LIESBETH LIST" arrives at Harlingen Haven from Leeuwarden on 24 April 2012. **David Haydock**

GTW 2/6 & GTW 2/8   3/4-SECTION DMUS

These units have 2+2 seating in both classes. Numbers are in a single series but starting with "2" for a 2-section and "3" for a 3-section unit. If a unit is lengthened, the prefix changes.

3-section unit 228 has cars numbered 10228A + 10228C (power car) + 10228B and so on.
4-section units are 10301A + 10301D + 10301C (power car) + 10301B and so on.
Units are named after illustrious people born in the region – yes, even Mata Hari!

Built: 2006–07.   **Builder:** Stadler.
Engine: One 12 cylinder MTU 12V183 TDE2 of 550 kW at 2100 rpm.
Transmission: Electric. Two ADtranz Type 6R1A 4548 three phase asynchronous traction motors.
Maximum Speed: 140 km/h.

Disc brakes. Magnetic track brakes.

* Fitted with retractable steps for operating into Germany.

GTW 2/6. 3-section units.

Length over Couplers: 18.195 + 4.500 + 18.195 m = 40.89 m.
Wheel Arrangement: 2-Bo-2.   **Weight:** 68 tonnes.
Accommodation: 16/32 (7) 1TD + –/56 († 16/20 (12) 1TD + – /56 with space for more bikes).

228	*	JAN UITHAM	239	†	PIET OBERMAN
229	*	SJOUKJE DIJKSTRA	240	†	EISE EISINGA
230	*	EDE STAAL	241	†	GER VADERS
231		HOTZE SCHUIL	242	†	SAMUEL VAN HOUTEN
232		FOPPE DE HAAN	243	†	EGBERT WAGENBORG
233		LIESBETH LIST	244	†	Anthony Winkler Prins
234		FEDDE SCHURER	247	†	Mata Hari
235		JAN DE ROOS	248	†	Evert van Bentheim
236		TONNY VAN LEEUWEN	249	†	Jan Pellevoer
237	†	MARIANNE TIMMER	250	†	Johan van Veen
238	†	FOPPE INNE BROUWER	251	†	Belcampo

On order. New units have MAN 16.0 V8 TCD engines of 600 kW and weigh 71 tonnes. Accommodation is 8/40 (12) + –/52 (4).

252	259
253	260
254	261
255	262
256	263
257	264
258	

GTW 2/8. 4-section units.

Length over Couplers: 18.195 + 4.500 + 15.047 + 18.195 m = 55.937 m.
Wheel Arrangement: 2-2-Bo-2.   **Weight:** 87 tonnes.
Accommodation: 16/32 (7) 1TD + –/56 + –/56 († 16/20 (12) 1TD + –/56 + –/56 with space for more bikes).

302	*†	BASTIAAN JAN ADER	317	WILLEM BARENTSZ
303	*†	TINY MULDER	318	NIENKE VAN HICHTUM
304	*†	HANS ALDERS	319	MARTE RÖLING
305	*†	UBBO EMMIUS	320	CEES BIJLSTRA
306		GERRIT KROL	321	PIET PAALTJENS
307		FRITS ZERNIKE	322	TITUS BRANDSMA
308		HEIKE KAMERLINGH ONNES	323	WILLEM ALBERT SCHOLTEN
309		HENDRIK NICOLAAS WERKMAN	324	SICCO MANSHOLT
310		ABE LENSTRA	325	J. J. NOOITGEDAGT
311		HANS WIEGEL	326	M.C.ESCHER
312		M. VASALIS	327	JELLE ZIJLSTRA
313		ALETTA H. JACOBS	345	Ruurt Hazewinkel
314		JOPIE HUISMAN	346	Pieter Jennes Troelstras
315		ABEL TASMAN		

On order. New units have MAN 16.0 V8 TCD engines of 600 kW and weigh 89 tonnes.

Accommodation: 8/32 (12) + –/52 (3) + –/52 (4).

EVN: 95 84 5012 **365**-c <u>NL</u>-ARR and so on.
Coaches are numbered 11365A + 15365D + 12365B and so on.

365	371
366	372
367	373
368	374
369	375
370	

GTW 2/6 & GTW 2/8   3/4-SECTION EMUS

Built: 2008 for Dordrecht–Geldermalsen. Details as for DMUs (above) except engine replaced by electrical equipment and accommodation details.

Power rating: 1100 kW.
Weight: GTW 2/6 68 tonnes. GTW 2/8 86 tonnes.
Accommodation: –/36 (17) + –/56 + –/56.

GTW 2/6. 3-section unit. Red/cream livery.

Accommodation: –/36 (17) + –/56.

407	Frank Wels		408	Trijntje

On order for Zwolle–Emmen. New units have detailed differences. Blue/cream livery.

Accommodation: 16/21 (11) 1TD + –/52 (3).

411	414
412	415
413	416

GTW 2/8. 4-section units. Red/cream livery.

Accommodation: –/36 (17) + –/56 + –/56.

501	Ronald Bandell		505	Andries Dirk Copier
502	Baron van Verschuer		506	Maarten Schakel
503	Adriaan Volker		509	Jan van Arkel
504	Ida Gerhardt		510	Hendrik Hamel

On order for Zwolle–Emmen. New units have detailed differences. Blue/cream livery.

Accommodation: 16/21 (11) 1TD + –/48 (2) + –/52 (3).

517	521
518	522
519	523
520	524

4.2. CONNEXXION

Connexxion was formed in 1999 from a merger of four Dutch public transport companies. In 2007 it became a holding owned 75% by French company Transdev, which merged with Veolia in 2011.

UTRECHT SNELTRAM

On behalf of *Bestuur Regio Utrecht* the company operates the Utrecht light rail system which departs from outside the main rail station and was formerly operated by NS. The system is sometimes known as *Sneltram Utrecht – Nieuwegein/IJsselstein* or SUNIJ. Qbuzz, a bus company 49% owned by NS, has won the contract to operate the Sneltram from December 2013 for ten years – replacing Connexxion.

Line operated:
• Utrecht Centraal Station–Nieuwegein Stadscentrum–Nieuwegein Zuid/Ijsselstein Zuid.

CLASS E6   2-SECTION ARTICULATED TRAMS

These former Wien light rail vehicles were brought in to cope with peak traffic in 2011. They formerly operated on Line U6 which is classed as a metro line but which has tram-like vehicles. These operate with former Wien Class c6 trailers 1932, 1935 and 1941. They remain in the classic Wien red and white livery. Tram 4901 plus four trailers were sold to Kraków in Poland.

Built: 1979–91.
Builder–Mechanical Parts: Rotax.
Traction Motors: Four of 95 or 110 kW.
Width: 2.31 m.
Wheel Arrangement: B-2-B.
Weight:

Builder–Electrical Parts: Kiepe.
Length over Couplers: 20.10 m.
Floor Height:
Accommodation: 31 + 72 standees.
Maximum Speed: 80 km/h.

| 4905 | 4917 | 4932 | | 4943 | 4946 | 4948 |
| 4913 | 4929 | 4941 | | | | |

▲ 5007 + 5022 stand beside 4941 + 1941 + 4929 at Nieuwegein Zuid on 2 July 2012.
Raimund Wyhnal

2-SECTION ARTICULATED TRAMS

These trams were originally finished in NS yellow livery, then later were turned out in Connexxion blue and green. During a recent light refurbishment they have regained a yellow livery, with black window panels. Tram 5018 was named Alexander Tchernoff in 2003. In 2010 this tram was involved in an accident and will probably be too expensive to rebuild.

Built: 1981–83.
Builder–Mechanical Parts: SIG.
Builder–Electrical Parts: BBC.
Traction Motors: Two BBC 228 kW.　　**Length over Couplers:** 29.80 m.
Width: 2.65 m.　　**Floor Height:** 920 mm.
Wheel Arrangement: B-2-B.　　**Accommodation:** 80 + 160 standees.
Weight: 37.5 tonnes.　　**Maximum Speed:** 80 km/h.

Disc brakes. Magnetic track brakes.

5001	5006	5011	5016		5020	5024
5002	5007	5012	5017		5021	5025
5003	5008	5013	5018	(U)	5022	5026
5004	5009	5014	5019		5023	5027
5005	5010	5015				

▲ Connexion Protos EMU 5033 is seen at Harselaar with a service to Amersfoort on 23 August 2012.
David Haydock

HEAVY RAIL

Connexxion operates the Amersfoort–Ede-Wageningen line with a fleet of Protos electric units. The producer of Protos EMUs went bankrupt and Connexxion could not obtain an additional set to cope with traffic, so the company has ordered one Stadler GTW 2/8 EMU. The Almelo–Mariënberg line is operated with two LINT 41s by Syntus in a red livery for the Twente transport authority.

Lines operated:
• Amersfoort–Ede-Wageningen (34 km, electrified).
• Almelo–Mariënberg (19 km, diesel-operated).

Depot: Amersfoort (owned by subsidiary TSN).

PROTOS   2-CAR EMUS

Unique EMUs produced by a company in eastern Germany, which later went bankrupt. Units are in a light blue livery with white front ends.

Built: 2007.
Builder: FTD.
Length over Couplers: 27.25 + 27.25 m.
Wheel Arrangement: 2-Bo + Bo-2.
Accommodation: 16/68 (62) + –/76 (10). These units have 2+2 seating in both classes.
Weight: 56 + 59 tonnes.

Traction Motors: Two of 335 kW per car.
Floor Height: 810 /1020 mm.

Maximum Speed: 160 km/h.

Disc brakes. Magnetic track brakes.

5031	5033	5035	Marijke van Haare
5032	5034		

GTW 2/8   4-SECTION EMU

One unit on order. See Arriva GTW 2/8 sets for technical details.

HERMES

Hermes is a bus company in the south-east of the Netherlands – a wholly-owned subsidiary of Connexxion. Hermes has won the concession to operate services, from December 2012, from Arnhem to Nijmegen from Stadsregio Arnhem Nijmegen. The service will be marketed as "Breng", a branding already used by Connexxion, Hermes and Novio bus services in this area. The Hermes service will combine with the Arriva (also from December 2012) Arnhem–Winterswijk service to give four trains an hour between Arnhem and Doetinchem. Hermes is not a railway undertaking so will operate under Connexxion's operating licence, safety certificates and infrastructure access agreement.

Services will be operated with nine Stadler GTW 2/8 DMUs, being delivered in late 2012.

GTW 2/8   4-SECTION DMU

Details as Arriva GTW 2/8 units 365–375.

5041	5043	5045	5047	5048	5049
5042	5044	5046			

▲ Hermes' first GTW 2/8 DMU 5041 is seen on a test trip from Nijmegen to Venlo at Meerlo-Tienray on 5 September 2012.											**Luc Peulen**

▼ EETC shunter 501, formerly ACTS 6004, is seen shunting DB Autozug stock at Amsterdam Watergraafsmeer on 10 August 2012.										**Quintus Vosman**

4.3. EURO-EXPRESS TREINCHARTER   EETC

Euro-Express Treincharter operates the *Ski-Trein* during the winter from Utrecht, 's Hertogenbosch and Venlo to Zell am See, the *Alpen Expres* (the winter ski train from Utrecht to Brig, Bischofshofen and Landeck) and the *AutoSlaap Trein* (summer motorail service from 's Hertogenbosch to Alessandria and Livorno in Italy). The coaches used are mainly ex-NS Internationaal, which finished operating overnight services in 2002. Maintenance is carried out by NedTrain at Watergraafsmeer. Locos are generally in a chestnut brown livery with yellow ends.

ELECTRIC LOCOMOTIVES

CLASS 1250   Co-Co

Former NS Class 1200. Class 1200 were constructed as "kit-form" locomotives with the bogies being supplied by Baldwin and electrical components by Westinghouse, the classic American styling clearly showing their design origin. The locos are used by EETC for empty stock workings at Amsterdam and may be used in future on the domestic stretch to Venlo. All are on long term hire to EETC, with the first three owned by Laurens Pit and Harry Schneider.

Built: 1951–53.
Builder–Mechanical Parts: Werkspoor.
Builder–Electrical Parts: Heemaf.
Traction Motors: 6 x Heemaf TM94 axle-hung. **One Hour Rating:** 2360 kW.
Weight: 108 tonnes.
Maximum Tractive Effort: 194 kN. **Length over Buffers:** 18.085 m.
Driving Wheel Diameter: 1100 mm. **Max. Speed:** 130 km/h.

Multiple working fitted.

Number/name	Built	Works no.	Notes
1251	1952	939	ex NS 1215
1252	1952	949	ex NS 1225
1254 ir J. HOEKWATER	1952	938	ex NS 1214
1255	1952	945	KLOK, ex NS 1221

DIESEL LOCOMOTIVES

LEW TYPE V60D   D

These are 0-8-0 diesel shunters used by DB Schenker as Classes 345 to 347 (former DR Classes 105 to 107) but also built in large numbers in East Germany for industry and other Eastern Bloc countries. Used at Rotterdam Kleiweg, Amsterdam Watergraafsmeer and 's Hertogenbosch.

501 and 502 were ex-ACTS 6004 and 6005 (503, or 6003, is being used for spares) while 504, 505 were ex-Volker Rail 106-1 "Knabbel" and 106-2 "Babbel" (formerly with ShortLines as 1001 and 1002) – named after the chipmunks known as "Chip 'n' Dale" in English-speaking countries.

Builder: LEW.
Engine: 12KVD21VW of 478 kW.
Transmission: Hydraulic. Pirna. **Wheel Diameter:** 1100 mm.
Maximum Tractive Effort: 175 kN. **Length over Buffers:** 10.88 m.
Weight: 55 tonnes. **Maximum Speed:** 60 km/h.

No.	Built	Works No.	EVN	Origin
501 (6004)	1979	16539	NL EETC 98 84 82 84 501-9	Severokámen Koštálov
502 (6005)	1982	18001	NL EETC 98 84 82 84 502-7	Heizwerk Varnsdorf 716 511
503 (6003) (U)	1983	18105	NL EETC 98 84 82 84 503-5	SaZ Sázava
504	1980	16144	NL EETC 98 84 82 84 504-3	MCHZ Ostrava
505	1982	17699	NL EETC 98 84 82 84 505-1	ACHP Trebíc-Sedlec

In 2012, EETC also had ex-NS English Electric shunter 661 on hire from preservation group VSM.

4.4. SYNTUS

Syntus operates a number of non-electrified routes in the Gelderland province and bought a fleet of Alstom Lint 41 DMUs for this purpose. These are now owned by NS Financial Services. It also uses DM'90 units hired from NS Financial Services, those used permanently having Syntus numbers. It was expected that SNCF subsidiary Keolis, originally only part-owner, would take full control of the company in 2012. Trains are in a yellow, white and blue livery. Syntus will lose all of these lines to Arriva in December 2012 except for Hengelo to Bad Bentheim and Zutphen. This will mean most of the trains listed below will be returned to NS Financial Services.

Lines operated:
• Tiel–Arnhem (44 km) **DM'90**.
• Arnhem–Winterswijk (64 km) **DM'90**.
• Winterswijk–Zutphen (43 km).
• Hengelo–Oldenzaal–Bad Bentheim (26 km).
• Hengelo–Zutphen (45 km).

Depot: Trains are maintained by Voith at Blerick.

CORADIA LINT 41　　　　　　2-SECTION ARTICULATED DMUS

A standard design of DMU built by Alstom for Germany (Class 648) and Denmark as well as the Netherlands.

Built: 2000–01.
Builder: Alstom Salzgitter, Germany.
Engine: Two 6-cylinder MTU 6R 183TD 13H engines of 315 kW each at 1900 rpm.
Transmission: Hydrodynamic.
Floor Height: 780 mm.
Accommodation: –/68 (5) + –/68 (5).
Maximum Speed: 120 km/h.
Length over Couplers: 20.905 + 20.905 m.
Wheel Arrangement: B-2-B.
Weight: 68 tonnes.

Disc brakes. Magnetic track brakes.

21		Masha Bijlsma	33		Berend van Hackfort
22		Hans Keuper	34		Wim Rijkenbarg
23	(U)	Ernst Daniel Smit	35		
24		Hendrickje Stoffels	36		
25		Spoorjan Willink	37		Gerard te Broke
26		Gerrit Komrij	38		Jovink en the Voederbietels
27		A.C.W. Staring	39		Monique Wolbert
28		Bennie Jolink	40		Johan de Bondt
29		Sandra Vanreijs	41		H. Kuipers-Rietberg
30		Nout Wellink	42		Bert Haanstra
31		Erik Breukink	43		Willem Wilmink
32		Berd Westerveld			

In red livery for use by Connexxion.

44		45	Hennie Kuiper

CLASS DM'90　　　　　　　　　　2-CAR DMUS

Units hired from NS Financial services. Details as for NS section except:

Accommodation: 48 (22) + –/68 (1).

50	(3450)	52	(3452)	54	(3441)	56	(3440)	58	(3439)	60	(3448)
51	(3451)	53	(3453)	55	(3442)	57	(3438)	59	(3437)	61	(3449)

▲ Syntus LINT 41 DMU 44, in red livery for the Twente transport authority, and operating on behalf of Connexxion, leaves Mariënberg for Almelo on 23 August 2012.   **David Haydock**

▼ Veolia GTW 2/6 DMU 202, in advertising livery, plus others of the same type, are seen stabled at Venlo on 22 August 2012.   **David Haydock**

4.5. VEOLIA TRANSPORT NEDERLAND

Veolia, part of a French conglomerate, has operated two lines in the Limburg province since 2006. DMUs and EMUs can operate in multiple with each other. Trains are finished in a white and red livery.

Lines operated:
• Roermond–Venlo–Nijmegen (84 km, diesel-worked).
• Maastricht–Heerlen–Kerkrade (33 km, electrified).

Depot: Trains are maintained by Voith at Blerick.

GTW 2/6 & GTW 2/8   3/4-SECTION DMUS

These units have 2+2 seating in first class and 3+2 in second class. Units 207 to 210 were extended and became 357 to 360. Coach numbers are 7201A + 7201C + 7201B for set 201, for example. Owned by leasing company CB Rail.

Built: 2007–08.   **Builder:** Stadler.
Engine: One 12-cylinder MTU 12V183 TDE2 of 550 kW at 2100 rpm.
Transmission: Electric. Two ADtranz Type 6R1A 4548 three phase asynchronous traction motors.
Floor Height: 830/996 mm.
Maximum Speed: 140 km/h.
EVN: 201 = 95 84 5 03 0001-6 + 95 84 5 03 2001-4 + 95 84 5 03 1001-5 NL-VTN and so on.

GTW 2/6. 3-section units.

Length over Couplers: 18.195 + 4.500 + 18.195 m.
Wheel Arrangement: 2-Bo-2.   **Weight:** 68 tonnes.
Accommodation: 16/27 (11) 1TD + –/66.

201	JAN VAN KUYC		204	MAT VESTJENS
202	PATER KAREL		205	JAN KLAASSENS
203	BART BRENTJENS		206	JAN LINDERS

GTW 2/8. 4-section units.

Length over Couplers: 18.195 + 4.500 + 15.047 + 18.195 m.
Wheel Arrangement: 2-2-Bo-2.   **Weight:** 87 tonnes.
Accommodation: 16/27 (11) 1TD + –/66 + –/66.

351	WILLEM NIJHOLT		356	CHRIET TITULAER
352	JORIS IVENS		357	GÉ REINDERS
353	JACK POELS		358	PIERRE CNOOPS
354	TITUS BRANDSMA		359	PIERRE CUYPERS
355	CONNIE PALMEN		360	WILHELM TELL

GTW 2/6 & GTW 2/8   3/4-SECTION EMUS

Built: 2008 for Maastricht–Kerkrade line.
Power and weight as Arriva EMUs. Accomodation as Veolia GTW DMUs.
Owned by leasing company Railpool.

GTW 2/6. 3-section units.

501	PIEKE DASSEN		504	SINT SERVAES
502	JO COENEN		505	SJENG KREMERS
503	BEPPIE KRAFT			

GTW 2/8. 4-section units.

651	SJEF DIEDERENS		653	ANDRÉ RIEU
652	JAC. P. THIJSSE			

5. DB SCHENKER RAIL NEDERLAND

DB Schenker Rail Nederland was formerly known as Railion Nederland and before that was NS freight department NS Cargo. The company has lost some traffic to competitors in the past few years but remains the biggest rail freight operator in the Netherlands. All locos are maintained by Shunter Tractie unless shown. Since the last edition DB has stopped using Class 204 and 232 locomotives in the Netherlands and has withdrawn its mP postal EMUs.

5.1. ELECTRIC LOCOMOTIVES

CLASS 1600   B-B

For details see NS Class 1800. The locomotives work freight trains over all principal lines except the 25 kV AC electrified Rotterdam *Havenspoorlijn* and *Betuweroute*. All in NS yellow livery unless shown otherwise; some names have been removed. Most stored locos are at Rotterdam Waalhaven. DB Schenker has hired or sold four locos to HTRS.

EVN: 91 84 100 **1601**-c <u>NL</u>-RN, and so on

1601		(S)	AMSTERDAM	1613			ROERMOND
1602	R		Schiphol	1614	R		SCHIEDAM
1603		(S)	ZUTPHEN	1615	R		ZANDVOORT
1604	R		DORDRECHT	1616	R		OLDENZAAL
1607		(S)	VLISSINGEN	1617		(S)	ASSEN
1608		(S)	'S-HERTOGENBOSCH	1618		(S)	ALMELO
1611	R		VENLO	1620		(S)	ARNHEM
1612	R		GOES				

▲ Former NS 1611, now in DB livery, heads very short freight 61072 from Kijfhoek to Sloeheven at Zevenbegse Hoek on 14 May 2012. **Carlo Hertogs**

CLASS 189   ES64F4   Bo-Bo

Electric locomotives for use on the *Betuweroute*. Siemens Type ES64F4 version VJ capable of operating in the Netherlands and Germany. The list shows only those DB Class 189 equipped with signalling to operate into the Netherlands. They mainly shuttle between Maasvlakte and Oberhausen but those with auto couplers head 5000 tonne ore trains from Maasvlakte, via the Rhine and Mosel valleys, to Dillingen, near Saarbrücken. For technical details see Section 6.1.

All equipped with ETCS Level 2 for operation over the *Betuweroute*.

k   equipped with Type AK automatic couplings for Rotterdam–Germany iron ore trains.

189 023	**R**		NN2	189 038	**R**	k	NN2	189 053	**R**		NN2	189 077	**R**	NN2
189 024	**R**		NN2	189 039	**R**	k	NN2	189 054	**R**		NN2	189 078	**R**	NN2
189 025	**R**		NN2	189 040	**R**	k	NN2	189 065	**R**		NN2	189 079	**R**	NN2
189 026	**R**		NN2	189 041	**R**	k	NN2	189 066	**R**		NN2	189 080	**R**	NN2
189 027	**R**		NN2	189 042	**R**	k	NN2	189 067	**R**		NN2	189 081	**R**	NN2
189 028	**R**		NN2	189 043	**R**	k	NN2	189 068	**R**		NN2	189 082	**R**	NN2
189 029	**R**		NN2	189 044	**R**	k	NN2	189 069	**R**		NN2	189 083	**R**	NN2
189 030	**R**	k	NN2	189 045	**R**	k	NN2	189 070	**R**		NN2	189 084	**R**	NN2
189 031	**R**	k	NN2	189 046	**R**	k	NN2	189 071	**R**		NN2	189 085	**R**	NN2
189 032	**R**	k	NN2	189 047	**R**	k	NN2	189 072	**R**		NN2	189 086	**R**	NN2
189 033	**R**	k	NN2	189 048	**R**		NN2	189 073	**R**		NN2	189 087	**R**	NN2
189 034	**R**	k	NN2	189 049	**R**		NN2	189 074	**R**		NN2	189 088	**R**	NN2
189 035	**R**	k	NN2	189 050	**R**		NN2	189 075	**R**		NN2	189 089	**R**	NN2
189 036	**R**	k	NN2	189 051	**R**		NN2	189 076	**R**		NN2	189 100	**R**	NN2
189 037	**R**	k	NN2	189 052	**R**		NN2							

▲ DB Schenker 189 074 heads a train of empty car carriers towards Germany at Harselaar, just east of Amersfoort, on 23 August 2012.   **David Haydock**

5.2. DIESEL LOCOMOTIVES

CLASS 6400   Bo-Bo

Thyristor-controlled locomotives for trip freights and shunting. Following electrification, and with DB losing traffic to competitors, many locos have been stored. Locos go into and out of store quite frequently. This is not well documented but at the time of writing over 50 were stored, mostly at Amersfoort. Locos are now all maintained by Shunter. Loco utilisation is conditioned by how the loco is equipped. 6421–6442 are found on the Rotterdam port line from Kijfhoek to Maasvlakte. Belgian-equipped locos work in Terneuzen plus daily via Gent and Antwerpen to Kijfhoek.

6456 and 6457 were sold to Eurotunnel which has similar locos and have been renumbered 0006 and 0007. 6415 and 6514 were withdrawn after a collision.

Built: 1988–94.   **Builder:** MaK.
Engine: MTU 12V396 TC 13 of 1180 kW at 1800 rpm.
Transmission: 4 x three phase BBC traction motors.
Maximum Tractive Effort: 290 kN.   **Weight:** 80 tonnes.
Driving Wheel Diameter: 1000 mm.   **Length over Buffers:** 14.40 m.
Maximum Speed: 120 km/h.
EVN: 92 84 200 **6401**-c and so on.

b   Equipped for working into Belgium.
d   Equipped for working into Germany.
e   Equipped with European Train Control System (ETCS).
h   Equipped for hump shunting at Kijfhoek yard.
i   Can work into Germany as centre loco of a three loco set only.
n   Fitted with ATP-NG ("New generation") automatic train protection.
p   On hire to Prorail as rescue locos at Amsterdam, Utrecht and Roosendaal.

No	R	f	(S)	Name	No	R	f	(S)	Name	No	R	f	(S)	Name
6401			(S)	Mijndert	6433		e		Han	6467		d	(S)	
6402			(S)	Marinus	6434	R	e		Henk	6468		d	(S)	
6403			(S)	Gijs	6435		e		Joop	6469		d		
6404	R	i	(S)	Jo	6436	R	e		Willem	6470		d	(S)	
6405	R	i	(S)	Jan	6437		e		Arie	6471		d	(S)	
6406		i	(S)	Tonnie	6438	R	e		Henk	6472		d		Frank
6407		i	(S)	Henk	6439	R	e		Geert	6473	R	d	(S)	
6408	R	i	(S)	Gerard	6440	R	e		Jaap	6474		d	(S)	
6409		i	(S)	Herman	6441		e		Joyce	6475		d		Ed
6410		i	(S)	Toon	6442	R	e			6476	R	h		
6411	R	n		Oliver	6443			(S)		6477	R	h		
6412	R	n		Hans	6444			(S)		6478		h		Eeltje
6413		n		Foeke	6445				Wijbo	6479		h		
6414	R	n		Sander	6446				Jo	6480			(S)	
6416		n		Arie	6447			(S)	Maurits	6481			(S)	Lies
6417	R	n		Bob	6448			(S)	Rein	6482			(S)	
6418	R	n		John	6449			(S)	John	6483			(S)	
6419			(S)	Willem	6450				Hanja	6484			(S)	
6420			(S)	Horst	6451		p		Daan	6485			(S)	
6421	R	e		Sebe	6452				Rein	6486			(S)	
6422	R	e		Wim	6453			(S)	Frans	6487			(S)	
6423		e		Chris	6454	R		(S)	Wim	6488			(S)	Gerard
6424	R	e		Dirk	6455				Klaas Abel	6489			(S)	
6425		e		Chris	6458		p		Harry	6490				
6426		e		Niko	6459				Anton	6491	R		(S)	
6427	R	e		Hans	6460				Leo	6492	R		(S)	
6428		e		Dirk	6461		d			6493			(S)	Joke
6429		e		Hans	6462		d		Olga	6494	R	d	(S)	
6430	R	e		Jan	6463		d	(S)	Theo	6495	R	d	(S)	
				Adrianus	6464		d		Jan	6496	R	d	(S)	Herman
6431	R	e		Antonius	6465		d	(S)	Lammert	6497	R	d	(S)	
6432		e		Hendrikus	6466		d			6498	R	d	(S)	

6499	**R** d			6506	**R** b			6513	**R** b		
6500	i	(S)		6507	**R** b			6515	**R** b	(S)	
6501	i	(S)	Edo	6508	**R** b		Karla	6516	**R** b p		Wouter
6502	i	(S)		6509	b			6517	**R**		
6503	i	(S)		6510	**R** b			6518	**R** b		
6504	**N**	(S)		6511	**R** b			6519	**R** b		
6505	b	(S)		6512	**R** b		Peter	6520	**R** b		

CLASS 363   C

The standard DB 0-6-0 shunter; formerly Class 361. These locomotives are ballasted to give greater adhesion for shunting these heavy trains. Mainly found in the Venlo area.

Built: 1955–64.
Builder: MaK/Henschel.
Engine: Caterpillar 3412 E D1-TTA of 485 kW (650 hp).
Transmission: Hydraulic. Voith L27z Ub, L37z Ub or L217.
Maximum Tractive Effort: 138 kN.   **Weight:** 53 tonnes.
Driving Wheel Diameter: 1250 mm.   **Length over Buffers:** 10.45 m.
Maximum Speed: 60 km/h.
EVN: 98 84 8**363 633**-c <u>D</u>-DB and so on.

363 633-9 **R**	363 716-2 **R**	(S)	363 729-9 **R**	363 833-5 **R**
363 712-1 **R**	363 723-5 **R**	(S)	363 825-1 **R**	

▲ DB Schenker 6453 heads a trip freight from the Lage Weide industrial estate near Utrecht on 31 March 2009.   **Quintus Vosman**

NOTES ON PRIVATE OPERATORS

The Benelux countries, particularly the Netherlands, have an increasing number of private freight operators. The Dutch freight market is open to any EU-approved train operator once the company has a safety certificate. There are cases of companies starting up using the safety certificate from another company and locomotives may also be borrowed or hired. Activity of all freight operators is concentrated around the port of Rotterdam which generates most freight in the Netherlands.

All of the companies here have very "light" operating methods – few have their own train maintenance depot and most use the services of locomotive leasing companies or builders. Vossloh diesel locos usually go to Moers in Germany for major attention.

The following railway undertakings have an operating licence, a safety certificate and a track access contract for operations in the Netherlands. Some of these are full open access freight operators while others are more concerned with track maintenance and, at the time of writing, do not operate "real trains". However, they may become active in the currency of this book and other companies may appear on the Dutch network either having gained the necessary licence and so on, or using the licence of another operator.

Company	Activity	Note
BAM Rail	Track maintenance	
Bentheimer Eisenbahn	Freight	
B-Logistics (Belgian Railways)	Freight	
Captrain Benelux	Freight	SNCF subsidiary
Crossrail Benelux	Freight	Formerly DLC
CTL Logistics	Freight	
DB Schenker Rail Nederland	Freight	Formerly Railion.
ERS Railways	Freight	
Eurailscout	Track inspection	
HGK (RheinCargo)	Freight	See German Railways book 2.
HSL Logistik	Freight	
Husa Transport Rail Services	Freight	Formerly known as ACTS
ITL Benelux	Freight	Now owned by SNCF/Captrain.
Kombirail	Freight	
Lloyd's Register Rail	Train testing	Owns no trains itself.
LOCON	Freight	
Metrans Rail	Freight	
PKP Cargo	Freight	
ProRail	Track equipment	
Rail Transport Services	Freight	
Rotterdam Rail Feeding	Freight	
RTB Cargo / TrainsporT	Freight	See German Railways book 2.
SBB Cargo	Freight	
Spitzke Spoorbouw	Track maintenance	See German Railways book 2.
Strukton Railinfra Materieel	Track maintenance	
TX Logistik	Freight	
VolkerRail	Track maintenance	
Arriva (ex-Prignitzer Eisenbahn)	Passenger	See German Railways book 2.
Arriva Trains Nederland	Passenger	
Connexxion	Passenger	
DB Autozug	Passenger	See German Railways book 1.
DB Regio NRW	Passenger	See German Railways book 1.
Euro-Express Treincharter	Passenger	
NS Reizigers	Passenger	
Syntus	Passenger	
Veolia Transport Nederland	Passenger	
Zuid Limburgse Stoomtrein	Heritage passenger	See Preserved section.

Since the last edition, Veolia Cargo has been bought by SNCF and is part of Captrain.

6. OTHER FREIGHT OPERATORS & LEASING COMPANIES

6.1. ROLLING STOCK LEASING COMPANIES

Most railway undertakings operating freight trains in the Benelux countries lease some or all of their locomotives. All leasing companies have growing fleets but many of their locomotives are not equipped to operate in Belgium, Luxembourg or the Netherlands. Only locomotives which are equipped to operate in the Benelux countries are listed below. The leasing companies involved in main line operations are:

A **ALPHA TRAINS**
Formerly known as Angel Trains Cargo. Although headquartered in Antwerpen many of Alpha Train's locomotives, in particular the electric locos, are not equipped to operate in Belgium or other Benelux countries.

Livery: Pale grey body with blue (earlier) or green (later) cabs. Locos have white frontal panels specifically for operation in the Netherlands.

B **ASCENDOS LEASING**
A company created after the division of CB Rail's fleet.

Livery: Brunswick green with a yellow front end.

C **CB RAIL**
Owned by Lloyd's Banking Group. CB Rail took over Porterbrook's continental European fleet, thus the first numbers starting in PB.

Livery: Mainly pale grey with a yellow front end.

D **DEUTSCHE LEASING**

E **BEACON RAIL LEASING**

F **FORTIS LEASING**
Owned by the Fortis bank company.

K **KBC LEASE**
A Belgian company involved in leasing almost anything, including cars.

M **MITSUI RAIL CAPITAL EUROPE (MRCE)**
This company started operating as a leasing company in its own right then, in 2006 took over Siemens' subsidiary Dispolok. As with Alpha Trains, by no means all locomotives are equipped to operate into Belgium and/or the Netherlands.

Livery: Black, plus white warning panel for Netherlands.

R **RAILPOOL**
A company created in 2008 by kfw IPEX-Bank and HSH Nordbank.

Livery: Silver with blue vertical stripe.

S **RAILMOTION**
Part of the HUSA Transportation group. Hires out Class 1600 locos to its own subsidiary HTRS.

V **VOSSLOH LOCOMOTIVES**
A subsidiary of the loco builder which hires out a small number of its own products.

Livery: Silver grey and apple green.

Z **COMMERZ LEASING**
Part of Commerz Real, a German company based in Düsseldorf which also leases cars.

6.1.1. ELECTRIC LOCOMOTIVES

BOMBARDIER TRAXX (CLASS 186)   Bo-Bo

Bombardier produces its modular TRAXX electric locomotives in three basic versions – DC which is configured for 3000 V DC and is known as Class E.483 in Italy, AC for 15/25 kV AC, usually for Germany and Austria and numbered as Class 185 and MS (Multi System) which can operate off 1500 and 3000 V DC plus both 15 and 25 kV AC. The MS loco, known as Class 186, is only configured for whichever voltages the customer specifies and operating capability is conditioned by which signalling systems are installed. 186 111–125 will be used on Fyra services in the Netherlands until all V250 high speed trains are in service. During this period they will be finished in a red livery with white frontal panels. Based at Amsterdam Watergraafsmeer (WG). 2801 to 2803 should go to SNCB Logistics once the V250s are operating properly.

Builder: Bombardier Transportation, Kassel.   **Weight:** 86 tonnes.
Continuous Rating: 5600 kW (4000 kW at 1500 V DC).
Length over Buffers: 18.90 m.   **Maximum Tractive Effort:** 300 kN.
Maximum Speed: 140 km/h (160 km/h 186 111–125).
Systems: 1500/3000 V DC, 15/25 kV AC.

EVN: These have not been included as all have the same six-figure endings from 186 101 upwards.

Note: 186 161–180, 301–320 and 341–345 are operated by Euro Cargo Rail whilst 186 321–340 are owned by DB Schenker. All of these are equipped for France, Belgium and Germany and are shown in the Platform 5 book FRENCH RAILWAYS. Other Class 186 locos are not equipped to operate in Benelux and are therefore not the concern of this publication.

Version DACHINL (Germany, Austria, Switzerland, Italy and the Netherlands). Built: 2006/07.

Number	Works No	Leasco	Hired to/Number	Number	Works No	Leasco	Hired to/Number
186 101	34299	R	IGT (DE)	186 107	34327	R	RTB Cargo
186 102	34300	R	Lokomotion (DE)	186 108	34325	R	SBB Cargo DE
186 103	34317	R	SBB Cargo	186 109	34328	R	Lokomotion
186 105	34319	R	Kombirail	186 110	34330	R	RTB Cargo
186 106	34320	R	Lokomotion				

Version DANLBE (Germany, Austria, Belgium and the Netherlands). Built 2006–08

*   sub-leased from NS Hispeed.
§   owned by CB Rail but sub-hired to Railpool.

Number	Works No	Leasco	Hired to	Number	Works No	Leasco	Hired to
186 111	34303	A	NS Hispeed	186 144	34376	C	LOCON
186 112	34304	A	NS Hispeed	186 148	34340	C	Captrain BE
186 113	34302	A	NS Hispeed	186 149	34344	C	Captrain BE
186 114	34310	A	NS Hispeed	186 150	34348	C	Captrain BE
186 115	34309	A	NS Hispeed				
186 116	34311	A	NS Hispeed	186 181	34411	R	Metrans Rail
186 117	34321	A	NS Hispeed	186 182	34412	R	Metrans Rail
186 118	34322	A	NS Hispeed	186 183	34833	R	Metrans Rail
186 119	34323	A	NS Hispeed	186 187	34835	R	Metrans Rail
186 120	34331	A	NS Hispeed				
186 121	34339	A	NS Hispeed	186 236	34436	R §	NS Hispeed
186 122	34342	A	NS Hispeed	186 237	34441	R §	LTE NL
186 123	34312	A *	SNCB 2801	186 238	34442	R §	LTE NL
186 124	34313	A *	SNCB 2802	186 239	34448	R §	CRS
186 125	34316	A *	SNCB 2803	186 240	34457	R §	RTB Cargo
186 142	34373	C	Captrain BE				

SIEMENS TYPE ES64F4 (CLASS189) Bo-Bo

This locomotive is a four-voltage design which, like the TRAXX MS, can be equipped as required to operate in many countries. DB Schenker Rail (see section 5 of this book) owns 90 of the type as Class 189, most of them equipped to operate into the Netherlands. All of the locos below are owned by MRCE. All EVNs carry the same Class 189 number as shown below.

Builder: Siemens, München Allach.
Weight: 86 tonnes.
Wheel Diameter: 1250 mm.
Maximum Tractive Effort: 300 kN.

Continuous rating: 6400 kW.
Length over Buffers: 19.58 m.
Maximum Speed: 140 km/h.

189 090–099 are Version VJ, capable of operating in the Netherlands and Germany. They were purchased from Railion Deutschland and also carry the numbers ES64F4 990–999 which can cause confusion with 189 990–999!!

Number	Works No.	Built	Hired to:		Number	Works No.	Built	Hired to:
189 090	21076	2005	HTRS		189 095	21081	2005	Kombirail
189 091	21077	2005	ERS		189 096	21082	2005	HTRS
189 092	21078	2005	HTRS		189 097	21083	2005	ERS
189 093	21079	2005	DE (Captrain)		189 098	21084	2005	ERS
189 094	21080	2005	DE (Captrain)		189 099	21085	2005	ERS

189 101–115 are Version VE and capable of operating in the Netherlands, Germany, Austria, Switzerland, Italy, Slovenia and Croatia.

189 101	21501	2009	DB Autozug		189 109	21512	2009	DE (Captrain)
189 102	21502	2009	TXL		189 110	21514	2009	ERS
189 103	21503	2009	CFI (IT)		189 111	21515	2009	Captrain DE
189 104	21505	2009	BCB (Captrain)		189 112	21517	2009	Captrain BE
189 105	21506	2009	TXL		189 113	21518	2009	TXL
189 106	21508	2009	BoxXpress (DE)		189 114	21520	2009	HTRS
189 107	21509	2009	SBB Cargo		189 115	21521	2009	DB Autozug
189 108	21511	2009	BCB (Captrain)					

189 200–213 are Version VO and can operate in the Netherlands, Germany and Poland. 189 200–207, 209 were converted from 189 906, 911, 913, 919, 921, 922, 925, 929 and 933 respectively.

189 200	20719	2004	Kombirail		189 207	21241	2006	HTRS
189 201	20980	2004	CTL "Zabrze"		189 208	21482	2008	ERS
189 202	20986	2005	TXL		189 209	21246	2006	CTL
189 203	20756	2004	TXL		189 210	21483	2008	ERS
189 204	21234	2006	stored after accident		189 211	21484	2008	HTRS
					189 212	21485	2008	ERS
189 205	21235	2006	PKP Cargo		189 213	21486	2008	TXL
189 206	21238	2006	LOCON					

189 280–290 are Version VK and can operate in the Netherlands and Germany.

189 280	21487	2008	TXL		189 286	21493	2009	ERS
189 281	21488	2008	TXL		189 287	21631	2009	TXL
189 282	21489	2008	HTRS		189 288	21632	2009	HTRS
189 283	21490	2008	TXL		189 289	21633	2009	HTRS
189 284	21491	2009	Kombirail		189 290	21634	2009	ERS
189 285	21492	2009	ERS					

189 982–999 are Version VE as 189 101–115. They also carry numbers ES64F4 082–099.

189 982	21635	2009	HTRS		189 991	20739	2004	NIAG (DE)
189 983	21636	2009	Captrain		189 992	20721	2004	TXL
189 984	21637	2009	LOCON		189 993	20723	2004	NordCargo (Italy)
189 985	21638	2009	DB Schenker		189 994	20695	2003	BCB (Captrain)
189 986	21639	2009	TXL		189 995	20698	2003	TXL
189 987	21640	2009	ISC (IT)		189 996	20701	2003	TXL
189 988	20732	2004	BCB (Captrain)		189 997	20704	2004	TXL
189 989	20734	2004	NordCargo (IT)		189 998	20707	2004	TXL
189 990	20736	2004	BCB (Captrain)		189 999	20730	2004	Nordcargo (IT)

6.1.2. DIESEL LOCOMOTIVES

VOSSLOH TYPE G1206 (CLASS 275)   B-B

Vossloh's most popular off-centre-cab type which can be found right across Europe. A small number of locos have MTU engines but none of these were used in the Benelux countries at the time of writing. This list does not include G1206 locos **owned** by Benelux railway companies.

Builder: Vossloh.
Engine: Caterpillar 3512 B DI-TA of 1500 kW.
Transmission: Hydraulic. Voith L5r4 zU2.   **Wheel Diameter:** 1000 mm
Maximum Tractive Effort: 254 kN.   **Length over Buffers:** 14.70 m.
Weight: 87.3 tonnes.   **Maximum Speed:** 100 km/h.

e   Equipped with ETCS for use on the Betuweroute

Works No.	Built	Leasco.	Hired to:	Number/Name	EVN
1001374 e	2003	A	ERS	1201 "Sandra"	92 84 2275 101-8 F-ERS
1001375 e	2003	A	ERS	1202 "Corina"	92 80 1275 617-c D-ATLD
5001505 e	2004	A	Captrain	1505	92 80 1275 612-0 D-ATLD
5001506 e	2004	A	HTRS	1506	92 80 1275 613-c D-ATLD
5001507 e	2004	A	HTRS	1507	92 80 1275 614-c D-ATLD
5001508 e	2004	M	ERS	1508	92 80 1275 615-3 D-DISPO
5001510	2006	M	HTRS	7106	92 80 1275 624-5 D-DISPO
5001511 e	2006	M	LOCON	1511	92 80 1275 627-8 D-DISPO
5001553	2004	M	HTRS	7101	92 80 1275 618-7 D-DISPO
5001554 e	2004	M	Captrain DE	7102	92 80 1275 619-5 D-DISPO
5001555 e	2005	M	Captrain	1555	92 80 1275 620-3 D-DISPO
5001571 e	2006	M	Captrain DE	500 1571	92 80 1275 625-2 D-DISPO
5001572 e	2005	M	HTRS	7110	92 80 1275 621-1 D-DISPO
5001601 e	2005	M	ERS	1203 "Monique"	92 80 1275 622-9 D-DISPO

▲ G 1206 diesels 5001510 (HTRS 7106) and 5001798 (HTRS 1798) stand outside the older Shunter Tractie depot at Waalhaven Zuid on 23 August 2012.   **David Haydock**

5001627 e	2005	M	Captrain	1627	92 80 1275 623-7 D-DISPO
5001648 e	2006	M	DE (Captrain)	1648	92 80 1275 628-6 D-DISPO
5001796	2008	V	HTRS	7108	92 80 1275 632-8 D-VL
5001797	2008	V	LOCON	-	92 80 1275 633-6 D-ACTS
5001798	2008	V	HTRS	1798	92 80 1275 634-4 D-VL

VOSSLOH TYPE G 2000 (CLASSES 272 & 273)   B-B

Vossloh's biggest diesel-hydraulic type which is used across Europe. Originally known as the G2000 BB now the MaK 2000 BB. Produced in five versions. The G2000-1 has unusual asymmetrical cabs but only 20 were built. The G2000-2 is a version for Italy with a cab for two drivers. Most locos seen in the Benelux countries are the G2000-3 version. The fourth and fifth versions, which have 2700 kW MTU 20V4000 engines, were only prototypes at the time of writing.

Builder: Vossloh.
Engine: Caterpillar 3516 B-HD of 2240 kW.
Transmission: Hydraulic. Voith L620 re U2.   **Wheel Diameter:** 1000 mm.
Maximum Tractive Effort: 283 kN.   **Length over Buffers:** 17.40 m.
Weight: 87.3 tonnes.   **Maximum Speed:** 120 km/h.

These locos are all equipped to operated in the Netherlands and Germany and have been or are being equipped with ETCS. Those marked as such can also operate in Belgium.

*   Also equipped to operate in Belgium (also in France for locos from 5001615).

Class 273 Type G2000-1 (asymmetrical cabs, all equipped with ETCS)

Works No.	Built	Leasco.	Hired to:	Number	EVN
1001029	2001	A	HGK	DH 59	92 80 1273 101-6 D-HGK
1001034	2001	A	HGK	DH 58	92 80 1273 105-7 D-HGK
1001035	2001	A	HGK	DH 751	92 80 1273 106-5 D-HGK
1001038	2002	A	HGK	DH 752	92 80 1273 107-3 D-HGK
1001039	2002	A	HGK	DH 754	92 80 1273 103-2 D-HGK
1001042	2002	A	HTRS	-	92 80 1273 014-1 D-ATLD
1001043	2002	A	HTRS	1043	92 80 1273 102-4 D-ATLD
1001326	2002	A	HGK	DH 753	92 80 1273 104-0 D-HGK
1001384	2002	A	ERS	1384	92 80 1273 019-0

Class 272 Type G2000-3

1001324 e	2003	A	Captrain DE	2002	92 80 1272 201-5 D-CTD
1001445 e*	2004	A	RRF	1103	92 80 1272 401-1
1001446 e*	2004	A	HTRS	1446	92 80 1272 402-9 D-CTB
1001457	2004	M	RTS	-	92 80 1272 204-9 D-DISPO
1001458	2004	M	RTS	1458	92 80 1272 205-6 D-DISPO
5001604 *	2005	A	RRF	1101	92 80 1272 403-7 D-RRF
5001605 e*	2005	A	Captrain DE	2006	92 80 1272 404-5 D-CTD
5001606 e*	2005	A	Railtraxx	2007	92 80 1272 405-2 D-CTb
5001607 *	2005	M	HTRS	1607	92 80 1272 406-0 D-DISPO
5001608 *	2005	M	RTS	V202	92 80 1272 407-8 D-DISPO
5001615 *	2006	A	Europorte	1615	92 88 2272 004-3 B-EPF
5001616 *	2006	A	Europorte	1616	92 88 2272 005-0 B-EPF
5001617 *	2006	A	SNCB	5703	92 87 0002 012-8
5001618 *	2006	A	SNCB	5704	92 87 0002 013-3
5001634	2008	A	RRF	1102	92 88 2272 001-9 B-RRF
5001637 *	2007	A	Euro Cargo Rail	-	92 87 0002 006-0
5001640 *	2007	A	SNCB	5709	92 87 0002 007-8
5001641 *	2007	A	Euro Cargo Rail	-	92 87 0002 008-6
5001669 *	2007	A	SNCB	5707	92 87 0002 009-4
5001670 *	2007	A	SNCB	5708	92 87 0002 010-2
5001750	2007	A	Colas Rail	-	92 80 1272 607-3
5001751	2007	A	Colas Rail	-	92 80 1272 608-1
5001755	2008	A	Europorte	1755	92 87 0002 014-4 F-EPF
5001756 *	2008	A	Europorte	1756	92 87 0002 015-1 F-EPF
5001757 *	2008	A	SNCB	5701	92 87 0002 019-3
5001758	2008	A	SNCB	5705	92 87 0002 002-1

EMD TYPE JT42CWR (CLASS 266) Co-Co

These locos are known in most countries as Class 66 after their British classification. This type is now used extensively in the Benelux countries. From 2006, locos delivered have been Type JT42CWRM, M meaning Modified, the locos having improved cabs and engines.

Builder: EMD.
Engine: JT42CWR: General Motors Type 12N-710G3B-EC of 2238 kW.
 JT42CWRM: General Motors Type 12N-710G3B-T2 of 2238 kW.
Transmission: Electric. Six General Motors D43TR traction motors.
Wheel Diameter: 1120 mm.
Maximum Tractive Effort: 409 kN. **Length over Buffers:** 21.35 m.
Weight: 126 tonnes. **Maximum Speed:** 120 km/h.

Works No.	Built	Leasco	Leasco No.	Hired to:	Number	EVN
20008254-1	2001	B	PB 01	RTB Cargo	V264	92 80 1 266 003-3 D-RTB
20008254-2	2001	B	PB 02	HGK	DE 676	92 88 0 266 004-1 D-HGK
20008254-3 and 4 are HHPI 29001 and 29002 and not equipped for Benelux.						
20008254-5	2001	B	PB 03 *Mireille*	Crossrail	PB 03	92 80 1 266 018-1 D-XRAIL
20008254-6	2001	B	PB 04	HGK	DE 63	92 80 1 266 063-7 D-HGK
20008254-7	2001	B	PB 05	Captrain	6609	92 80 1 266 009-0 B-CTB
20008254-8	2001	B	PB 06	HGK	DE 64	92 80 1 266 064-5 D-HGK
20008254-9	2001	B	PB 07	Captrain	6601	92 88 0 266 001-1 B-CTB
20008254-10	2001	B	PB 08	Captrain	6602	92 88 0 266 002-9 B-CTB
20008254-11	2002	B	PB 09	Captrain	6603	92 88 0 266 003-7 B-CTB
20008254-12	2002	B	PB 10	RTB Cargo	V266	92 80 1 266 014-0 D-CBRL
20008254-13 is HHPI 29003 and not equipped for Benelux.						
20018360-1	2002	B	PB 11	Captrain	6605	92 80 1 266 016-5 D-CTB
20018360-2	2002	B	PB 12	Crossrail	-	92 80 1 266 017-3 D-XRAIL
20018360-3	2002	B	PB 13	Crossrail	-	92 80 1 266 098-1 D-XRAIL
20018360-4	2002	B	PB 14	Crossrail	-	92 80 1 266 065-2 D-XRAIL
20018360-5	2002	B	PB 15	Crossrail	-	92 80 1 266 066-0 D-XRAIL
20018360-6	2002	B	PB 16	OHE	-	92 80 1 266 067-8 D-XRAIL
20018360-7	2002	B	PB 17	RTB Cargo	V267	92 80 1 266 021-5 D-RTB
20018360-8	2002	B	PB 18	ITL	-	92 80 1 266 022-3 D-ITL
20018360-9	2002	B	PB 19	HGK	DE 678	92 80 1 266 023-6 D-HGK
20018360-10	2003	B	PB 20	Railtraxx	RL 002	92 80 1 266 024-9 D-
20028453-1	2002	E		HGK	DE 668	92 80 1 266 068-6 D-HGK
20028453-2	2002	E		HGK	DE 669	92 80 1 266 069-4 D-HGK
20028453-3	2002	E		HGK	DE 670	92 80 1 266 070-2 D-HGK
20028453-4	2002	E		HGK	DE 671	92 80 1 266 071-0 D-HGK
20028453-5	2002	E		HGK	DE 672	92 80 1 266 072-8 D-HGK
20038513-1	2003	E	ER 1	Captrain		92 80 1 266 025-6 D-BRLL
20038513-2	2003	E	ER 2	LWB (DE)		92 80 1 266 026-4 D-BRLL
20038513-3, 4 and 5 are HHPI 29004, 29006 and 29005 and not equipped for Benelux.						
20038513-6	2003	K	ER 6	Crossrail	DE 6301	92 80 1 266 133-1 D-XRAIL
20038513-7	2003	K	ER 7	Crossrail	DE 6302	92 80 1 266 034-8 D-XRAIL
20038513-8	2004	M	ER 8	RRF	513-8	92 80 1 266 035-5 D-DISPO
20038513-9	2004	M	ER 9	-	513-9	92 80 1 266 036-3 D-DISPO
20038513-10	2004	M	ER 10	RRF	513-10	92 80 1 266 037-1 D-DISPO
20038545-1	2004	D	EC 1	-	-	92 80 1 266 030-c
20038545-2	2004	C	EC 2	Captrain	6606	92 80 1 266 031-4 D-CTB
20038545-3	2004	C	EC 3	CFL cargo DK	-	92 80 1 266 032-2 D-CBRL
20038561-01	2004	M	EM 1	HGK	DE 673	92 80 1 266 038-9 D-HGK
20038561-02	2004	M	EM 2	HGK	DE 674	92 80 1 266 039-7 D-HGK
20038561-03	2004	M	EM 3	ERS	6611	92 80 1 266 040-5 D-DISPO
20038561-04	2004	M	EM 4	ERS	561-04	92 80 1 266 041-3 D-DISPO
20038561-05	2004	M	EM 5	ERS	561-5	92 80 1 266 042-1 D-DISPO

JT42CWRM sub type (known as Class 77 in France)

20048653-01	2005	M	JT-1	HGK	DE 675	92 80 1 266 111-4 D-DISPO
20048653-02	2005	M	JT-2	ERS "Kayden"	6615	92 80 1 266 112-2 D-DISPO
20048653-03	2005	M	JT-3	ERS "Lauryn"	6614	92 80 1 266 113-0 D-DISPO
20048653-04	2005	M	JT-4	HTRS	653-4	92 80 1 266 114-8 D-DISPO
20048653-05	2005	M	JT-5	HTRS	653-05	92 80 1 266 115-5 D-DISPO

20048653-06 was scrapped in 2011 after an accident.

20048653-07	2005	M	JT-6	ERS	6617	92 80 1 266 116-3 D-DISPO
20048653-08	2005	M	JT-7	Captrain "Wessel"	653-08	92 80 1 266 117-1 D-DISPO
20048653-09	2005	M	JT-8	OHE		92 80 1 266 118-9 D-DISPO
20048653-10	2005	M	JT-9	OHE		92 80 1 266 119-7 D-DISPO

20058725-01	2006	B	EU 1	HGK	DE 677	92 80 1 266 107-2 D-DB

20058725-02 to 05 are Freightliner PL locos in Poland, not equipped for Benelux.

20058725-06	2006	B	EU 06	Captrain	CB 1000	92 80 1 266 105-6 D-RCHEM
20058725-07	2006	B	EU 07	Captrain	CB 1001	92 80 1 266 106-4 D-RCHEM
20058725-08	2006	K	EU 08	Crossrail	DE 6306	92 80 1 266 101-5 D-DLC
20058725-09	2006	K	EU 09	Crossrail	DE 6307	92 80 1 266 102-3 D-DLC
20058725-10	2007	K	EU 10	Crossrail	DE 6308	92 80 1 266 103-1 D-DLC
20058725-11	2007	K	EU 11	Crossrail	DE 6309	92 80 1 266 104-9 D-DLC

20078968-001	2008	F		Crossrail "Griet"	DE 6310	92 80 1 266 280-7 D-XRAIL
20078968-002	2008	F		Crossrail "Hana"	DE 6311	92 80 1 266 281-5 D-XRAIL
20078968-003	2008	F		Crossrail "Alix"	DE 6312	92 80 1 266 282-3 D-XRAIL

20078968-004, 006, 007 ordered by Crossrail but never accepted. Now sold to GB Railfreight.

20078968-005	2008	F		Crossrail "Hanna"	DE 6314	92 80 1 266 284-9 D-XRAIL

▲ HGK Class 66 DE 668 is seen at Biezenmortel on the 's-Hertogenbosch–Tilburg line on 10 May 2008, with the Linz shuttle, from Linz to Maasvlakte in the port of Rotterdam. **Quintus Vosman**

NBE RAIL

NBE Rail is a German company (NBE stands for Nordbayerische Eisebahngesellschaft) based in Aschaffenburg and hires V100 locos to Dutch operators, amongst others. Livery is light blue, white and orange. Only the following locos have been noted in the Netherlands.

LEW TYPE V100 B-B

These shunting and trip freight locomotives were built for DR as Classes 108 and 110 to 114 then became DB Classes 201, 202, 204 and 298. Most locos are ex DB and have been re-engined and modernised by Alstom Locomotive Service at Stendal works. Some are hired out by ALS. Modernised locos are generally known as Class 203. At the end of 2007, there were 25 Type V100 in service in the Netherlands (RRF has the biggest fleet), plus V100 093 preserved by VSM. This has been hired for main line work in the past.

Builder: LEW.
Engine (original): VEB-MWJ 12KVD 18/21 AII of 736 kW (Classes 201 & 298); 12KVD 21AL-3 of 853 kW (Class 202); 12KVD 21AL-4 of 1104 kW (Class 204).
Engine (new): MTU 12V4000 R10 of 1380 kW or Caterpillar 3512B DI-TA of 1305 kW.
Transmission: Hydraulic. Pirna.   **Wheel Diameter:** 1000 mm.
Maximum Tractive Effort: 206 kN.   **Length over Buffers:** 14.24 m.
Weight: 72 tonnes.   **Max. Speed:** 100 km/h.

NBE no.	Ex DB no.	Works no.	EVN
203 160	202 637	13955	92 80 1203 160-7 D-NBEG
203 163	202 613	13931	92 80 1203 163-1 D-NBEG

▲ Shunter Tractie's two V100 diesels 203 101 and 102 are seen between hire contracts at the company's Rotterdam Zuid depot on 23 August 2012. **David Haydock**

SHUNTER TRACTIE

Shunter was founded in 2003 in order to supply maintenance facilities to other operating companies and now carries out work for almost all freight operators, including DB Schenker Rail Nederland. Shunter also hires out shunting locomotives including two Class 203 (V100) main line diesels from Alstom. The company is also a fully licenced RU to allow movement of stock around the country.

Depots: Geleen Lutterade, Roosendaal (wagon works), Rotterdam Zuid, Waalhaven (two depots – north side of yard, running maintenance; south side, heavy repairs).

LEW TYPE V100 B-B

For technical details, see NBE Rail.

No.	Name	Ex DB no.	Works No.	Built	EVN
203 101	"Robert"	202 850	15235	1976	92 84 2203 101-5 NL-SHTR
203 102	"Arnold"	202 341	12850	1971	92 84 2203 102-3 NL-SHTR

SHUNTING LOCOMOTIVES

No.	Name	Axles	Builder	Works No.	Year	Type	Power	Notes
202	Nicky	B	O&K	26707	1971	MB125N	92 kW	ex ENKA, Ede.
203	Roos (S)	B	O&K	26618	1967	MB5N	92 kW	ex Aluchemie, Botlek.
204	Faye	B	O&K	26795	1974	MB200N	147 kW	ex EBO, Bad Orb.
205	Sara	B	O&K	26811	1977	MB200N	147 kW	ex WRS, Duisburg.
206	Nancy	B	O&K	26773	1972	MB170N	125 kW	ex Degussa, Frankfurt.
(207)	Kelly	B	O&K	26730	1972	MB170N	149 kW	ex BfB, Nürnberg.
208	Maya	B	O&K	26764	1972	MB125N	92 kW	ex Rethe-Speicker, Hamburg
209	Maura	B	O&K	26810	1975	MB200N	149 kW	ex Holzmann, Weisenbach
-	Lyondell	B	O&K	26535	1965	MB7N	92 kW	ex DETAG, Witten
301	Monica	B	Vollert	93 1073	1993	DR6000	180 kW	ex ?
303	Andrea	B	O&K	26659	1968	MB9N	184 kW	ex Combinatie Havenmond.
304	Myrthe	B	O&K	26656	1968	MB9N	184 kW	ex Holcim, Untervaz.
305		B	O&K	26703	1971	MB9N	184 kW	ex Pfleiderer, Neumarkt.
306		B	O&K	26667	1969	MB9N	184 kW	ex Ford, Köln.
307		B	O&K	26684	1970	MB9N	184 kW	ex Ford, Köln.
308		B	O&K	26702	1971	MB9N	190 kW	ex Ford, Genk.
401	Klm	B	O&K	26555	1965	MB11N	190 kW	ex O&K, Amsterdam.
402		B	O&K	26762	1972	MB360N	195 kW	ex Deutsche Shell, Monheim.
481	Jansen	B	Windhoff	260007/1	1981	RW110DH	94 kW	Cabless loco
482	Jansen	B	Windhoff	260007/2	1981	RW110DH	94 kW	Cabless loco
501	Sharon	B	O&K	26777	1973	MC500N	318 kW	ex FTE, Emden.
502	Key-Leigh	B	O&K	26584	1967	MC14N	250 kW	ex Papierfabrik, Albbruck.
503	Caitlin	B	O&K	26630	1967	MC14N	250 kW	ex Papierfabrik, Albbruck.
601	Annemiek	C	O&K	26954	1980	MEC502	510 kW	ex DE 761
602	(U)	C	O&K	26955	1980	MEC502	510 kW	ex DE 762
603	Evy	C	O&K	26957	1980	MEC502	510 kW	ex DE 764

6.2. BENELUX FREIGHT OPERATORS

Like the traffic generated by the Benelux ports, the number of freight train operators is in continual expansion, especially in the Netherlands where the port of Rotterdam is a honeypot. Almost all of these companies work closely together and often sub-hire traction to each other. Unless shown otherwise, none of them have their own maintenance facilities.

BENTHEIMER EISENBAHN   BE

This German company, owned by the local authorities in the area, runs the 76 km line from Bad Bentheim, just over the border in Germany, to Coevorden in the Netherlands where the company operates a container terminal. After years of contracting other companies to operate trains from this terminal to Rotterdam, BE bought electric loco 1835 from NS Reizigers in late 2011. BE also intends to have its diesel loco D20 approved for use in the Netherlands. BE shunts the terminal with one of its bigger German locos. These can be found in our book *German Railways: Part 2 Private Railways*. In summer 2012 MaK loco D 22 was doing the honours.

Depots: Bad Bentheim, Nordhorn, Nordhorn Süd.

CLASS 221   B-B

These popular locomotives are former DB Type V200.1. They look like British "Warships" from the exterior but the more powerful engines made them the equivalent of the "Westerns". Several were preserved and 20 sold to Greece, then most were brought back to Germany 13 years later in 2002. 221 147 was Greek Railways (OSE) 416 for a while. The loco was re-engined during overhaul in 2008 by Arriva in Neustrelitz. The loco is in a superb black, yellow and red livery.

Built: 1965.   **Builder:** Krauss-Maffei (works number 19267).
Engines: Two MTU DM 12V4000R41 of 1500 kW each.
Transmission: Hydraulic. MTU K184U.   **Maximum Tractive Effort:** 245 kN.
Weight in working order: 78 tonnes.   **Driving Wheel Diameter:** 950 mm.
Length: 18.44 metres.   **Maximum Speed:** 140 km/h.

D20 (EVN 92 80 **1221 147**-2 D-BE)

▲ On 14 May 2012 Captrain 186 150 works a container train from Germany over the *Betuweroute* to the port of Rotterdam near Hardinxveld-Giessendam.   **Carlo Hertogs**

CLASS 1800 B-B

See NS Reizigers for technical details.

1835

CAPTRAIN BENELUX

In 2007 French Railways' freight arm Fret SNCF expanded its operations to the ports of Antwerpen and Rotterdam using the name SNCF Fret Benelux. The company then took over ITL of Germany and Veolia Cargo's operations (Veolia had absorbed rail4chem in 2008), then created the branding Captrain. Captrain Benelux encompasses SNCF Fret Benelux, ITL Benelux and Captrain Netherlands. ITL originally owned four former DR V100 diesel locos but was selling these to Trainsupport in mid 2012.

Fret SNCF itself operates Class BB 67400 diesels and BB 36000 electrics from northern France into Belgium, mainly to Gent and Antwerpen. BB 36000 also operate steel trains from Dunkerque and Berguette-Isbergues to the Liège and Charleroi areas.

DIESEL LOCOMOTIVES

TYPE V100 B-B

See NBE Rail for technical details.

No.	Built	Works No.	Former number	EVN
101	1971	12877	Ex DB 202 368	92 80 1203 137-5 D-ITL

Captrain also operates Class 186 and 189 electrics plus G1206, G2000 and Class 66 diesels. See Section 6.1.

CONTINENTAL RAIL SERVICES CRS

This company was set up in 2009 by German company AR-Logistics Consulting and has so far only operated by using traction from other RUs as well as hiring one Class 186 for Hungary–Rotterdam cereals traffic. In late 2012 the company started crewing trains in connection with Austrian company LTE which had also hired one Class 186. See Section 6.1.

CROSSRAIL BENELUX XRAIL

Crossrail was created through the merger of DLC, the first Belgian open access operator, with the Swiss operator Crossrail, which had been created from the freight arm of Regionalverkehr Mittelland. The company is now a major operator of intermodal services on the Benelux–Germany–Switzerland–Italy route. These services are all hauled by Class 66 within Belgium and the Netherlands, although the company has a fleet of Class 185 and 186 TRAXX locos used from the German border.

Crossrail operates leased EMD Class 66 locomotives. See Section 6.1.

CTL LOGISTICS CTL

This is a Polish company with a subsidiary in Germany which operates intermodal trains between the Netherlands and Poland using leased Class 189 locomotives. See Section 6.1.

▲ CRS mainly works cereal trains between the port of Rotterdam and Germany with its locomotive 186 239. On 27 May 2012 such a train is seen near Hardinxveld-Giessendam on the Betuweroute.
Carlo Hertogs

▼ Crossrail Class 66 PB 03 is seen with a rather light load at Putkappel on the Aarschot–Leuven line on 26 July 2012.
Thierry Nicolas

DORTMUNDER EISENBAHN   DE

This is a German company which operates a major local network serving industry around Dortmund, and now operates main line services. Captrain Deutschland (see above) now owns 65% of the company. DE works with Captrain on traffic such as biodiesel from Germany to Rotterdam and coal from Amsterdam and Rotterdam to Germany, mostly using Class 189 locos. See Section 6.1.

ERS RAILWAYS   ERS

European Rail Shuttle was a joint venture involving shippers Maersk, Sealand, Nedlloyd and P&O, set up in 1994, which started open access operations in 2002 after establishing subsidiary ERS Railways. The company is now wholly owned by Maersk. After a period of operating only container trains for its shareholders, ERS is now operating trains of any sort for all and sundry and Maersk is giving contracts to other operators.

ERS operates leased Vossloh G1206, G2000 and EMD Class 66 locomotives. See Section 6.1.

EUROPORTE

This company is based in France but operates freights into Belgium using Vossloh G2000 and Euro 4000 locomotives. Details of these can be found in our French Railways stock book.

HSL LOGISTIK   HSL

This company, which has its headquarters in Hamburg, Germany, started operations in November 2010, hauling cereals from Germany to Oss and Rotterdam. The company initially hired in traction, then bought NS Reizigers 1832 in mid 2012. Livery is a black-and-white chess board pattern.

CLASS 1800   B-B

See NS Reizigers for technical details.

1832

HUSA TRANSPORTATION RAIL SERVICES   HTRS

Husa is a transport conglomorate which is expanding in order to carry out Europe-wide logistics services. The company absorbed ACTS in late 2010 then started to apply its own logos and a blue and orange livery in early 2011. The company also owns Rent-a-Rail in Germany.

ACTS was formed in 1989 and originally specialised in the transport of household waste in special containers (thus the name *Afzet Container Transport Systeem*) then started operating its own trains in March 1998. ACTS also hires out containers and carries out maintenance of railway rolling stock. Since the last edition of this book, and before absorption by HTRS, ACTS got rid of its Class 1200 electrics and its Class 58, 60 and 67 diesel locos. HTRS now mainly hires traction.

CLASS 1600   B-B

These are former NS (later Railion) locos and are actually owned by HTRS leasing company Railmotion. They are all in HTRS orange/blue livery and can be found on freight anywhere on the 1500 V DC network.

| 1606 | | 1609 | | 1619 | | 1621 |

HTRS also operates leased traction. See Section 6.1.

▲ ERS loco 189 098 (a.k.a ES 64 F4 998) is seen at Helmond heading for the port of Rotterdam on 10 March 2010.   **Paul Conlan**

▼ HSL Logistik's remarkable livery for loco 1832 was first displayed on 1 October 2012 at Rotterdam IJsselmonde.   **Luc Peulen**

HVLE

Havelländerische Eisenbahn Aktiengesellschaft is a German RU which has occasionally operated into the Netherlands – Voith Maxima V 490.1 worked a train to Veendam in 2012. The company's locomotives can be found in Platform 5 Publishing's book German Railways Part 2.

KOMBIRAIL EUROPE (KOMBIVERKEHR)

Kombirail Europe is a subsidiary of German company Kombiverkehr and operates frequent container shuttles between Dutch ports and Germany, particularly the Ruhr area – there are no less than 40 departures a week between the Ruhr and Rotterdam. The company uses hired electric locos. See section 6.1.

LLOYD'S REGISTER RAIL

This company arrived in the Netherlands in October 2006 when it took over Nedtrain Consulting, the engineering consultancy division of Netherlands Railways. LRR is involved in approving new traction types and therefore requires an operating licence but does not have any locos of its own at the time of writing.

▲ In the port of Rotterdam HTRS G 1206 7101 – still in the ACTS Portfeeders livery – runs alongside the Oude Maas with a heavy oil train on 27 May 2012. The diesel will take the train from Vondelingenplaat to Kijfhoek where an electric locomotive will take over. **Carlo Hertogs**

LOCON BENELUX

This is the Benelux subsidiary, set up in early 2011, of German company Logistik & Consulting AG which is based in Berlin-Brandenburg. The company also has some Vossloh G1206 diesels on hire and hires V100 locos from other companies – in the past Spitzke and Volker Rail – as required. The company also had a V100 on hire from German company Nordbayerische Eisenbahngesellschaft in 2012. See Section 6.1.2. Livery is orange with a white band.

CLASS 189   Bo-Bo

For details, see Section 6.1. Built 2012.

189 820 (LOCON 501) | 189 821 (LOCON 502)

TYPE V100   B-B

See NBE Rail for technical details.

No.	Built	Works No.	Former number	Notes
LOCON 220	1973	13933	Ex DB 202 615	Owned by LOCON.
203 161	1973	13931	Ex DB 202 613	Hired from NBE Rail.

CLASS 9800   Bo-Bo

These former SNCB locomotives were originally brought to the Netherlands by ACTS. As they are not equipped with Dutch ATP they will be used for "last mile" operations. SNCB 6392 was renumbered 6704 but later scrapped. See SNCB Class 62 for technical details.

6701 A	1966	-	for spares, ex SNCB 6321
9802 A	1966	-	ex SNCB 6325, ex ACTS 6702
6703 A	1966	-	ex SNCB 6391
6705 A	1966	-	ex SNCB 6393

CLASS 9900   B-B

See NS Reizigers Class 1800 for technical details. 9903 does not exist.

9901 (1827) | 9902 (1834) | 9904 (1831) | 9905 (1836)

LTE NEDERLAND

This is a subsidiary of an Austrian freight operator which started running trains to the Netherlands in September 2012, initially using CRS's licence and leasing locos 186 237 and 238 (see section 6.1.).

METRANS RAIL

This is a Czech company, formerly known as Railtransport, working trains through to Rotterdam using Class 186 locos on hire. See Section 6.1.

PKP CARGO

PKP Cargo is Polish State Railways' freight operating arm. Hired Class 189 locos in PKP Cargo livery now operate to Rotterdam and the company is expected to work through to Antwerpen in future. See Section 6.1.

▲ LOCON electric loco 9905, formerly NS 1836, is seen at Nieuwstadt while hauling Connexxion EMU 919 from Amersfoort for repair at Maastricht on 10 September 2012. **Luc Peulen**

PRORAIL

ProRail is the State-owned infrastructure manager which manages the whole of the Netherlands rail network except the *Betuweroute* freight-only line and the *Havenspoorlijn* which runs from Kijfhoek yard to Maasvlakte serving the port of Rotterdam. ProRail is a licensed railway undertaking, able to operate its own trains. The company has just two locos at present.

CLASS 600   C

These ex-NS locomotives are similar to the British Class 08. The loco shunts at Crailoo track depot.

Built: 1950–57.
Builder: English Electric.
Engine: English Electric 6KT of 294 kW at 680 rpm.
Transmission: Electric. Two EE 506 4B axle-hung traction motors.
Weight in Full Working Order: 47 tonnes.
Maximum Tractive Effort: 143 kN.
Length over Buffers: 9.07 m.
Driving Wheel Diametrer: 1230 mm.
Max. Speed: 30 km/h.

No.	Built	Works No.
647	1956	2144

CLASS V100   B-B

See NBE RAIL for technical details. This former DR loco was initially preserved by VSM, then sold to ProRail in 2008.

No.	Built	Works No.	Former number	EVN
V100 093	1968	11931	Ex DB 201 093	-

RAILTRAXX

This is a Belgian company set up by Ronny Dillen, one of the partners who started DLC which grew into Crossrail. The company started operation of freights from Belgium to Romania in 2011 and has so far leased one Class 66, one G2000 and an Alpha Trains Class 186 – the latter subleased from SNCB! At the time of writing, locos were not in a special livery; only the G2000 was marked Railtraxx. See Section 6.1 for details.

RHEINCARGO

RheinCargo is the merger of the rail freight operators Häfen und Güterverkehr Köln (HGK) and Neusser Eisenbahn (NE), which stems from the merger, announced in early 2012, of the port authorities at Köln and Neuss-Düsseldorf on the river Rhein in Germany. At the time of writing, the two railways had not started to be rebranded. HGK has been active in the Netherlands, on services from Germany, for several years. NE has occasionally loaned its G2000 to operators in the Netherlands.

HÄFEN & GÜTERVERKEHR KÖLN   HGK

This company started as the river port rail network operator in Köln but expanded in recent years to become an open access operator. Full details of the fleet are given in the Platform 5 German Railways handbook Part 2. Only part of the fleet is equipped to operate in the Netherlands – all but one Class 66 loco (DE 61 , 63 and 64, DE 668 to 674 plus hired locos) plus three MaK Type DE 1002 locos DE 81 to DE 83. The use of HGK Class 66s and G2000s in the Netherlands is daily but incursions by the DE 1002s are now rare.

HGK also operates leased Vossloh G2000 and EMD Class 66 locomotives. See Section 6.1.

DIESEL LOCOMOTIVES

EMD JT42CWR (CLASS 66)   Co-Co

HGK owns two Class 66 locos, DE 61/62. However DE 62 has no equipment to work into the Netherlands. For technical details see Section 6.1.

No.	Built	Works No.	Notes
DE 61	1999	998101-1	Originally to be EWS 66154.

MaK TYPE DE 1002   Bo-Bo

Basically very similar to NS Class 6400. Only DE 81 to DE 83 are equipped with Dutch ATB equipment. Being equipped with new Cummins engines.

Built: 1987/93.
Engine: MWM TBD604BV12 of 1320 kW.
Transmission: Electric.
Weight: 90 tonnes.
Length over Buffers: 13.00 m.

Builder: MaK.

Wheel Diameter: 1000 mm.
Maximum Tractive Effort:
Maximum Speed: 90 km/h.

DE 81	1993	1000882
DE 82	1993	1000883
DE 83	1993	1000884

▲ Railtraxx Vossloh G 2000 diesel 5001606, the first loco to receive the company's branding, is seen shunting on 2 August 2012 in Rhodesië yard in the port of Antwerpen. **Carlo Hertogs**

NEUSSER EISENBAHN NE

NE operates just over the border from the Netherlands in Germany and has hired its one G2000 to Netherlands railway undertakings several times. Full details of the fleet are given in the Platform 5 German Railways handbook Part 2.

VOSSLOH TYPE G2000 B-B

For technical details, see Section 6.1.

No.	Built	Works No.
NE 9	2002	1001040

ROTTERDAM RAIL FEEDING RRF

This company started operations in 2004 and both hauls its own trains and provides services to other train operators. The company was bought by US company Genesee & Wyoming in April 2008 and has since expanded operations to other areas including Amsterdam and Antwerpen. Although the company is still officially known as Rotterdam Rail Feeding, locos working elsewhere carry the words "Rail Feeding" on the side; operations in Belgium are by subsidiary Belgium Rail Feeding. The original livery was green but this has been replaced by G&W orange and black.

RRF also has two Vossloh G2000 diesels on long term hire, in the company's orange livery, plus Class 66s on hire. See Section 6.1.

DIESEL LOCOMOTIVES

CLASS 600   C

See ProRail for technical details. Some of the locos, plus ex NS 640, have been noted stored at Rotterdam Botlek.

No.	Built	Works No.	EVN	Notes
1	1956	2124		ex NS 684 (ex 626)
2	1956	2149		ex NS 689 (ex 652)
3	1955	2108		ex NS 676 (ex 611)
4	1955	2113		ex NS 679 (ex 616)
5	1956	2118		ex NS 683 (ex 621)

TYPE V100   B-B

See NBE Rail for technical details. All equipped with ETCS Level 2 for the Betuweroute. They are leased from Sumitomo. 16 was involved in an accident and probably will not run again.

16 (U)	1971	12930	ex DB 202 421
17	1974	14383	ex DB 202 682
18	1975	15091	ex DB 202 819
19	1971	12832	ex DB 202 323
20	1974	14431	ex DB 202 730
21	1972	12916	ex DB 202 407
22	1973	13566	ex DB 202 527
23	1972	13493	ex DB 202 454
24	1975	14476	ex DB 202 775

▲ On 30 March 2009 Rotterdam Rail Feeding shunter no. 2 (former NS 689) moves ex-NS Type DH railcars 3226+3110+3222+3105 from the RHB docks to Waalhaven Zuid yard. **Quintus Vosman**

CLASS 73   C

Ex SNCB Class 73. See SNCB section for details.

101		ex-SNCB 7382
102		ex SNCB 7394
103		ex SNCB 7391
104	98 84 8283 733-9 NL-RRF	ex SNCB 7395
105		ex SNCB 7378
106		ex SNCB 7387
107		ex SNCB 7390
108		ex SNCB 7392

RAIL TRANSPORT SERVICE (Swietelsky)

An Austrian track company which opened an office in the Netherlands in early 2010. The company has so far used two leased Vossloh G2000 in the Netherlands. See Section 6.1.

RTB CARGO

Rurtalbahn (RTB), based in Düren, Germany, operates into the Netherlands and Belgium, in concert with Belgian operator TrainsporT, in which RTB holds 97% of shares. RTB Cargo traction which only operates in Germany is shown in the Platform 5 book German Railways Part 2.

RTB Cargo also operates leased Class 186 and EMD Class 66 locomotives. See Section 6.1.

TYPE G1206   B-B

See Section 6.1 for technical details. V152 to V154 were hired locos, now returned.

RTB number	Built	Works No.	EVN
V151 "Josy"	2004	5001490	92 80 1275 118-8 D-RTB
V155	2009	5001652	92 80 1275 636-9 D-RTB
V156	2009	5001654	92 80 1275 637-7 D-RTB

TYPE G2000   B-B

See Section 6.1 for technical details. V201, V202 and V205 were hired locos, since returned.

V203	2008	5001752	92 80 1272 408-6 D-RTB
V204	2008	5001753	92 80 1272 409-4 D-RTB
V206	2009	5001760	92 80 1272 410-2 D-RTB

SBB CARGO DEUTSCHLAND

Swiss Federal Railways now operates a large number of freight services from Switzerland through to Aachen West in Germany, but at the time of writing did not continue through to Antwerpen. The company also works a small number of services into the Netherlands, using leased Class 186 electric locos – just two at the time of writing. See Section 6.1.

TrainsporT

TrainsporT is the Belgian subsidiary of Rurtalbahn and holds the contracts for rail traffic between Belgium and Germany, although operation is effectively by RTB Cargo (see above). TrainsporT still owns former SNCB Class 59 diesels 5922 and 5930, stored at Düren, but is trying to sell them.

▲ On 26 April 2012 RTB Cargo G 2000 diesel V206 pushes a very long train loaded with new Ford cars towards the Grimaldi terminal in the port of Antwerpen. **Carlo Hertogs**

TRAINSUPPORT

This company is part of the TrainGroup, created by Martijn Loois, formerly of rail4chem then Captrain Nederland. TrainSupport supplies "last mile" services. The company started operations in late 2011, under HTRS's licence and infrastructure agreement, and hiring V100 diesels, then started to buy the same type from Captrain in 2012. A third V100 was expected in late 2012 plus two G1206s on hire from HTRS. Loco livery is orange and white.

TYPE V100 B-B

See NBE Rail for technical details.

TG-102	1971	12878	Ex DB 202 369	Ex Captrain/ITL 102
TG-103	1975	14658	Ex DB 202 777	Ex Captrain/ITL 103

TX LOGISTIK TXL

This is a German company now wholly owned by Italian State Railways (FS). TXL works various freight trains between the Netherlands and Germany using Class 189 locos hired from MRCE – but without TXL identification – see Section 6.1.1.

6.3 TRACK MAINTENANCE COMPANIES

BAM RAIL   BAM

This is a track maintenance firm, part of a large group, with its headquarters in Breda and offices in Eindhoven, Rotterdam and Dordrecht. The company has no locos of its own and hires them in when necessary. A V100 hired from RRF was marked with the company's name.

EURAILSCOUT INSPECTION & ANALYSIS

Eurailscout is owned by Strukton Rail and SNCF Infrastructure and is engaged in track inspection. The company has inspection trains but no locomotives or rolling stock. Eurailscout hires Class 2200 locos from Strukton on a semi-permanent basis.

DIESEL LOCOMOTIVES

NS CLASS 2200   Bo-Bo

These ex-NS locos are hired by Strukton to Eurailscout. The locos are now equipped with lights and cameras to video the track and labelled *VideoSchouwTrein*. 2270 is being cannibalised for spares.

Built: 1955–58.
Builder: Allan (2201–2300), Schneider (2301–2350).
Engine: Stork-Schneider Superior 40C-Lx-8 of 670 kW at 1100 rpm.
Transmission: Electric. 4 Heemaf TM98 traction motors.
Weight in Full Working Order: 72 tonnes.
Maximum Tractive Effort: 181 kN.   **Length over Buffers:** 14.10 m.
Driving Wheel Dia.: 950 mm.   **Max. Speed:** 100 km/h.

302270 (U)	Berta	ex NS 2270	VST07-1	EVN 92 84 028 4 220-0
302282	Anneke	ex NS 2282	VST07-3	EVN 92 84 028 4 222-5
302328	José	ex NS 2328	VST07-2	EVN 92 84 028 4 221-c

ELECTRIC POSTAL CARS

CLASS 3000   mP

These former NS single units, formerly used for postal traffic, are now in service use. "Jules", converted from 3032, is used to test Dutch ATB and "Jim", converted from 3024, to test ETCS/ERTMS and GSM-R. 3031 is preserved at the NSM.

Built: 1965–66.
Builder-Mechanical Parts: Werkspoor.
Builder-Electrical Parts: Smit.   **Weight:** 54 tonnes.
Traction Motors: 4 x Heemaf 145 kW.   **Length over Couplers:** 26.40 m.
                                               Maximum Speed: 140 km/h.

BRT-91 "Jules"	EVN 80 84 978 1 003-2
BRT-08 "Jim"	

▲ Spitzke V100 SP 004 (ex DB 202 690) is seen at Molenweg on 2 April 2009. **Paul Conlan**

▼ Strukton Rail's G 1206 "Carin" is seen passing Amersfoort station with a few wagons on 3 July 2012. **Raimund Wyhnal**

SPITZKE SPOORBOUW

Spitzke is a German track maintenance company based in Grossbeeren which has now started to work regularly in the Netherlands having taken over Dutch company GTI Infra in 2006. The Dutch headquarters is in Houten. Only three of the fleet (shown in bold) are actually with Spitzke's Dutch subsidiary but the other V100s may appear one day. Spitzke also has ex DB Class 228 and 232 locos plus shunters but these are not shown. They can be found in Platform 5's German Railways Book 2. Livery is light blue with white line and front end.

TYPE V100   B-B

For technical details, see NBE Rail.

Number/name/EVN number	Built	Works No.	Notes
V100-SP-001	1976	15231	ex DB 202 846
V100-SP-003	1974	14378	ex DB 202 677
V100-SP-004 "Mariëlle"	**1974**	**14391**	**ex DB 202 690**
V100-SP-005 "Truus"	**1974**	**14445**	**ex DB 202 744**
V100-SP-006 "Marieke"	**1971**	**12849**	**ex DB 202 340**
V100-SP-007	1973	13575	ex DB 202 536
V100-SP-008 92 80 1203 128-4 D-SLG	1973	13568	ex DB 202 529
V100-SP-009 92 80 1203 129-2 D-SLG	1973	13567	ex DB 202 528

STRUKTON RAIL

Strukton's origins go back to the 1920s but the company only started to expand in its present form after the reorganisation of Dutch railways in 1997. Strukton Groep grew out of NS's rail-related construction projects but NS sold the whole group to engineering company Oranjewoud in 2010. Strukton is also active in Belgium, Denmark, Germany, Sweden and Italy, where the company has a 40% stake in CLF of Bologna. The company abandoned activities in Norway in 2012.

Strukton is a fully licensed RU and owns track maintenance machines as well as diesel locomotives, for movement of equipment around the network and shunting. Strukton also offers workshop services to third parties. Strukton has a 50% share in Eurailscout Inspection & Analysis (see above), which operates track inspection vehicles. Since the last edition, the company has parted with its former NS Class 600 shunters.

Livery: All over yellow. Ex NS locos carry their old numbers preceded by 30 or 300.
Depots: Zutphen (Strukton built a new depot here in 2012; it is shared with Arriva), Maarsen.

TYPE G1206   B-B

For details see Section 6.1. 303001 was delivered to Angel Trains Cargo then bought by Strukton in 2003.

303001	Carin	2002	1001147	-
303002	Willy	2003	1001173	-
303007	Danique	2008	5001681	-
303008	Demi	2008	5001724	-

OTHER LOCOMOTIVES

Number	Name	Axles	Builder	Year	Works No.	Type	Notes
300201	Tiny	B	O&K	1963	26256	MC14N	ex BPM, Pernis No. 1
300202	Herma	B	O&K	1967	26620	MB9N	ex H& B, Hoek van Holland
303005	Ankie	B-B	Deutz	1961	57187	DG1200BBM	ex HGK DH 31
303006	Irene	B-B	Deutz	1961	57188	DG1200BBM	ex HGK DH 32
1322320	Janine	B-B	Deutz	1963	57471	DG1200BBM	ex HGK DH 36
1322321	Monique	B-B	Deutz	1966	57983	DG1200BBM	ex HGK DH 38

VOLKER RAIL

This company is part of large Dutch construction group Volker-Wessels. The company has a safety certificate to operate in Germany as well as the Netherlands and is also active in Poland and Estonia. The company's two V60D locos were sold to EETC in 2011. Volker Rail was hiring most of its V100 locos out to freight train operators – mainly LOCON and TrainSupport in 2012.

Livery is a reverse of Alpha Trains diesel livery – white cab and blue bonnets, but with a yellow front end.

Depot: Dordrecht Zeehaven.

TYPE V100 B-B

See NBE Rail for technical details.

Number	Name	Built	Works No.	Notes
203-1	Tom	1973	13578	Ex DB 202 539
203-2	Jerry	1974	14392	Ex DB 202 691
203-3	Spike	1975	14840	Ex DB 202 783
203-4	Butch	1971	12922	Ex DB 202 413
203-5	Tyke	1973	13557	Ex DB 202 518

OTHER LOCOS

No.	Name	Axles	Builder	Built	Works No.	Type	Power	Notes
209	Robin	C	Henschel	1961	30319	DH500Ca	370 kW	ex RAG 429.

▲ Volker Rail's V100s 203-2 "Jerry" and 203-3 "Spike" are seen at Amsterdam Westhaven on 9 April 2007.
Quintus Vosman

7. INTERNATIONAL HIGH SPEED TRAINS

7.1. TRAINS À GRAND VITESSE (TGVs)

EUROSTAR THREE CAPITALS   9-CAR HALF-SETS

Eurostar Three Capitals sets mainly work services through the Channel Tunnel from London to Paris and Brussels. The three-voltage sets (750 V DC third rail equipment was removed after opening of HS1, the London–Channel Tunnel high speed line) also work London–Bourg St. Maurice ski trains in winter and London–Avignon in summer. 3203/4 and 3225–8 are not used on Channel Tunnel services, being restricted to Paris–Lille–Tourcoing.

Eurostars are based on the TGV concept, and the individual cars are numbered like TGVs. Each train consists of two 9-coach half sets back-to-back with a power car at the outer end. They normally operate in pairs 3001/2, and so on. All sets are articulated with an extra motor bogie on the coach next to the power car. Coaches are referred to by their position in the set viz. R1–R9 (and in traffic R10–R18 in the second set). Coaches R18–R10 are identical to R1–R9.

Units are being refurbished for a second time from 2012 and will appear in a new livery.

TGV + TGVZBD + 4 TGVRB + TGVRr + 2 TGVRA + TGVRAD.

Systems: 3000 V DC/25 kV AC (v + 1500 V DC).
Built: 1992–93.
Builders: GEC-Alsthom/Brush/ANF/De Dietrich/BN/ACEC.
Axle Arrangement: Bo-Bo + Bo-2-2-2-2-2-2-2-2-2.
Accommodation: 0 + –/48 2T + –/56* 1T + –/56* 2T + –/56* 1T + –/56* 2T + bar/kitchen + 39/– 1T + 39/– 1T + 25/– 1T. *Non refurbished sets 3203/4, 3225/6, 3227/8 and 3101/2 are –/58 1T.
Length: 22.15 + 21.845 + (7 x 18.70) + 21.845 m.
Weight: 68.5 + 44.6 + 28.1 + 29.7 + 28.3 + 29.2 + 31.1 + 29.6 + 32.2 + 39.4 tonnes.
Continuous Rating: 12 x 240 kW (25 kV AC); 5700 kW (1500 and 3000 V DC).
Maximum Speed: 300 km/h.
Cab Signalling: TVM 430.

Class Specific Livery: S White with dark blue window band roof and yellow bodysides.

Trailer cars are numbered in the following sequence:

Set nnnn: 37nnnn1/37nnnn2/37nnnn3/37nnnn4/37nnnn5/37nnnn6/37nnnn7/37nnnn8/37nnnn9.

Set	Owner	Power Car								
3001	EU	3730010	S	TI	3101	SNCB	3731010	S		FF
3002	EU	3730020	S	TI	3102	SNCB	3731020	S		FF
3003	EU	3730030	S	TI	3103	SNCB	3731030	S		FF
3004	EU	3730040	S	TI	3104	SNCB	3731040	S		FF
3005	EU	3730050	S	TI	3105	SNCB	3731050	S		FF
3006	EU	3730060	S	TI	3106	SNCB	3731060	S		FF
3007	EU	3730070	S	TI	3107	SNCB	3731050	S		FF
3008	EU	3730080	S	TI	3108	SNCB	3731060	S		FF
3009	EU	3730090	S	TI						
3010	EU	3730100	S	TI	3201	SNCF	3732010	S	v	LY
3011	EU	3730110	S	TI	3202	SNCF	3732020	S	v	LY
3012	EU	3730120	S	TI	3205	SNCF	3732050	S		LY
3013	EU	3730130	S	TI	3206	SNCF	3732060	S		LY
3014	EU	3730140	S	TI	3207	SNCF	3732070	S	v	LY
3015	EU	3730150	S	TI	3208	SNCF	3732080	S	v	LY
3016	EU	3730160	S	TI	3209	SNCF	3732090	S	v	LY
3017	EU	3730170	S	TI	3210	SNCF	3732100	S	v	LY
3018	EU	3730180	S	TI	3211	SNCF	3732110	S		LY
3019	EU	3730190	S	TI	3212	SNCF	3732120	S		LY
3020	EU	3730200	S	TI	3213	SNCF	3732130	S	v	LY
3021	EU	3730210	S	TI	3214	SNCF	3732140	S	v	LY
3022	EU	3730220	S	TI	3215	SNCF	3732150	S	v	LY

3216	SNCF	3732160	S	v	LY
3217	SNCF	3732170	S		LY
3218	SNCF	3732180	S		LY
3219	SNCF	3732190	S		LY
3220	SNCF	3732200	S		LY
3221	SNCF	3732210	S		LY
3222	SNCF	3732220	S		LY
3223	SNCF	3732230	S	v	LY

3224	SNCF	3732240	S	v	LY
3229	SNCF	3732290	S	v	LY
3230	SNCF	3732300	S	v	LY
3231	SNCF	3732310	S		LY
3232	SNCF	3732320	S		LY

Spare Power Car

3999	EU	3739990	S	TI

Names:

3001/02	Tread Lightly / Voyage Vert
3003/04	Tri-City-Athlon 2010
3007/08	Waterloo Sunset
3009/10	REMEMBERING FROMELLES

3013/14	LONDON 2012
3207/08	MICHEL HOLLARD
3209/10	THE DA VINCI CODE

▲ Eurostar set **3218** + **3217** is seen at Marcq on **23** October **2012** heading at top speed towards Brussels with train **9132** from London St Pancras.   **Carlo Hertogs**

THALYS PBKA   8-CAR FOUR-VOLTAGE SETS

This is basically a four-voltage version of TGV-Réseau but with the new generation of power car with a central driving position as first seen with TGV Duplex. Trailer cars are exactly the same as Thalys PBA sets 4532–4540 (see below). The power car includes all equipment necessary for operation in France, Belgium, the Netherlands and Germany including German Indusi and LZB cab signalling. With all this extra equipment, it was necessary to design a lighter transformer in order to keep the power car weight to 68 tonnes because of the 17 tonne axle load limit on French high-speed lines.

These sets work Paris–Brussels–Köln/Amsterdam services. Sets can operate in multiple with TGV Réseau sets but normally only run with each other and PBA sets. The sets belong to the four railways concerned and are based and maintained at Brussels Forest. Units were refurbished internally and received ETCS equipment from 2008 to 2011.

Systems: 1500 V DC/25 kV AC 50 Hz/3000 V DC/15 kV AC 16.7 Hz.
Built : 1996–98.
Builder-Mechanical Parts: GEC-Alsthom/De Dietrich/Bombardier Eurorail.
Builder-Electrical Parts: GEC-Alsthom/ACEC/Holec.
Axle arrangement: Bo-Bo + 2-2-2-2-2-2-2-2 + Bo-Bo.
Weight: 67 + 43 + 28 + 28 + 28 + 28 + 28 + 28 + 43 + 67 tonnes.
Length: 22.15 + 21.845 + 18.7 + 18.7 + 18.7 + 18.7 + 18.7 + 18.7 + 21.845 + 22.15 m.
Accommodation:
0 + 42/– 1T + 39/– 1T + 39/– 1T + –/16 bar + –/56 2T + –/56 2T + –/56 1T + –/73 2T + 0
Continuous Rating: 3680 kW (1500 V DC and 3000 V DC); 8000 kW (25 kV AC); 5120 kW (15 kV AC).
Maximum Speed: 300 km/h.
Cab Signalling: TVM 430 & ETCS.
Class-specific Livery: S Metallic grey with red front end and roof.

Trailer cars are numbered in the following sequence, prefixed TGVR:

Set nnnn: nnnn1 + nnnn2 + nnnn3 + nnnn4 + nnnn5 + nnnn6 + nnnn7 + nnnn8

Set	Owner	Power Car 1	Power Car 2	Livery	Depot
4301	SNCB	TGV 43010	TGV 43019	S	FF
4302	SNCB	TGV 43020	TGV 43029	S	FF
4303	SNCB	TGV 43030	TGV 43039	S	FF
4304	SNCB	TGV 43040	TGV 43049	S	FF
4305	SNCB	TGV 43050	TGV 43059	S	FF
4306	SNCB	TGV 43060	TGV 43069	S	FF
4307	SNCB	TGV 43070	TGV 43079	S	FF
4321	DB	TGV 43210	TGV 43219	S	FF
4322	DB	TGV 43220	TGV 43229	S	FF
4331	NS	TGV 43310	TGV 43319	S	FF
4332	NS	TGV 43320	TGV 43329	S	FF
4341	SNCF	TGV 43410	TGV 43419	S	FF
4342	SNCF	TGV 43420	TGV 43429	S	FF
4343	SNCF	TGV 43430	TGV 43439	S	FF
4344	SNCF	TGV 43440	TGV 43449	S	FF
4345	SNCF	TGV 43450	TGV 43459	S	FF
4346	SNCF	TGV 43460	TGV 43469	S	FF

▲ Thalys PBKA sets are used on services from Paris via Brussels to both Amsterdam and Köln. This is set 4304, officially owned by SNCB, at Dordrecht Zuid in the Netherlands, with an Amsterdam–Paris service on 24 July 2012. **Thierry Nicolas**

▼ Thalys PBA set 4532 is seen at Duffel, just south of Antwerpen, on 26 July 2012 with train 9364 15.16 Amsterdam–Paris Nord. **Thierry Nicolas**

TGV RÉSEAU (TGV-R)　　　　8-CAR THREE-VOLTAGE SETS

Apart from their three-voltage capabilities, these sets are identical to TGV-Réseau two-voltage sets 501–550 (see French Railways Handbook) and were designed to operate Belgium–south of France services on which they often work in multiple with Duplex sets south of Lille. Sets 4501–4506 were later equipped to work into Italy and started operating Paris–Torino–Milano services from September 1996 so they are not included here.

In 2006, set 4530 was converted for use as a high-speed test train and travels all over the TGV network on these duties, including to Brussels. The set is no longer numbered but is known as "Iris 320" and carries a special silver livery with red lines.

Sets 4507 to 4509 were split up in 2007, the power cars going to SNCF Réseau-Duplex sets 613 to 615 and their trailers to Réseau sets 551 to 553.

Set 4551 was formerly Thalys PBA set 4531 and was refurbished as a standard TGV Réseau set in 2008. This was part of a deal under which SNCF allocates capacity to Air France on Brussels–Roissy–south of France services.

All sets were refurbished in the late 2000s.

Built: 1994–96.　　　　　**Systems:** 1500 V DC/3000 V DC/25 kV AC.
Builder–Mechanical Parts: GEC-Alsthom/De Dietrich.
Builder–Electrical Parts: Francorail-MTE.
Continuous Rating: 3680 kW (1500 & 3000 V DC); 8800 kW (25 kV AC).
Traction Motors : 8 x FM 47 synchronous of 1100 kW each.
Axle Arrangement: Bo-Bo + 2-2-2-2-2-2-2-2-2 + Bo-Bo.
Accommodation:
0 + 42/- 1T + 39/- 1T + 39/- 1T + -/16 bar + -/56 2T + -/56 2T + - /56 1T + -/73 2T + 0
Weight: 65 + 43 + 28 + 28 + 28 + 28 + 28 + 43 + 65 tonnes
Length: 22.15 + 21.845 + 18.7 + 18.7 + 18.7 + 18.7 + 18.7 + 21.845 + 22.15 m.
Maximum Speed: 320 km/h.
Cab Signalling: TVM 430.

Class-specific Livery: S Metallic grey with dark blue window band.
C: New standard "Carmillon" livery (2012) – silver-grey with black window band, white power cars plus red doors and lining.

Trailers are numbered in the following sequence, prefixed TGVR:

Set nnnn: 38nnnn1 + 38nnnn2 + 38nnnn3 + 38nnnn4 + 38nnnn5 + 38nnnn6 + 38nnnn7 + 38nnnn8

Set	Power Car 1	Power Car 2	Livery	Depot	Set	Power Car 1	Power Car 2	Livery	Depot
4510	TGV 380019	TGV 380020	S	FF	4522	TGV 380043	TGV 380044	C	FF
4511	TGV 380021	TGV 380022	S	FF	4523	TGV 380045	TGV 380046	S	FF
4512	TGV 380022	TGV 380023	S	FF	4524	TGV 380047	TGV 380048	S	FF
4513	TGV 380024	TGV 380025	S	FF	4525	TGV 380049	TGV 380050	S	FF
4514	TGV 380027	TGV 380028	S	FF	4526	TGV 380051	TGV 380052	S	FF
4515	TGV 380029	TGV 380030	S	FF	4527	TGV 380053	TGV 380054	S	FF
4516	TGV 380031	TGV 380032	S	FF	4528	TGV 380055	TGV 380056	S	FF
4517	TGV 380033	TGV 380034	S	FF	4529	TGV 380057	TGV 380058	S	FF
4518	TGV 380035	TGV 380036	S	FF	"Iris"	TGV 380059	TGV 380060	S	LY
4519	TGV 380037	TGV 380038	S	FF	4551	TGV 380061	TGV 380062	S	FF
4520	TGV 380039	TGV 380040	S	FF					
4521	TGV 380041	TGV 380042	C	FF	Spare Power Car		TGV 380081	S	PE

Named:

4511　　　Villeneuve d'Ascq

THALYS PBA
8-CAR THREE-VOLTAGE SETS

The final ten TGV Réseau three-voltage sets – 4531 to 4540 – were equipped with a special pantograph and Dutch ATB automatic train protection in order to operate Paris–Brussels–Amsterdam Thalys services. Because of this they are known as Thalys PBA sets. These units also have a completely different "Thalys" livery and improved interiors with red moquette seats throughout. They work in multiple with each other and Thalys PBKA sets. Units were refurbished internally and received ETCS equipment from 2008 to 2011. In 2007, set 4531 was transferred to SNCF for use on Brussels–south of France services and renumbered 4551.

Details as TGV sets 4510–4530 except:

Cab signalling: TVM 430 & ETCS.
Class-specific Livery: S Metallic grey with red front end and roof.

4532	TGV 380063	TGV 380064	S	FF	4537	TGV 380073	TGV 380074	S	FF
4533	TGV 380065	TGV 380066	S	FF	4538	TGV 380075	TGV 380076	S	FF
4534	TGV 380067	TGV 380068	S	FF	4539	TGV 380077	TGV 380078	S	FF
4535	TGV 380069	TGV 380070	S	FF	4540	TGV 380079	TGV 380080	S	FF
4536	TGV 380071	TGV 380072	S	FF					

7.2. INTERCITY EXPRESS (ICE)

ICE-3M
8-CAR MULTI-VOLTAGE EMUs

These four-voltage units work the Amsterdam–Köln–Frankfurt(–Basel) and Brussels–Köln–Frankfurt services. They have proven unreliable and cancellations were rife at the time of writing. DB therefore intends to introduce its Class 407 ICEs, at least on the Brussels service, as soon as possible – this is unlikely before 2014. The missing units in the 4601–4611 series were modified to operate into France and renumbered in the 4680 series. They only operate the Frankfurt–Paris service so are not included here. 4654 was damaged in an accident, rebuilt with power cars from damaged 4681 and sold to DB.

Systems: 1500/3000 V DC/25 kV AC 50 Hz/15 kV AC 16.7 Hz.
Built: 1998–2000.
Builders: Siemens/ADtranz/Alstom/Bombardier. **Continuous Rating:** 8000 kW (AC), 4300 kW (DC).
Axle arrangement: Bo-Bo + 2-2 + Bo-Bo +2-2 +2-2 + Bo-Bo +2-2 + Bo-Bo.
Accommodation: 46/– + 43/– 2T + 45/– 2T + 24 dining + –/44 1T 1TD + –/68 2T + –/66 2T + –/60.
Total Weight: 465 tonnes.
Length: 25.675 + (6 x 24.775) + 25.675 m.
Maximum Speed: 330 km/h (AC), 220 km/h (DC).

Livery: White with red stripe under windows.

These units use the DB numbering system where each vehicle is separately numbered. Trains also carry set numbers 4601–4611, 4651–4654.

4601	406 001	406 101	406 201	406 301	406 801	406 701	406 601	406 501	DB	I	FGM
4602	406 002	406 102	406 202	406 302	406 802	406 702	406 602	406 502	DB	I	FGM
4603	406 003	406 103	406 203	406 303	406 803	406 703	406 603	406 503	DB	I	FGM
4604	406 004	406 104	406 204	406 304	406 804	406 704	406 604	406 504	DB	I	FGM
4607	406 007	406 107	406 207	406 307	406 807	406 707	406 607	406 507	DB	I	FGM
4610	406 010	406 110	406 210	406 310	406 810	406 710	406 610	406 510	DB	I	FGM
4611	406 011	406 111	406 211	406 311	406 811	406 711	406 611	406 511	DB	I	FGM
4651	406 051	406 151	406 251	406 351	406 851	406 751	406 651	406 551	NS	I	WG
4652	406 052	406 152	406 252	406 352	406 852	406 752	406 652	406 552	NS	I	WG
4655	406 053	406 153	406 253	406 353	406 853	406 753	406 653	406 553	NS	I	WG
4654	406 081	406 154	406 254	406 354	406 854	406 754	406 654	406 581	DB	I	FGM

Names:

4603	Mannheim	4611	Düsseldorf
4607	Hannover	4651	Amsterdam
4610	Frankfurt am Main	4652	Arnhem

▲ DB ICE 3M set 4604 is seen on the Vesdre bridge in Goffontaine, Belgium, on 13 June 2009. This was the last day ICEs used Line 37 – the day after, high speed trains started running over high speed Line 3 between Aachen and Liège.   **Carlo Hertogs**

▼ Fyra set 4802, on Belgian Line 12, passes Antwerpen Luchtbal yard on 8 August 2012, with the first test run of that evening to Antwerpen-Centraal.   **Carlo Hertogs**

ICE VELARO D   8-CAR MULTI-VOLTAGE EMUs

15 more multi-voltage ICE 3 sets (Class 406) were ordered from Siemens in November 2007 for service from December 2011, again for use from Germany to the Netherlands, Belgium and France. Like previous orders the run-on order turned into a new type – Class 407. The trains are based on the Siemens Velaro model which has been exported (Spain, China, Russia) and thus this type is Velaro D (D= *Deutschland*). Although only 15 sets were initially ordered there will in fact be 17 as an extra one was later ordered to make up for an accident-damaged Class 406 whilst another one is being provided by Siemens as compensation for late delivery. The sets are intended to strengthen the fleet for working into other countries with the priority being to help out on Frankfurt–Paris services and the launch of Frankfurt–Köln–Brussels–London and Amsterdam–Brussels–London services, currently slated for 2015. The first units were not expected in service before December 2012, and then only on domestic services. Class 407 are expected to be able to work in multiple with Classes 403 and 406. A change to previous ICEs is that Class 407 is a Siemens product whereas all previous sets have been constructed by consortia. Certain equipment is now located on the roof (e.g. air conditioning). Low level three phase asynchronous motors with cage rotors are provided but it is understood that set 17 will have synchronous motors. Interestingly (as this is likely to cause trouble, and may lead to a change), sets numbers are the same as TGV Euro Duplex sets which also work Paris–Frankfurt services. The units will almost certainly be allocated to Frankfurt Griesheim.

Built: 2009–12.
Systems: 15 kV AC 16.7 Hz, 25 kV AC 50 Hz, 1500, 3000 V DC.
Wheel arrangement: Bo-Bo + 2-2 + Bo-Bo + 2-2 + 2-2 + Bo-Bo + 2-2 + Bo-Bo.
Continuous rating: 8000 kW (AC), 4200 kW (DC).
Maximum Tractive Effort: 300 kN.   **Maximum Speed:** 320 km/h (AC), 220 km/h (DC).
Length over couplings: 25.735 + 24.175 x 6 + 25.735 m. = 200.72 m. in total.
Wheel Diameter: 1250 mm.   **Weight:** 454 tonnes empty.
Accommodation: 42/– + 51/– 2T + 18/– (+ –/16 in Bistro) 2T + –/45 1 TD + –/76 2T + –/76 2T + –/76 2T + –/64.

Livery: White with red stripe under windows.

4701	407 001	407 101	407 201	407 301	407 801	407 701	407 601	407 501
4702	407 002	407 102	407 202	407 302	407 802	407 702	407 602	407 502
4703	407 003	407 103	407 203	407 303	407 803	407 703	407 603	407 503
4704	407 004	407 104	407 204	407 304	407 804	407 704	407 604	407 504
4705	407 005	407 105	407 205	407 305	407 805	407 705	407 605	407 505
4706	407 006	407 106	407 206	407 306	407 806	407 706	407 606	407 506
4707	407 007	407 107	407 207	407 307	407 807	407 707	407 607	407 507
4708	407 008	407 108	407 208	407 308	407 808	407 708	407 608	407 508
4709	407 009	407 109	407 209	407 309	407 809	407 709	407 609	407 509
4710	407 010	407 110	407 210	407 310	407 810	407 710	407 610	407 510
4711	407 011	407 111	407 211	407 311	407 811	407 711	407 611	407 511
4712	407 012	407 112	407 212	407 312	407 812	407 712	407 612	407 512
4713	407 013	407 113	407 213	407 313	407 813	407 713	407 613	407 513
4714	407 014	407 114	407 214	407 314	407 814	407 714	407 614	407 514
4715	407 015	407 115	407 215	407 315	407 815	407 715	407 615	407 515
4716	407 016	407 116	407 216	407 316	407 816	407 716	407 616	407 516
4717	407 017	407 117	407 217	407 317	407 817	407 717	407 617	407 517

7.3. NS HISPEED

V2590 FYRA 8-CAR EMUS

These new high speed trains are for use on the Amsterdam–Rotterdam–Breda and Amsterdam–Rotterdam–Brussels "Fyra" services operated by the High Speed Alliance and SNCB. The first of 19 sets was outshopped in 2009 – after the trains were supposed to enter service, in late 2007. Passengers were not carried in revenue service until autumn 2012 and it was hoped that full deployment would by in late 2012. When first presented to the public, the trains were nicknamed "Albatros", something which they turned out to be. Three of the sets are owned by SNCB, the others by NS Financial Services. The original agreement between HSA and SNCB included a 20th set to be purchased by Belgian Railways, and an infrequent Brussels–Breda–Den Haag service, but this is now in doubt. When first delivered, the "Belgian" trains were numbered in the 4880 series, but were subsequently renumbered. Trains will be managed in a pool and maintained at NedTrain's Amsterdam Watergraafsmeer depot. Coach numbering is not yet determined.

Built: 2009–12. **Builder:** AnsaldoBreda.
Systems: 1500/3000 V DC, 25 kV 50 Hz AC. **Power rating:** 5500 kW.
Axle arrangement: Bo-Bo + 2-2 + Bo-Bo + 2-2 + 2-2 + Bo-Bo + 2-2 + Bo-Bo.
Accommodation: 127/419.
Total Weight: 423 tonnes.
Length over Couplers: 26.95 m + 6 x 24.50 m + 26.95 m = 200.90 m.
Maximum speed: 250 km/h.

Livery: Fyra colours of white, red and pink stripes.

4801	WG
4802	
4803	
4804	WG
4805	WG
4806	WG
4807	
4808	WG
4809	
4810	
4811	WG
4812	
4813	
4814	
4815	
4816	
4817	
4818	
4819	

8. PRESERVED LOCOMOTIVES & RAILCARS

This section contains details of all known locomotives **from former national railways** which are preserved in the Benelux countries. For space reasons stock from other sources is not included.

STATUS CODES

A   Active (location could vary).
P   Plinthed.
K   Retained for special excursions.
M   Museum or Museum line loco.
R   Under restoration (perhaps at another place).
S   Stored or for spares.

For society and railway abbreviations see the "Museums and Museum Lines" section.

8.1. BELGIUM

SPECIAL NOTE

At the time of writing, SNCB had just started building a railway museum known as Train World next to Schaarbeek station, and is to create a small exhibition at Oostende station. These will be completed in 2014. SNCB has decided to retain only a quarter of the vehicles in its "collection". The remainder will either be donated to associations or scrapped. The need to empty the reserve at Leuven (to build a car park) means that all of the items there are to be moved by the end of July 2013. This means that many SNCB items will be in temporary quarters – either stored or being restored – until 2014. Below we show the 2014 destination as well as the temporary storage point where known. All stock from Leuven destined for Oostende will be temporarily housed at Stienbrugge (Brugge)

8.1.1. STEAM LOCOMOTIVES

Number	Type	Built	Status	Location
2	2-2-2ST	1842	M	SNCB. Brussels Nord > Train World.
MF 72	0-8-0T	1859	MS	(ex Nord Belge 615) SNCB. FLV > SDP.
336A	0-4-0VB	1877	MP	Starucca House, Susquehanna, PA, USA.
5620	0-8-0T	1906	MS	(53.320). SNCB. FLV > Oostende.
1.002	4-6-2	1935	M	+ tender 38.134. SNCB. Treignes museum > Oostende.
7.039	4-6-0	1921	MS	+ tender 24.365. SNCB. FLV. Reserve for active stock.
10.018	4-6-2	1911	MS	+ tender 31.031. FLV > NK > Train World.
12.004	4-4-2	1939	MS	+ tender 24.640. SNCB. FLV > Train World.
16.042	4-4-2T	1907	MS	SNCB. Treignes museum.
18.051	4-4-0	1905	MS	+ tender 18.020. SNCB. FLV > Gentbrugge > Train World.
29.013	2-8-0	1945	MA	+ tender 235.217. SNCB. FSR.
29.164	2-8-0	1946	MS	+ tender 29.194. SNCB. Haine St Pierre > Train World.
41.195	0-6-0	1910	MS	+ tender 17.115. SNCB. Haine St. Pierre > SCM.
44.225	0-6-0	1907	MS	+ tender 13.332. SNCB. FLV > Oostende.
64.045	4-6-0	1918	MS	+ tender 22.153. SNCB. FLV > Oostende.

8.1.2. ELECTRIC LOCOMOTIVES

Number	Type	Built	Status	Location
1503	Bo-Bo	1962	MS	SNCB. Haine St Pierre > Train World.
1504	Bo-Bo	1962	MS	PFT. St Ghislain.
1602	Bo-Bo	1966	MS	SNCB. FSR > Oostende.
1608	Bo-Bo	1966	MS	PFT. FSR.
1805	C-C	1974	MA	PFT, St Ghislain.
2201	Bo-Bo	1953	MS	PFT. St Ghislain.

2383	Bo-Bo	1957	MA	To be preserved by SNCB.
2551	Bo-Bo	1960	MS	PFT. St Ghislain.
2629	B-B	1970	M	PFT. St Ghislain.
2801	Bo-Bo	1949	M	SNCB. La Louvière > Train World.
2912	Bo-Bo	1949	MS	(as 101.012). SNCB. Treignes museum.
2913	Bo-Bo	1949	M	SNCB. FSR. > PFT.

8.1.3. DIESEL LOCOMOTIVES

5117	Co-Co de	1961	M	PFT, St. Ghislain (as 5001).
5120	Co-Co de	1961	MA	CFV3V. Treignes.
5128	Co-Co de	1962	MA	PFT, St. Ghislain.
5142	Co-Co de	1962	MS	SNCB. NK > Train World.
5149	Co-Co de	1961	MA	PFT, St. Ghislain.
5166	Co-Co de	1963	MA	SNCB, FNND.
5183	Co-Co de	1963	MA	PFT. Spontin.
5215	Co-Co de	1955	MS	PFT. St Ghislain (for spares).
5217	Co-Co de	1955	M	PFT. St Ghislain.
5404	Co-Co de	1956	MA	SNCB. FNND.
5910	Bo-Bo de	1955	MA	(as 201.010). SNCB, FNND.
5917	Bo-Bo de	1955	MS	SNCB. Haine St. Pierre (for spares).
5926	Bo-Bo de	1955	MS	PFT, FSR (for spares).
5927	Bo-Bo de	1955	MR	PFT. FSR.
5941	Bo-Bo de	1955	MA	PFT. St. Ghislain.

▲ PFT electric locomotives 1504 and 1805, plus diesel 5941 behind them, are seen at an open day event at St Ghislain station on 26 June 2010. **David Haydock**

6010	Bo-Bo de	1965	MS	PFT. FSR.
6019	Bo-Bo de	1965	MA	PFT, St. Ghislain.
6041	Bo-Bo de	1965	MA	SNCB. NK.
6077	Bo-Bo de	1965	MA	PFT. Spontin (as 210.077).
6086	Bo-Bo de	1965	MA	CFV3V. Mariembourg.
6106	Bo-Bo de	1965	MA	PFT, St. Ghislain.
6289	Bo-Bo de	1966	MA	PFT, St. Ghislain.
6306	Bo-Bo de	1966	MA	SNCB. NK.
6406	B-B dh	1962	MS	(as 211.006). SNCB. FLV > Train World.
7005	Bo-Bo de	1955	MA	PFT, St. Ghislain (as 270.005).
7103	D dh	1957	MS	SNCB. FLV > PFT.
7209	D dh	1956	MS	SNCB, FNND > Stad Antwerpen.
7304	C dh	1965	MA	CFV3V. Mariembourg. Named "CUBITUS"
7305	C dh	1965	MA	PFT. Ciney.
7309	C dh	1965	MA	Train 1900, Fond de Gras, Luxembourg.
7324	C dh	1965	MA	PFT. St Ghislain.
7408	C dh	1977	MA	SCM. Maldegem.
8040	C dh	1961	MR	SCM, Maldegem.
8051	C dh	1961	MS	PFT. St Ghislain (for spares).
8061	C dh	1963	MA	PFT. St Ghislain.
8062	C dh	1963	MA	Museum Küstenbahn Ostfriesland, Germany.
8213	C dh	1965	MA	Kohlenspoor. As.
8219	C dh	1965	MA	SNCB. NK > Stienbrugge.
8319	C dh	1956	MA	SNCB. Haine St Pierre > CFV3V. Mariembourg.
8320	C dh	1956	MA	PFT, St. Ghislain.
8428	0-6-0 dh	1962	MR	PFT, St. Ghislain.
8441	C dh	1962	M	SNCB. FNND > Oostende.
8463	0-6-0 dh	1959	MR	SDP.
8467	0-6-0 dh	1959	MA	SDP.
8509	0-6-0 dh	1955	MA	SDP.
8516	0-6-0 dh	1955	MS	SDP.
8524	0-6-0 dh	1957	MA	PFT, St. Ghislain.
9008	0-4-0 dh	1961	MA	CFV3V. Treignes (Disguised former industrial).
9151	0-4-0 dh	1964	M	PFT. St Ghislain (for spares).
9206	0-6-0 dh	1960	P	FAZ.
9209	0-6-0 dh	1960	MA	PFT, St. Ghislain.

8.1.4. DIESEL RAILCARS

Number	Type	Built	Status	Location
4001	3-car dhmu	1957	MS	PFT, St. Ghislain.
4006	3-car dhmu	1957	MS	SNCB, FLV > PFT. St Ghislain.
4302	2-B dhmu	1954	MA	SDP.
4309	2-B dhmu	1954	MS	SDP, Basrode (as ES409 for spares).
4333	2-B dhmu	1955	MA	PFT, Spontin.
4403	B-2 dhmu	1954	MA	SCM, Maldegem.
4407	B-2 dhmu	1954	MA	CFV3V, Mariembourg.
4505	A1-1A dhmu	1955	MS	SNCB. Haine St Pierre > Oostende.
4506	A1-1A dhmu	1954	MA	PFT, St. Ghislain.
4601	1A-A1 dhmu	1952	MR	SNCB. NK > SCM.
4602	1A-A1 dhmu	1952	MA	PFT. Ciney.
4603	1A-A1 dhmu	1952	P	Charleroi Sud.
4604	1A-A1 dhmu	1952	P	Club ULM-Ath, Isières. Used as clubhouse.
4605	1A-A1 dhmu	1952	MR	PFT. FSR.
4608	1A-A1 dhmu	1952	M	CFV3V, Mariembourg.
4610	1A-A1 dhmu	1952	MS	AFSA, Maubeuge. Treignes.
4611	1A-A1 dhmu	1952	MA	CFV3V, Mariembourg (as 554.11).
4614	1A-A1 dhmu	1952	P	Maredsous station as restaurant/buffet.
4616	1A-A1 dhmu	1952	MA	CFV3V, Mariembourg.
4618	1A-A1 dhmu	1952	MA	PFT, St. Ghislain (as 554.18).
4620	1A-A1 dh	1952	MA	SCM, Maldegem.
4903	1A-A1 dm	1942	MS	SNCB. FLV > SCM.

4905	A1-1A dm	1942	MS	SNCB. FLV > scrap.
4906	1A-A1 dm	1942	MR	PFT. FSR. (as 553.29).
551.26	A-A dmmu	1939	MR	Overpelt. PFT (ex ES308)
551.48	A-A dmmu	1939	MS	SNCB. FLV > Train World.
608.05	1A-A1 dmmu	1939	MS	SNCB. Treignes museum.
654.02	1/3 demu	1936	MS	SNCB. FLV > PFT, St Ghislain.
ES 102	Single car	1949	MA	PFT. Spontin.
ES 106	Single car	1949	MA	BVS
ES 202	Single car	1974	MA	SCM Maldegem.
ES 205	Single car	1974	MS	SDP.
ES 206	Single car	1974	MS	LSV, Winterslag.
ES 208	Single car	1974	MS	BVS.
ES 301	B dm	1939	MS	(551.34) SNCB. FLV > SDP.
ES 303	B dm	1939	MR	SCM, Maldegem (551.15).
ES 409	2-B dh	1955	MS	SDP. Spares for 4302.

8.1.5. ELECTRIC MULTIPLE UNITS

002	2-car	1939	MS	SNCB, Haine St. Pierre.
002	2-car postal	1935	MS	SNCB, Haine St. Pierre > PFT, St Ghislain.
027	2-car	1950	MS	SNCB, Haine St. Pierre > PFT, St Ghislain.
039	2-car	1953	MS	SNCB, Haine St. Pierre > scrap.
082	2-car	1954	MR	FSR, PFT.
902	2-car	1957	MR	(Benelux) SNCB. FLV > loan in Netherlands.
7.312/7.724	4-car	1935	MS	SNCB. FSR > Train World (one car).

▲ PFT preserved diesel shunters 8428, 8524 and 9209 are seen at St Ghislain depot on 26 June 2010. **David Haydock**

8.1.6. FOREIGN LOCOMOTIVES & RAILCARS

Railway	Number	Type	Built	Status	Location
CFR	230 084	4-6-0	1919	MA	PFT, St. Ghislain (as "SNCB 64.169").
DR	50 3696	2-10-0	1939	MA	CFV3V. Mariembourg.
ÖBB	52 3314	2-10-0	1944	MS	CFV3V. Treignes.
DR	52 8200	2-10-0	1943	MS	CFV3V. Mariembourg (as 52 467).
PMPPW	Ty2-3554	2-10-0	1943	MS	PFT. FSR. (as "26.101").
PMPPW	Ty2-7173	2-10-0	1943	MR	PFT. FSR. To be plinthed at Oostmalle.
DB	64.250	2-6-2T	1933	MA	CFV3V. Mariembourg.
DR	310 778	B dm	1939	P	Shop "Chez Jacky". Lontzen.
DB	795 662	A1 dmmu	1955	MA	CFV3V (as 551.662).
PKP	OI49.12	2-6-2	1952	MA	SCM, Maldegem.
PKP	TKt48.87	2-8-2T	1952	MA	CFV3V. Mariembourg.
SNCF	BB 12120	Bo-Bo e	1959	M	CFV3V. Treignes.
SNCF	BB 63123	Bo-Bo de	1955	MA	CFV3V. Treignes (as CFL "914").
SNCF	BB 63149	Bo-Bo de	1954	MA	CFV3V. Mariembourg.
SNCF	X 3998	B-2 dmmu	1957	MA	CFV3V. Mariembourg.
SNCF	Y 5130	B de	1961	MA	CFV3V. Mariembourg. Named "IDEFIX"
SNCF	Y 6502	B de	1956	MA	CFV3V. Mariembourg.
SNCF	Y 6563	B de	1957	MA	CFV3V. Treignes.

8.2. LUXEMBOURG

8.2.1 LOCOMOTIVES & RAILCARS

Number	Type	Built	Status	Location
Z 105	1A-A1 dmmu	1949	MA	GAR. Luxembourg.
Z 151	A-1 dmmu	1951	MR	AMTF. Fond de Gras.
201 + 211	2-car dmmu	1956	MA	CFV3V. Mariembourg
208 + 218 *	2-car dmmu	1956	MA	SSMN. Luxembourg (numbered 208A + 208B).
455	C dh	1955	MS	CFL. Luxembourg depot.
804	Bo-Bo de	1954	MS	CFL. Pétange works.
805	Bo-Bo de	1954	MA	CFL. Luxembourg depot.
806	Bo-Bo de	1954	MA	PFT. Pétange works.
856	Bo-Bo de	1956	MS	CFL. Fond de Gras.
1011	B dh	1964	MA	CFL. Luxembourg depot.
1602	Co-Co de	1955	MA	PFT. Spontin (B) (as "202.020").
1603	Co-Co de	1955	MA	PFT. Spontin (B).
1604 *	Co-Co de	1955	MA	GAR. Pétange works. Named 'FOND-DE-GRAS'.
2001	B dh	1957	MA	AMTF. Fond de Gras.
3602	Bo-Bo e	1958	M	Bahnpark, Augsburg, Germany.
3608	Bo-Bo e	1958	MR	CFL. Luxembourg.
5519	2-10-0	1947	MA	5519 asbl. Luxembourg depot.

* Preserved by CFL as a "listed national monument".

8.2.2 FOREIGN LOCOMOTIVES & RAILCARS

Railway	Number	Type	Built	Status	Location
ÖBB	52 3504	2-10-0	1943	MR	GAR, Luxembourg depot. (as CFL 5621).
DB	795 669	A-1 dmmu	1955	MA	AMTF. (as "551 669").

▲ Preserved CFL GM Bo-Bo diesel 804 with 2-car DMU 208 and single railcar Z 105 prepare to leave Pétange on 20 May 2011 with a special to the open day at Koblenz Lützel in Germany.

Mike Wohl

▼ Steam locos 89 "NESTOR", 326 and 13 – all 2-4-0s – are seen at the Spoorwegmuseum in Utrecht on 2 July 2012.

Raimund Wyhnal

8.3. NETHERLANDS

8.3.1. STEAM LOCOMOTIVES

Number	Type	Built	Status	Location
13	2-4-0	1865	M	NSM, Utrecht.
89 "NESTOR"	2-4-0	1880	M	NSM, Utrecht.
107	4-4-0	1889	M	NSM, Utrecht.
326	2-4-0	1881	M	NSM, Utrecht.
657	0-4-0T	1901	MA	MBS (Lok 7), Haaksbergen.
2104	4-4-0	1914	M	NSM, Utrecht.
3737	4-6-0	1911	M	NSM, Utrecht.
5085	2-10-0	1945	M	NSM, Utrecht (ex WD 73755).
6317	4-8-4T	1931	M	NSM, Utrecht .
"6513"	0-4-0T	1887	MR	SHM. Hoorn. (Neuhoffnungshütte II, disguised)
7742	0-6-0T	1914	MA	SHM, Hoorn "BELLO".
8811	0-6-0ST	1943	MA	SSN, Rotterdam Noord. (ex WD 75080).
8815	0-6-0ST	1944	MA	Ribble Steam Railway, Preston, UK.
8826	0-6-0ST	1944	MR	ZLSM, Simpleveld. (ex WD 75115)

8.3.2. DIESEL & ELECTRIC LOCOMOTIVES

No.	Type	Built	Status	Location
103	4w dm	1930	M	NSM, Utrecht.
116	4w dm	1931	MR	VSM, Beekbergen.
122	4w dm	1931	MR	SDL, Goes.
125	4w dm	1931	M	MBS (Lok 15), Haaksbergen.
137	4w dm	1932	MS	NSM, Blerick.
145	4w dm	1932	M	MBS (Lok 14), Haaksbergen.
162	0-4-0 dm	1941	MA	Stichting 162, Hoorn (Ex WD 33, 70033).
204	Bo de	1934	MA	STAR, Stadskanaal.
209	Bo de	1934	M	SEIN, Roosendaal.
210	Bo de	1934	MS	SDL, Watergraafsmeer.
211	Bo de	1934	MA	SDL, Blerick.
213	Bo de	1934	M	SEIN.
214	Bo de	1935	MS	SEIN, Nijmegen.
217	Bo de	1935	P	Tini van Laaden, Uden.
218	Bo de	1935	MR	VSM, Beekbergen.
222	Bo de	1935	MA	SEIN, Haarlem.
225	Bo de	1935	MA	VSM, Beekbergen.
228	Bo de	1935	MA	SSN, Rotterdam Noord.
230	Bo de	1935	P	Onnen.
231	Bo de	1935	MR	Private owner, Nijmegen yard.
232	Bo de	1935	P	Private owner, Haarlem.
234	Bo de	1935	P	Shunter, Rotterdam Waalhaven.
238	Bo de	1935	P	Uithoorn, former station.
242	Bo de	1935	MA	MBS, Haaksbergen.
243	Bo de	1935	MA	SHD, Amersfoort (no number).
244	Bo de	1935	M	Museum Vliegbasis, Deelen.
246	Bo de	1935	MA	HIJSM, Haarlem.
247	Bo de	1935	MR	SEIN, Nijmegen.
248	Bo de	1935	MA	ZLSM, Simpelveld.
249	Bo de	1935	MR	STAR, Stadskanaal.
250	Bo de	1935	MR	STAR, Stadskanaal.
252	Bo de	1935	MA	SDL, Amersfoort.
253	Bo de	1935	P	Mr Vermeulen, Horn.
254	Bo de	1936	P	Private owner, Amersfoort.

259	Bo de	1936	MA	MBS, Haaksbergen.
262	Bo de	1936	MA	SGB, Goes.
264	Bo de	1936	MA	SGB, Goes.
265	Bo de	1936	MR	VSM, Apeldoorn.
267	Bo de	1936	P	Maastricht depot.
270	Bo de	1936	P	GOLS, Winterswijk.
271	Bo de	1936	MA	SHM, Hoorn.
274	Bo de	1936	P	Nedtrain, Haarlem Works.
276	Bo de	1936	MA	SDL, Amersfoort.
282	Bo de	1936	M	SHM, Hoorn.
283	Bo de	1938	P	ESM, Kaatsheuvel.
285	Bo de	1938	MA	SDL, Nederlands Openluchtmuseum, near Arnhem.
286	Bo de	1938	MS	Private owner, Blerick.
288	Bo de	1938	MA	SHM, Hoorn.
289	Bo de	1938	MA	VSM, Beekbergen.
291	Bo de	1938	P	Perron 3 restaurant, Tynaarlo.
292	Bo de	1938	P	Partycentrum 't Hoefslag, Barneveld.
293	Bo de	1938	MA	MBS, Haaksbergen.
294	Bo de	1938	MS	Blerick.
297	Bo de	1938	P	Deventer.
299	Bo de	1938	M	SEIN, Roosendaal.
300	Bo de	1938	M	SEIN, Roosendaal.
301	Bo de	1938	MA	SHD, Amersfoort.
306	Bo de	1938	MA	VSM, Apeldoorn.
307	Bo de	1938	MS	H Tyres warehouse, Woudenberg.
309	Bo de	1940	MA	VSM, Beekbergen.
311	Bo de	1940	MA	NSM, Utrecht.
314	Bo de	1940	MR	GSS, Nijmegen yard.
316	Bo de	1940	MA	CSY, Beverwijk.
319	Be de	1940	M	Tini van Laaden, Uden.
320	Bo de	1940	M	SNFLS, Morra.
321	Bo de	1940	MA	VSM, Beekbergen.
323	Bo de	1949	P	MSM, Sneek.
326	Bo de	1950	P	Partycentrum 't Hoefslag, Barneveld.
327	Bo de	1950	MS	GSS, Nijmegen yard.
329	Bo de	1950	P	Kreekweg, Dordrecht.
334	Bo de	1950	MA	SHD, Amersfoort.
335	Bo de	1950	P	Utrecht Zuilen (Werkspoor monument).
345	Bo de	1950	M	NSM, Utrecht.
347	Bo de	1950	M	SDL, Havenmuseum, Rotterdam Leuvehaven.
350	Bo de	1950	M	SEIN
352	Bo de	1950	P	Aalsmeer former station.
353	Bo de	1950	MA	STAR, Stadskanaal.
354	Bo de	1951	P	Private owner, Waterhuizen.
355	Bo de	1951	P	Den Haag Zuiderpark.
357	Bo de	1951	P	Hein Heun scrapyard, Enschede Binnenhaven.
359	Bo de	1951	MA	Private owner, Amersfoort.
360	Bo de	1951	P	Bechtold scrapyard, Winkel.
361	Bo de	1951	MA	SGB, Goes.
362	Bo de	1951	M	NSM, Utrecht.
363	Bo de	1951	MR	SEIN, Haarlem.
366	Bo de	1951	P	Ommedijkseweg, Valkenburg (ZH).
368	Bo de	1951	MA	MBS, Haaksbergen.
369	Bo de	1951	P	SEIN
451	C de	1956	MA	MBS (Lok 11), Haaksbergen.
508	C de	1944	MS	NSM, Blerick. (WD 70269).
512	C de	1954	M	NSM, Utrecht.
521	C de	1953	MA	SGB, Goes.
532	C de	1954	MA	VSM, Beekbergen.
604	C de	1955	MS	VSM, Beekbergen.
609	C de	1955	M	STAR, Stadskanaal.
618	C de	1956	MS	VSM, Beekbergen.
629	C de	1956	MA	NSM, Blerick.
636	C de	1956	MR	VSM, Beekbergen.

639	C de	1957	MR	ZLSM, Simpelveld.
650	C de	1957	M	VSM, Beekbergen.
658	C de	1957	MS	SSN, Rotterdam Noord.
660	C de	1957	M	MBS, Haaksbergen.
661	C de	1957	MA	VSM, Beekbergen.
663	C de	1957	M	NRM, Shildon, UK.
671	C de	1955	MR	Ribble Steam Railway, Preston, UK. (Originally 601).
673	C de	1955	M	NSM, Utrecht.
677	C de	1955	M	ZLSM (Lok 11), Simpelveld.
1010	1ABoA1 e	1949	M	STIBANS, NSM Utrecht.
1107	Bo-Bo e	1951	MS	NSM, Blerick.
1122	Bo-Bo e	1951	MA	KLOK, Kijfhoek.
1125	Bo-Bo e	1955	M	NSM, Utrecht. (Displayed as 1122).
1136	Bo-Bo e	1951	MS	SGB, Goes.
1145	Bo-Bo e	1952	MS	SGB, Goes.
1201	Co-Co e	1951	MR	KLOK, Den Haag.
1202	Co-Co e	1951	MA	NSM, Utrecht.
1211	Co-Co e	1954	MS	Bahnpark Augsburg, Germany. (NSM).
1218	Co-Co e	1954	MA	Werkgroep 1501. Operating with EETC as 1253.
1302	Co-Co e	1952	MS	NSM, Blerick.
1304	Co-Co e	1952	MS	KLOK (spares).
1312	Co-Co e	1956	MA	NSM, Utrecht.

▲ Former NS locos 1312 and 673, the latter with strange decorations, are seen at the Spoorwegmuseum in Utrecht on 2 July 2012.
Raimund Wyhnal

1315	Co-Co e	1956	MS	KLOK, Rotterdam Noord.
1501	Co-Co e	1954	MA	KLOK, Rotterdam.
1502	Co-Co e	1954	M	Midland Railway, Butterley, UK.
1505	Co-Co e	1954	M	Greater Manchester Museum of Science & Technology, UK.
1656	B-B e	1983	M	NSM, Utrecht.
2203	Bo-Bo de	1955	MA	VSM, Beekbergen.
2205	Bo-Bo de	1955	MR	SHD, Amersfoort (later 2226 then SNCB 7618).
2207	Bo-Bo de	1955	MA	VSM, Beekbergen.
2233	Bo-Bo de	1955	MA	VSM, Beekbergen (with parts from 2208).
2215	Bo-Bo de	1955	MA	NSM, Amsterdam.
2225	Bo-Bo de	1955	MR	SMMR, Rotterdam.
2264	Bo-Bo de	1956	MR	NSM, Blerick.
2275	Bo-Bo de	1956	MS	SHD, Zutphen (carries SNCB number 7608).
2278	Bo-Bo de	1957	MA	SMMR, Waalhaven.
2299	Bo-Bo de	1958	MA	VSM, Beekbergen.
2368	Bo-Bo de	1957	MA	SMMR, Waalhaven (originally 2296).
2412	Bo-Bo de	1956	MS	VSM, Beekbergen.
2459	Bo-Bo de	1956	MA	VSM, Beekbergen.
2498	Bo-Bo de	1956	M	NSM, Utrecht.
2530	Bo-Bo de	1957	MA	VSM, Beekbergen.

8.3.3. DIESEL MULTIPLE UNITS

No.	Type	Built	Status	Location
20	Bo-Bo de	1954	MA	NSM, Utrecht.
27	3-car de	1934	M	NSM, Utrecht.
41	Bo-Bo de	1954	M	NSM, Utrecht.
113	3-car de	1960	MA	SHD, Amersfoort.
114	3-car de	1960	MS	NSM, Blerick.
115	3-car de	1960	MA	Stichting de-III.
121	3-car de	1961	MR	SHD, Amersfoort.
164	2-car de	1954	M	Controversy Tram Inn, Hoogwoud.
179	2-car de	1954	MR	ZLSM, Simpelveld "Wil".
180	2-car de	1952	MA	WIJS, Haarlem.
186	2-car de	1954	MA	HSA, Winterswijk.

8.3.4. ELECTRIC MULTIPLE UNITS

No.	Type	Built	Status	Location
252	2-car	1938	M	STIBANS, Blerick.
273	2-car	1952	MA	NSM, Arnhem.
375	2-car	1962	M	Verkeerspark, Assen.
386	2-car	1962	M	NSM, Utrecht.
766	4-car	1960	MA	SM 54114, Amsterdam.
876	2-car	1972	MA	NSM Utrecht.
904	2-car	1973	MA	Stichting Mat'64. Enschede.
3031	Single car	1966	MA	NSM Utrecht.
9002	Single car	1924	MA	Werkgroep JAAP, Haarlem.
9006	Single car	1926	MS	STIBANS, Blerick . (Also known as "JULES")
9107	Single car	1927	MA	NSM, Utrecht.
9911	Single car	1908	M	NSM, Utrecht.

8.3.5. FOREIGN LOCOMOTIVES & RAILCARS

Railway	Number	Type	Built	Status	Location
DB	01 1075	4-6-2	1937	MA	SSN.
DB	23 023	2-6-2	1952	MR	SSN.
DB	23 071	2-6-2	1956	MA	VSM.
DB	23 076	2-6-2	1956	MA	VSM.
DB	41 105	2-8-2	1939	MR	SSN.
DB	41 241	2-8-2	1939	MR	SSN (on loan from DTO, Germany).
DB	44 1085	2-10-0	1942	MR	VSM, Beekbergen.
DR	44 1593	2-10-0	1943	MA	VSM.
DB	50 1255	2-10-0	1941	MR	SSN.
DR	50 3520	2-10-0	1943	MS	VSM.
DR	50 3564	2-10-0	1940	MA	VSM (as 50 307).
DR	50 3654	2-10-0	1942	MR	VSM.
DR	50 3645	2-10-0	1961	MS	STAR, Stadskanaal.
DR	50 3666	2-10-0	1961	MS	VSM, Beekbergen (as 50 0073).
DR	50 3681	2-10-0	1940	MS	VSM.
ÖBB	52 3879	2-10-0	1944	MA	VSM, Beekbergen.
DR	52 8010	2-10-0	1943	MS	VSM.
DR	52 8053	2-10-0	1943	MA	VSM.
DR	52 8060	2-10-0	1962	MS	STAR, Stadskanaal.
DR	52 8082	2-10-0	1943	MA	STAR, Stadskanaal.
DR	52 8091	2-10-0	1943	MS	VSM, Beekbergen.
DR	52 8139	2-10-0	1944	MA	VSM.
DR	52 8160	2-10-0	1943	MA	VSM (as 52 532).
DB	64 415	2-6-2T	1936	MA	VSM.
DB	65 018	2-8-4T	1956	MA	SSN.
DB	80 036	0-6-0T	1929	MR	VSM.
DB	94 1640	0-10-0T	1923	P	Gennep.
DB	323 036	B dh	1941	MA	STAR, Stadskanaal (as BE D10).
DB	323 542	B dh		MA	StFSM (to be sold as owner bankrupt).
DB	332 139	B dh	1964	MA	ZLSM, Simpleveld (as 332-6 "Conrad").
DB	332 187	B dh	1964	MA	ZLSM, Simpleveld (as 332-3 "SPANIOL").
DB	798 643	A-A dmr	1956	MA	SGB, Goes (as C909).
DB	798 647	A-A dmr	1956	MA	ZLSM (as 798-04).
DB	798 668	A-A dmr	1959	MA	ZLSM (as 798-09).
DB	798 680	A-A dmr	1959	MA	SGB, Goes (as C910).
SJ	E2 1040	2-8-0	1910	MR	ZLSM, Simpleveld.
SJ	E 1090	0-8-0	1911	MA	ZLSM, Simpleveld.
SJ	B 1220	4-6-0	1914	MR	ZLSM, Simpleveld.
SJ	B 1289	4-6-0	1916	MA	ZLSM, Simpleveld.
SJ	S6 1611	2-6-2T	1918	MS	STAR.
SZD	TE-5933	2-10-0	1943	MA	STAR, Stadskanaal.

9. MUSEUMS & MUSEUM LINES

Museums, museum collections and museum lines continue to evolve. The biggest upheaval since the last edition is in Belgium where an official railway museum, Train World, is now under construction and will open in 2014. As mentioned in Section 8, this is resulting in closure of De Mijlpaal, and the tiny national museum in Brussels Noord station, as well as the removal of stock from Haine Saint Pierre, Leuven and Schaarbeek depot. As well as Train World, there will be a new exhibition of stock at Oostende.

Otherwise, increasing numbers of diesel and electric locomotives are being preserved as old classes disappear.

9.1. BELGIUM

Buurtspoorwegmuseum Schepdaal   BS
Association pour le Musée du Tramway   AMUTRA

www.amutra.be (French but few details); www.trammuseum.net (Dutch,covering several sites, but no details of stock).

Ninoofsesteenweg 955, B-1703 Schepdaal. 600, 1000, 1435 mm.

A large collection of tramway equipment, 13 km west of Brussels, access being by bus N Brussels–Ninove. The museum is normally open Wednesday, Friday, Sunday and holidays April–October, 13.30–17.30. See META for details of the collection of stock.

▲ CFL 1603 and SNCB 202020 (which is actually former CFL 1602 in disguise, both locos owned by Belgian group PFT) are seen at Ciney with a special train on 30 June 2007. **Paul Conlan**

Association pour la Sauvegarde du Vicinal   ASVi

www.asvi.be

Rue du Fosteau 2A, 6530 Thuin.

Lobbes Pont du Nord–Thuin–Biesme-sous-Thuin. 5 km. 1000 mm.

Operates Sunday and holiday afternoons April to October plus Saturday July and August. Access: Train to Lobbes or Thuin then walk. Or trams 88 or 89 from Charleroi Sud to Anderlues Dépôt then Bus 91 to Thuin. First departure is 11.15 from Thuin museum.

1 steam tram loco, 3 diesel trams, 16 electric trams.

Chemin de Fer de Sprimont   CFS

www.cfs-sprimont.be

Rue du Mierdy 2b, 4140 Sprimont. 600 mm.

Damré Station–Damré Formation. I km.

This line is built on the trackbed of a former SNCV line and uses old mining diesel locos. Operates on demand and on certain a few special days at weekends June–September. Usually open for the *Journées du Patrimoine* (heritage days) in mid September. TEC bus routes 65 and 727 run daily from Liège and Pepinster/Verviers to Aywaille SNCB station via Sprimont.

17 diesels, of which five are static.

Chemin de Fer à Vapeur des Trois Vallées   CFV3V

http://insiteout.brinkster.net/0000064cfv3v/

Chaussée de Givet 49-51, 5660 Mariembourg.

Mariembourg–Treignes. 14 km.

The CFV3V now only operates between Mariembourg and Treignes where there is a fine museum building complete with shop and refreshment facilities. The museum is open 10.00–18.00 Tuesday to Sunday March to November, plus Mondays in July and August. Operations are at weekends April to end of October but with daily operation in July and August. There is a steam festival in late September.

27 steam, 2 electric, 22 diesel, 15 diesel railcars.

De Bakkersmolen ("the Baker's Mill")

www.bakkersmolen.be

Sint Jansstraat 238, 2910 Essen-Wildert.

Historic windmill and bakery with 600 mm railway circuit which operates 11.00–17.00 on Sundays April–September. About 1 km east of Wildert station.

1 steam, 1 diesel.

Kolenspoor

www.kolenspoor.be

Stationsstraat zn, 3665 As.

As–Eisden and As–Waterschei.

Operates As–Eisden on the first and third Sundays of May, June, September and October and to Waterschei on all Sundays in July and August. As can be reached by bus from Genk.

4 steam, 7 diesels.

Mobiliteits Erfgoed Tram en Autobus   META

www.metavzw.be

An umbrella organisation for all tram and bus collections in Vlaanderen. Sites include Schepdaal (see BS).

3 steam tram locomotives, 2 diesel trams, 26 trams and trailers.

Musée Ferroviaire de Kinkempois   MFK

www.museedekinkempois.be

3 rue du Chêne, 4031 Kinkempois.

This is a regional railway museum located at the SNCB depot. There is also a small museum in an old station building. Open 14.00–18.00 first and third Saturdays of the month, March–June and August–November.

4 diesels (at the depot, owned by SNCB).

Musée des Transports en Commun du Pays de Liège

www.musee-transports.be

Rue Richard Heintz 9, 4020 Liège.

An excellent collection of trams and buses in the former Natalis tram depot. The museum is on bus route 4 but the walk from Liège Guillemins is not long. The layout is very spacious and excellent for photography. Open March–November weekdays 10.00–12.00 and 13.30–17.00 but at weekends and in holidays 14.00–18.00.

1 steam, 18 trams.

Musée du Transport Urbain Bruxellois   MTUB

www.trammuseumbrussels.be

Avenue de Tervuren 364b, B-1150 Brussels.

This excellent tram and bus museum is located in the Brussels suburb of Woluwe St. Pierre at the old depot. Opens weekends and holidays April–mid October 13.30–19.00. Access is by tram Lines 36, 39, 44 to Musée du Tram or Line 42 to Woluwe. A preserved tram service is operated to Tervuren and Cinquantenaire-Jubelpark whilst on Sundays April to October there is a 35 km run around Brussels taking from 10.00 to 13.45.

More than 45 trams/trailers.

Patrimoine Ferroviaire Touristique   PFT

www.pfttsp.be

Musée du Rail. St. Ghislain.

PFT has taken over the old wagon shop at St. Ghislain where most of their stock is now located. It is now an official museum which is open for volunteer work on Saturdays. Some stock is still kept at Schaerbeek SNCB depot. The society continues to preserve many SNCB locos and railcars, doing a much better job than SNCB.

The organisation also operates a museum service on the Chemin de Fer du Bocq Ciney–Spontin–Purnode line on Sundays July–October.

2 steam, 3 electric, 30 diesel, 1 EMU, 11 DMU.

Rail Rebecq–Rognon   RRR

www.rail-rebecq-rognon.eu

Rue du Pont 82, 1430 Rebecq.

Rebecq–Rognon. 4 km. 600 mm.

Located near Tubize from where there is an infrequent bus service or a 4 km walk from Hennuyères station. The line serves a pleasant area along the River Senne. Operates afternoons on Sundays and holidays May–September plus Saturdays July to September.

3 steam, 2 diesel.

Stoomcentrum Maldegem   SCM

www.stoomcentrum.be

Stationsplein 8, 9990 Maldegem. 600 mm and 1435 mm.

A museum has been established alongside the old station at Maldegem and a 2 km narrow gauge line constructed. The society also operates over the line to Eeklo (10 km). Trains operate Sundays and holidays 1 May–30 September plus Wednesdays and Fridays in July and August, with a steam festival in early May. Traction engines and agricultural equipment are also present.

5 steam, 3 diesel, 1 battery electric (600 mm); 12 steam, 5 diesels, 5 diesel railcars (1435 mm).

Stoomtrein Dendermonde–Puurs   SDP

www.stoomtrein.be

Fabriekstraat 118, 9200 Baasrode (Dendermonde).

Dendermonde–Puurs. 14 km.

Operates over a closed NMBS line on Sundays in July and August with some extra operating days on certain Saturdays and holidays. Mixed steam and diesel operation. The stock is kept at Baasrode Noord. The line can be reached by SNCB train, most conveniently at Dendermonde.

7 steam, 11 diesel, 6 diesel railcar.

Train World

Schaarbeek station.

Belgian Railways (SNCB) is building a new railway museum next to Schaarbeek station, north of Brussels, which is due to open in 2014. The museum is expected to house a dozen preserved locomotives. Other exhibits will be displayed from 2013 or 2014 next to Oostende station. At the time of writing SNCB housed its collection at depots in Haine St Pierre (La Louvière Sud), Leuven and Schaarbeek which are not normally open to the public. Leuven depot is to be cleared by July 2013 and demolished. The other two stores are also to be emptied by the time Train World and its Oostende annexe open.

Tramway Touristique de l'Aisne   TTA

www.tta.be

Rue du TTA, 6997 Erezée.

Erezée–Dochamps. 12 km. 1000 mm.

An interesting preserved tramway deep in the Ardennes and rather inaccessible. Operates Sundays and holidays mid-April–mid-October and also Saturdays plus most Tuesdays to Fridays in July and August. It is not possible to reach Erezée by public transport during the operating periods.

3 steam, 6 diesel trams, 1 diesel loco.

Tramway Vicinal des Grottes de Han   TVGH

www.tramdehan.net

Han-sur-Lesse–Grottes de Han. 5.4 km. 1000 mm gauge.

This tramway runs from the village of Han to the famous caves nearby, the only remainder of the Wellin network of "Vicinal" lines in the Luxembourg province, although the route was significantly revised in 1968. It is possible to travel on the tram without visiting the caves. Runs daily April–August plus 26–31 December from 10.00 plus weekends in March.

5 diesel trams.

Vlaams Tram- en Autobusmuseum   VlaTAM

www.delijn.be/over/vlatam

Diksmuidelaan 42, 2600 Berchem.

The museum is located in the old Groenenhoek tram depot which is 500 metres from Antwerpen-Berchem station or accessed by tram Lines 8 and 11 and bus route 14. The museum is open on Saturdays, Sundays and holidays mid-April to mid-October 14.00–17.30 but is closed for restoration until May 2013.

1 steam tram loco, 1 diesel tram, 16 trams and trailers.

9.2. LUXEMBOURG

A very useful internet portal for Luxembourg is www.rail.lu. An excellent site with various links. Where no website is given below, use the portal then click on "Monuments - Musées".

Association des Musées et Tourisme Ferroviaires   AMTF

www.train1900.lu

Train 1900 Pétange–Fond de Gras–Bois de Rodange. 8 km.

This line runs through to Pétange station where there is easy interchange with CFL trains. The depot is at Fond de Gras. Operations are on Sundays and holidays May to September, with a mixture of steam and DMU workings.

14 steam, 8 diesel, 4 DMU.

CFL Luxembourg depot   CFL

A staff association here (5519 asbl) has restored CFL 5519 (a DR Class 42 *Kriegslok* 2-10-0) which is regularly used on excursions. CFL itself is building up a museum collection, but for the time being the locos are kept at the running depot.

1 steam, 4 diesel, 1 electric.

Groupement des Amis du Rail   GAR

www.gar.lu

This society is also based at the CFL depot and has a former ÖBB Class 52 2-10-0, numbered CFL 5621, diesel 1604 and diesel railcar Z 105 plus other items.

Minièresbunn **MBD**

http://minieresbunn.kohle-und-eisen.de

Fond de Gras–Doihl–Lasauvage–Saulnes. 700 mm.

This narrow gauge mining railway starts from Fond de Gras close to the Train 1900 station (see AMTF above). The train journey is in three parts. A steam locomotive works from Fond de Gras to the mine entrance at Doihl from where an electric locomotive goes through the mine to emerge at Lasauvage in France from where another diesel works to the end of the line at Saulnes. Well worth the effort of making a visit. Operates on the same Sundays and holidays May to September as Train 1900.

4 steam, 1 compressed air, 19 diesel, 7 electric plus 4 battery electric locomotives.

Musée National des Mines de Fer Luxembourgoises **MNM**

www.mnm.lu

Carreau de la Mine Walert, 3714 Rumelange.

Visits to this mining museum include a short train ride, the museum having a collection of about 30 diesel and electric locomotives. About 1 km north of Rumelange station. Open Thursday to Sunday from April to September 14.00–18.00.

Musée de Tramways et de Bus de la Ville de Luxembourg

www.vdl.lu

63 Rue de Bouillon, 1248 Luxembourg (Hollerich area).

This small museum is open Thursdays 13.30–17.30 plus Saturday, Sunday and holidays 10.00–18.00. Access by bus 17 from the city centre.

2 trams.

▲ Preserved former CFL 2-car DMUs 201 (owned by Belgian group CFV3V) and 208 (owned by SSMN of Luxembourg) are seen at Olloy sur Viroin on the CFV3V's Mariemburg–Treignes line in Belgium, on 26 September 2009. **Paul Conlan**

9.3. NETHERLANDS

Corus Stoom Ymuiden   CSY
www.csy.nl

Beverwijk.

This is a steam hauled excursion train around the vast Tata steelworks covering an 18 km return journey which takes around 1½ hours. Photo stops are made on the journey. Departure is from Velserbosch station at 10.45 and 13.00 on the last Sunday of the month May to November. Velserbosch station is near the steelworks – some 4 km from Beverwijk station.

2 steam, 5 diesel.

Decauville Spoorweg Museum   DSM
www.decauville.nl

Museumpark ISK, Otterloseweg 5, Harscamp.

This new organisation is located in a former military area and currently has a 1 km line. It can be accessed by bus 105 from Arnhem station or bus 107 from Ede station. It is open Monday–Friday 13.00–16.00 – fewer days outside high summer – but with limited operations.

3 steam, 2 steam outline diesel, 21 diesel, 1 electric.

Eerste Drentse Vereniging van Stoomliefhebbers   EDS
www.veenpark.nl

Veenpark, Berkenrode 4, 7884 TR Barger Compascuum.

2.5 km. 700 mm.

This operation is in the Veenpark (moorland park) and a short train journey is made through the old village. The park is open every day from April to October. The train rides are included in the entrance fee. The nearest railway station is Emmen then by bus No. 26.

2 steam, 9 diesel.

Electrische Museumtramlijn Amsterdam   EMA
www.museumtram.org

Haarlemmermeerstation, Amstelveenseweg 264, 1075 XV Amsterdam.

Amsterdam Haarlemmermeer–Bovenkerk 7 km.

This organisation operates museum trams on Sundays and holidays April–October and also Wednesdays in July and August. Reached by tram Lines 6/16. The EMA has a large collection of museum trams and trailers, not only from the Netherlands but also from Berlin, Bonn, Lisboa, Praha and Wien. Most of the stock is at the Karperweg depot but some may also be found at Havenstraat depot.

60 trams, 20 trailers, 4 electric locomotives, 5 diesel locomotives and numerous other tramway type equipment.

Efteling Stoomtrein Maatschaappij   ESM
www.efteling.com

Europalaan 1, Kaatsheuvel. 1.5 km. 600 mm.

This is a steam operation in a vast amusement park close to Tilburg. The park is open and trains run each day April to October 10.00–18.00.

3 steam, 2 diesel.

Gelderse Smalspoor Stichting GSS

www.smalspoor.nl

Steenbakkerij Randwijk, Renkumse Veerweg 5a, Heteren.

This narrow gauge group has only a 2 km line with 600/700 mm gauge stock. There are limited opening days. Access by bus No. 6 from Arnhem for Heteren alighting at Sprokkelenburg.

48 narrow gauge diesels.

Haags Openbaar Vervoermuseum HOVM

www.hovm.nl

Parallelweg 224, Den Haag.

Museum trams operate on Sundays April–October (and other odd dates) around Den Haag from this museum and depot. Entrance to the museum is free but a charge is made for rides. Tram Lines 9, 11, 12 from Den Haag HS or Line 9 from Den Haag CS.

Over 20 trams, 1 electric locomotive.

Stichting Historisch Streekvervoer Achterhoek HSA

www.stichting-hsa.nl

This group has preserved "Blue Angel" DE-II DMU 186 at Winterswijk station.

Industrieel Smalspoor Museum ISM

www.smalspoorcentrum.nl

Griendtsveenstraat 140, 7887 TK Erica. 700 mm.

This is a tourist line on a railway used for transporting peat. The nearest station is Emmen then take a No. 44 bus to Schoonbeek. The museum is open Wednesdays 13.00–16.30, Thursdays and Saturdays 10.00–16.30, and Sundays 11.00–16.30 May to mid-Octobber

About 70 diesels, 2 electric.

Stichting Klassieke Lokomotieven KLOK

www.werkgroep1501.nl

This is a new name for werkgroep1501 as the organisation now aims to preserve several types of NS main line electric locomotives.

4 electric.

Museum Buurt Spoorweg MBS

www.museumbuurtspoorweg.nl

Stationstraat 3, 7481 JA Haaksbergen.

Haaksbergen–Boekelo. 7 km.

The depot is located at Haaksbergen which is 9 km from Enschede and can be accessed by bus 53 from Hengelo and buses 20, 73 from Enschede. Operates Sundays April–October and Wednesdays and Thursday in July and August plus other odd days. Three round trips normally operate departing Haaksbergen at 11.00, 13.00 and 15.00.

7 steam, 11 diesel, 1 DMU.

Het National Modelspoormuseum MSM

www.modelspoormusem.nl

A model railway museum at Sneek station. One Sik shunter is plinthed outside.

Nederlands Openluchtmuseum NOM

www.openluchtmuseum.nl

Schelmseweg 89, 6800 AP Arnhem.

This well-established museum has a 1.7 km tramway and has acquired stock from various cities. Take bus no. 3 from Arnhem station towards Alteveer.

7 trams, 1 diesel.

Nederlands Spoorweg Museum
(now referred to as Het Spoorwegmuseum) NSM

www.spoorwegmuseum.nl

Maliebaanstation, Johan van Oldenbarneveldtlaan 6, 3581 XW Utrecht.

The NS museum has been completely rebuilt in recent years and new display areas opened but even so there is still not enough room to show everything and some stock is stored, mostly at Blerick. The museum is open Tuesday–Sunday 10.00–17.00 but also on Mondays during school holidays. There is a special hourly train service from Utrecht Centraal station to the museum.

11 steam, 7 electric, 15 diesel, 7 EMU, 4 DMU and trams.

NZH Vervoer Museum NZH

www.nzh-vervoermuseum.nl

Leidsevaart 396, 2014 HM Haarlem.

This small museum is dedicated to the former Den Haag "blue trams" (Noord-Zuid Hollandsche Vervoermaatschappij - NZH) undertaking. Open Saturdays 11.00–16.00. Free. Reached by bus no. 90 from Haarlem station.

4 trams.

Museum RTM Ouddorp RTM

www.rtm-ouddorp.nl

De Punt West, G.C. Schellingerweg 2, Ouddorp (ZH).

De Punt Remise–Scharendijke Dolfijn. 1067 mm. 5 km.

Steam and diesel trains run on this line in the dune area of Ouddorp in July and August with steam on Wednesdays and Thursdays and diesel on Saturdays. Trains also run on other odd days. There is a museum and depot at RTM De Punt-West. It can be reached by Connexxion Bus 104 from Spijkenisse metro station for Vlissingen, to Ouddorp De Punt.

4 steam, 5 diesel trams, 2 electric railcars.

Stichting 162

www.stichting162.nl

An association dedicated to preserving former NS shunter 162, built in Britain and former War Department loco 73755. The loco is now based at the SHM depot in Hoorn.

Stichting De Locomotor SDL

www.locomotor.nl

A society whose aim is to preserve the different forms of shunting tractors. They have no official museum but do work on restoring locomotives at the old wagon shops in Amersfoort. Some of their locomotives are on show at other centres.

7 diesels.

Stoomtrein Goes–Borsele SGB

www.destoomtrein.nl

Albert Plesmanweg, Goes.

Goes–Baarland 11km.

SGB uses a former NS line. The (former NS) depot is located at Goes station. Trains run on Sundays and holidays April–October, Sunday–Friday July and August with some Saturday running in the peak holiday period.

5 steam, 8 diesel, 2 electric, 1 tram, 2 railbuses.

Stichting Historisch Dieselmaterieel SHD

www.dieseltreinen.nl

Another new organisation whose aim is to preserve a selection of diesel locomotives. So far only two Class 2200 have been preserved.

2 diesels

▲ Preserved railway Stoomtrein Goes Borsele's former DB Uerdinger Schienenbüssen 798 680, now C910 and SGB C909 (798 643), have just left Hoedekenskerke with train 36 Baarland–'s-Gravenpolder and are seen being flagged across 's-Gravenpoldersestraat on 14 August 2011. **Quintus Vosman**

Museumstoomtram Hoorn–Medemblik SHM

www.museumstoomtram.nl

Van Dedemstraat 8, Hoorn.

Hoorn–Medemblik. 20 km.

This line is well established and a visit is recommended. The depot is adjacent to Hoorn NS station. It is possible to do a train–boat–train circular journey. During July/August operation is daily whilst at other times between April and October there is a daily except Monday service.

9 steam, 5 diesel, 1 diesel railcar.

Stichting Mat'54 Hondekop-vier SM54H4

www.mat54.nl

This group is behind the preservation of NS 4-car emu No. 766.

Stichting Mat'64

www.mat64.nl

An association dedicated to saving Mat'64 EMUs which owns unit 904 which is based in Enschede.

Stichting Museum Materieel Railion SMMR

www.smmr.nl

This foundation, dedicated to saving former Railion Nederland locos has not changed its name now that the company is called DB Schenker Rail Nederland. The main priority seems to be Class 2200 diesels, especially loco red-liveried 2225. Locos are usually found at Waalhaven.

Stichting Rijssens Leemspoor SRL

www.leemspoor.nl

Markeloseweg 78b, 7461 EE Rijssen. 600 mm, 1.2 km.

Operates every Saturday in July and August plus other odd days April–October. Nearest NS station is Wierden.

1 steam, 16 diesel, 3 electric

Stichting RoMeO

www.stichtingromeo.nl

This organisation is basically the Rotterdam tramway society which runs preserved trams over the network in Rotterdam. See also TMR.

12 trams.

Stadskanaal Rail STAR

www.stadskanaalrail.nl

Stationstraat 3, 9503 AD, Stadskanaal.

Veendam–Wildevank–Stadskanaal–Musselkanaal. 26 km.

This line started up when stock was acquired from a closed line in Germany. Since then it has continued to gain stock. Operating days are Sundays July, August, October plus some Wednesdays and Thursdays in July and August. Access is by Arriva train to Veendam on days when tourist trains operate that far. Buses to Stadskanaal from Veendam, Assen or Emmen stations.

5 steam, 10 diesel.

Stichting tot Behoud van af te voeren Nederlands Spoorwegmaterieel STIBANS

www.stibans.nl

This society is active in preserving old Dutch locomotives and rolling stock. Restoration work is carried out at Amsterdam and Blerick.

1 electric, 2 EMUs, 2 diesels.

Stoom Stichting Nederland SSN

www.stoomstichting.nl

Rolf Hartkoornweg 50, 3062 CA, Rotterdam.

SSN is now well established at its depot near Rotterdam Noord Goederen yard. The depot also houses a museum. The SSN does not have a museum line but is able to run its locos several times each year on excursion trains over the Dutch network. Most of the locos are ex DB. The depot is open each Wednesday 10.00–15.00 and Saturday 10.00–17.00. A ten minute walk from Bosdreef on bus routes 37 (Paradijsplein) and 38 (Kerkhoflaan)

8 steam, 3 diesel.

Stoomtrein Valkenburgse Meer SVM

www.smalspoormuseum.nl

Jan Pellenbargweg 1, 2235 SP Valkenburg (ZH).

3 km line.

This is the new location for the Nederlandse Smalspoorweg Stichting, previously at Katwijk. A completely new depot and workshop has been built to house their ever increasing fleet of stock. Operates each Saturday and Sunday mid-May to end September, also Thursdays in July and August. Access by bus No. 43 Leiden–Wassenaar–Den Haag.

18 steam, 77 diesels (700, 900 mm gauges).

Stichting Spoorweg-Maatschappij Zuid-Beveland   SZB
Trammuseum Rotterdam (Tramweg Stichting)   TMR/TS

www.tramwegstichting.nl

Kootsekade 19, 3051 PC Rotterdam.

Tramweg Stichting has preserved several Rotterdam trams. Their museum is open on Saturdays May–September 11.00–16.00. Tram 4 from Rotterdam Centraal to Heemraadsplein, or Metro Calandlijn, station Delfshaven.

TS also has a depot in Den Haag at Harstenhoekplein Scheveningen which is open on Mondays 11.00–15.00 and Wednesday evenings 19.00–22.00.

26 trams.

Veluwse Stoomtrein Maatschappij   VSM

www.stoomtrein.org

Dorpstraat 140 7361 AZ Beekbergen.

Apeldoorn–Dieren. 22 km.

Operates over a closed NS branch line on which the depot is located at Beekbergen. Main operating days are Mondays–Fridays in July and August. Uses mostly former DB locos.

22 steam, 28 diesel.

Zuid Limburgse Stoomtrein Maatschappij   ZLSM

www.zlsm.nl

Stationstraat 20-22, 6369 ZH Simpelveld.

Valkenburg–Schin op Geul–Simpelveld–Kerkrade. 23 km; Simpelveld–Vetschau. 6 km.

The ZLSM operates over a closed NS line using mostly Swedish steam locomotives, but also has an ex-DB railbus and trailer and in 1999 obtained NS railcar 179 which is very appropriate as these units used to work in this area. Operates Wednesdays and Sundays May–October plus Thursdays in July and August and Sundays in March, April and December. NS connections at Valkenburg and Kerkrade. Depot at Simpelveld.

5 steam, 8 diesel, 3 DMU.

KEEP RIGHT UP TO DATE WITH....

TODAY'S RAILWAYS

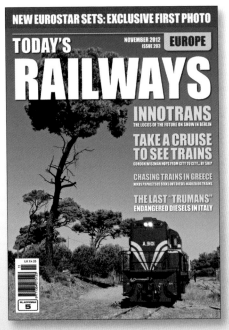

The only UK railway magazine exclusively devoted to events on Mainland Europe's railways.

Every issue is packed with the latest news, informative articles and comprehensive features, plus useful travel information, heritage news, light rail news, diary of events, readers letters and much much more!

On sale 4th Monday of EVERY MONTH

APPENDIX I. VEHICLE TYPE CODES FOR MULTIPLE UNITS

These are given in the continental system:

f*	Bicycle Van (Dutch – bicycles=fietsen)
k*	Vehicle with driving cab(s)
m*	Motor
s*	Driving Trailer
A	First Class
B	Second Class
D	Luggage, i.e., vehicle with luggage space and guard's compartment
R	Restaurant
K	Buffet Kitchen
P	Post, i.e., vehicle with compartment(s) for mail (and guard)

* NS only.

Examples:

BD	Second Class with luggage/guard's compartment
AB	Composite

Note: The continental system does not differentiate between open and compartment stock. The number of seats, toilet compartments and wheelchair spaces are shown as nF/nS nT nTD nW, e.g.: 24/36 1T 1TD 1W has 24 first class seats, 36 second class seats, two toilet compartments (one suitable for a disabled person) and 1 wheelchair space. The increasingly prevalent fold-up seats are shown in brackets.

APPENDIX II. DEPOT & LIVERY CODES

DEPOT CODES

SNCB

The SNCB has official depot codes as follows:

FHS	Hasselt		FSR	Schaarbeek
FKR	Merelbeke (Gent)		GCR	Charleroi Sud Quai
FNND	Antwerpen Noord		MKM	Stockem (Arlon)
FSD	Oostende		NK	Kinkempois (Liège)

NS & DB SCHENKER RAIL NEDERLAND

There are no official depot codes in the Netherlands, but the following unofficial depot codes are used:

LD	Leidschendam-Voorburg (Den Haag)		ON	Onnen
MT	Maastricht		WG	Watergraafsmeer (Amsterdam)
NN2	Nürnberg Rangierbahnhof (DB)			

(S) after the code denotes the vehicle is stored.

HIGH SPEED TRAINS

FF	Forest (Brussels)		PE	Paris Sud-Est
FGM	Frankfurt Griesheim		TI	Temple Mills (London)
LY	Le Landy (Paris)			

LIVERY CODES

Note: Where two colours are shown, the first mentioned is that on the lower half of the body.

SNCB

Unless a code is shown, electric locos are blue with a yellow band, diesel locos are yellow with a green band, shunters green with yellow bands and EMUs are Bordeaux red lined in white.

B Benelux push-pull livery (yellow & bordeaux red).
C CityRail livery. Similar to livery **N** but with CityRail logos and black panels on yellow front ends.
G Original green livery, with yellow stripes.
I New Infrabel of blue with yellow front ends and white stripes.
L New locomotive livery – white with blue stripe below and red stripe above bodyside grilles, plus yellow on upper front end.
M Silver with blue lower bodyside, red band and triangles plus yellow on front end.
N New standard multiple unit livery – white with red and blue lower bodyside stripes and red doors, plus yellow on front end.
S Class specific livery (refer to text).
Y Blue lower bodyside & yellow upper bodyside (locomotives) or departmental yellow.

NS & RAILION NEDERLAND

Where no code is shown against the individual vehicle, it is assumed that locomotives are yellow and NS multiple units are yellow with three blue trapeziums on the side. DB Schenker Class 6400 are dark grey with yellow ends and cabs and red cabside panels. Where two colours are shown, the first colour mentioned is the colour on the lower half of the body.

G Lime green with yellow ends (Class 700).
I NS Intercity livery – yellow with blue window bands.
N Non-standard livery (refer to text).
R Red (Railion or DB Schenker *Verkehrsrot*).
S New Sprinter livery – white with blue solebar and roof borders plus yellow doors and stripe.
Y Plain yellow.

APPENDIX III. BUILDERS

The following builder codes are used in this publication:

ABC	Anglo Belgian Corporation, Gent, Belgium.
ABR	Ateliers Belges Réunis, Familleureux, Belgium.
ACEC	Ateliers de Constructions Électriques de Charleroi, Belgium. Now Alstom.
ADtranz	ABB Daimler Benz Transportation, Germany. Now Bombardier.
AFB	Société Anglo-Franco-Belge des Ateliers de la Croyère, Belgium.
Allan	Allan & Co. Koninklijke Nederlandsche Fabrieken van Spoorwegmaterieel, NL.
Alsthom	Société Générale de Constructions Électriques et Mécaniques Alsthom, France.
Alstom	Alstom Transportation (various works), France.
ANF	Ateliers Construction du Nord de la France, Crespin, France. Now Bombardier.
Ansaldo	Ansaldo Trasporti, Napoli, Italy.
AnsaldoBreda	AnsaldoBreda, Pistoia & Napoli, Italy.
BBC	Brown Boveri & Cie., Switzerland. Now Bombardier.
BLC	Usines de Braine le Comte. Belgium
BM	Baume et Marpent SA, Morlanwelz, Belgium
BN	La Brugeoise et Nivelles, Belgium. Now Bombardier.
BND	La Brugeoise, Nicaise & Delcuve, Belgium.
Bombardier	Bombardier Eurorail or Bombardier Transportation (various works).
BREL	British Rail Engineering Ltd., Doncaster Works, England.
Breda	Società Italiana Ernesto Breda per Construzione Meccaniche, Milano, Italy.
Caterpillar	Caterpillar Rail Power Systems, Mossville, Illinois, USA.
CFCF	Constructions Ferroviaires du Centre, Familleureux, Belgium.
CMI	CMI, Seraing, Belgium

Cockerill	Cockerill-Ougrée, Seraing, Belgium.
Cummins	Cummins, Columbus, Indiana, USA.
CWFM	SNCB Central Workshops, Mechelen, Belgium.
De Dietrich	De Dietrich et Cie, Reichshoffen, France. Now Alstom.
Deutz	Klöckner, Humboldt, Deutz, Köln, Germany.
Donelli	Donelli, Poviglio, Reggio, Emilia, Italy.
Duewag	Duewag Uerdingen, Germany. Now Siemens.
EE	English Electric, Dick Kerr Works, Preston, UK.
EMD	General Motors Electro-Motive Division, later EMD, London, Ontario, Canada.
Fiat	Fiat, Torino, Italy.
FTD	Fahrzeugtechnik Dessau, Germany.
GEC-Alsthom	GEC-Alsthom, several plants, France.
GM	General Motors, La Grange, Illinois, USA.
Geismar	Société des Anciens Établissements L. Geismar, Colmar, France.
Germain	Ateliers Germain, Monceau, Belgium.
Heemaf	Heemaf, Hengelo, Netherlands.
Henschel	Henschel und Sohn GmbH, Kassel.
Holec	Holec-Riddekerk, Netherlands.
Jenbach	Jenbacher Werke, Jenbach, Austria.
Jung	Arnold Jung Lokomotivfabrik GmbH, Kirchen an der Sieg, Germany.
Kiepe	Kiepe Elektrik, Düsseldorf, Germany.
Krauss-Maffei	Krauss Maffei, München Allach, Germany.
LEW	Lokomotivbau-Elektronische Werke "Hans Beimler", Hennigsdorf, East Germany.
LKM	VEB Lokomotivbau Karl Marx, Babelsberg, Germany.
MaK	Maschinenbau Kïel GmbH, Kiel, Germany.
MAN	Maschinenfabrik Augsburg-Nürnberg, Germany.
Matisa	Matisa, Roma, Italy.
Maybach	Maybach Motorenbau, Friedrichshafen, Germany.
MTE	Société de Matériel de Traction Électrique, France. Now Alstom.
MTU	Motoren und Turbinen Union, Friedrichshafen, Germany.
MWM	MWM, Mannheim, Germany.
Niv.	Les Ateliers de Construction Métallurgiques, Nivelles, Belgium.
	October Revolution Locomotive Works, Voroshilovgrad, USSR
Oerlikon	Oerlikon, Zürich, Switzerland.
O&K	Orenstein & Koppel, Berlin-Drewitz, Germany
Ragheno	Usines Ragheno, Mechelen, Belgium.
Robel	Robel Bahnbaumaschinen, Freilassing, Germany.
Rotax	Rotax, Wien, Austria.
St. Eloi	Société Métallurgique d'Enghien-St Eloi, Enghien, Belgium.
Scania	Scania, Södertälje, Sweden.
Schneider	Société des Forges et Ateliers du Creusot, Usine Schneider, Le Creusot, France.
SEM	Société d'Électricité et de Mécanique, Charleroi, Belgium.
SEMG	Société d'Électricité et de Mécanique, Gent, Belgium.
Siemens	Siemens Transportation (various works).
SIG	Schweizerische Industrie Gesellschaft, Neuhausen am Rheinfall, Switzerland.
Smit	Smit, Slikkerveer, Netherlands.
Stadler	Stadler Rail, several works.
Stork	Gebroeders Stork, Hengelo, Netherlands.
Talbot	Waggonfabrik Talbot, Aachen, Germany. Now Bombardier.
VEB	VEB Motorenwerks, Johannisthal, Germany.
Voith	J. M. Voith, Heidenheim, Germany.
Vollert	Hermann Vollert, KG, Maschinenfabrik Weinsberg, Germany.
Vossloh	Vossloh Kiel, former Siemens Schienenfahrzeug Technik, GmbH, previously MaK.
Werkspoor	Werkspoor, Utrecht, Netherlands.
Windhoff	Windhoff AG, Rheine, Germany.

APPENDIX IV. VEHICLE NUMBERING

EUROPEAN VEHICLE NUMBERS

Whereas 12-digit numbers were applied systematically to hauled coaches and freight wagons in Europe under the UIC system until recently, the European Union introduced obligatory 12-digit European Vehicle Numbers (EVNs) for locomotives, railcars and multiple units from 2007 as part of its Technical Specifications for Interoperability. Each vehicle must be registered under this system and carry the number on the exterior **if the train operates into other countries** than that where registered. The owner and/or operator of the train can also use a shortened version of the number or any other system as well as the EVN for its own purposes.

In fact, the EVN is composed of 12 digits, the last being a "check digit" – used to check the other 11, and a Vehicle Keeper Marking (VKM) consisting of letters to show the country where the vehicle is registered then further letters to show the owner or operator of the vehicle. In principle, a locomotive retains the same 12-digits if it changes owners within a country, and if it has not been significantly rebuilt. However, the VKM will change. In the case of the locos changing country, a new EVN may be issued.

The 12 digit number is similar to that used previously under UIC rules with some differences:

(a) Digits 1 and 2. Include the type of traction unit:

90	Miscellaneous traction – used for steam locomotives, for example.
91	Electric locomotives faster than 99 km/h
92	Diesel locomotives faster than 99 km/h
93	High speed multiple units
94	EMUs
95	DMUs
96	Loose trailers
97	Electric locomotives with maximum speed under 100 km/h
98	Diesel locomotives with maximum speed under 100 km/h
99	Departmental vehicles

(b) Digits 3 and 4. These give the country of registration (these digits were used under the UIC system for owning railway):

80	DB (German Railways)
82	CFL (Luxembourg Railways)
84	NS (Netherlands Railways)
87	SNCF (French Railways)
88	SNCB (Belgian Railways)

(c) Digits 5 to 11. These can be used as required under (a) to register trains. in the case of the well-established DB system, digits 6 to 8 are the "class number" and 9 to 11 are serial numbers.

(d) Digit 12. This is the check digit which is calculated by multiplying the first 11 digits as follows:

Digit	1	2	3	4	5	6	7	8	9	10	11
x	2	1	2	1	2	1	2	1	2	1	2

Then by adding all resultant digits and subtracting the last digit of the resulting total from 10. This gives the check digit. For example:

	5	0	8	4	2	9	3	7	2	4	8
x	2	1	2	1	2	1	2	1	2	1	2
	1+0	+0	+1+6	+4	+4	+9	+6	+7	+4	+4	+1+6 = 53

Subtract 3 from 10 – check digit is 7.

Example:
Luxembourg Railways (CFL) Vossloh G 1206 diesel 1585 has EVN 92 80 1276 018-9 D-DISPO. 92 and 80 are explained above; 276 018 can be said to be the 6-digit number under the German system; D = Germany; DISPO = MRCE Dispolok, the leasing company which actually owns the loco. CFL has chosen to number all of its G 1206 locos in the 1500 series.

APPENDIX V. COMMON TERMS IN ENGLISH, FRENCH & DUTCH

English	French	Dutch
cancelled	annulé / supprimé	afgeschaft
to change (trains)	changer (de train)	overstappen
class (of vehicles)	la série	de serie / de reeks
connection	la correspondence	de aansluiting
depot	le dépôt	de stelplaats
DMU	l'autorail (diesel)	de (diesel)motorwagen
driver	le conducteur / la conductrice	de machinist / de bestuurder
EMU	l'automotrice (électrique)	het (elektrisch)motorstel
first class	la première classe	de eerste klas
freight wagon	le wagon (de marchandises)	de goederenwagen / de wagen
guard, conductor	le chef de train / controleur	de conducteur / de kaartjesknipper
late	en retard	de vertraging
locomotive	la locomotive	de locomotief (de loc)
marshalling yard	(la gare de) triage	het rangeerterrein (NL)
narrow gauge	la voie étroite	het smalspoor
passenger	le voyageur	de reiziger
passenger coach	la voiture (de voyageurs)	het rijtuig
platform	le quai (la voie)	het perron
power car	la motrice	de motorwagen
rail	le rail	de rail
railway	le chemin de fer	de spoorweg
rake, set	la rame	de compositie
second class	la deuxième classe	de tweede klas
shunter	le locotracteur	de kleinloc / de locotractor
sleeping car	la voiture-lits	het slaaprijtuig
stabling point	la remise	het afstelterrein
station	la gare	het station
steam	la vapeur	de stoom
stock	le materiel	het materieel
strike	la grève, le mouvement social	de staking
ticket	le billet	het kaartje
single	aller simple	de enkele reis
return	aller-retour	het dagretour (day return)
timetable	les horaires, l'indicateur	het spoorboekje
track	la ligne / la voie	het spoor
trailer car	la remorque	de aanhangwagen
train	le train	de trein
wheel	la roue	het wiel
workshop	les ateliers	de werkplaatsen